excellence in

Inventory Management

How to minimise costs and maximise service

excellence in

Inventory Management

How to minimise costs and maximise service

Stuart Emmett and David Granville

Contents

Abbreviations used in this book are as follows:

ATO	assemble to order
Av.D	average demand
BOM	bill of materials
CMI	co-managed inventory
CPFR	collaborative planning forecasting replenishment
CR	continuous review
DP	decoupling point
DPP	direct product profitability
DRP	distribution resource planning
DV	demand variability
ECR	efficient consumer response
EDI	electronic data interchange
EOQ	economic order quantity
EPOS	electronic point of sale
ERP	enterprise resource planning
EVA	economic value added
FE	forecast error
FIFO	first in first out
FOQ	fixed order quantity
FOT	fixed order time
FG	finished goods
FMS	fast, medium, slow
ICT	information communication technology
IT	information technology
ID	identification
IMS	inventory management system
JIT	just in time
KPI	key performance indicator
LCC	life cycle costs
LIFO	last in first out
LT	lead time
LTV	lead time variability
MAD	mean absolute deviation
MAE	mean absolute error
ME	mean error
MHE	mechanical handling equipment
MPE	mean percentage error
MRP	materials requirements planning
MRPII	manufacturing resources planning

MSE	mean squared error
MTO	make to order
MTS	make to stock
NDC	national distribution centre
OTIF	on time in full
PR	periodic review
Q	quantity
QR	quick response
RDC	regional distribution centre
RM	raw materials
RF	radio frequency
RFID	radio frequency identification
ROA	return assets
ROCE	return on capital employed
ROL	reorder level
ROP	reorder point
RP	requirements or resource planning
S&OP	sales and operating planning
SCM	supply chain management
SD	standard deviation
SE	standard error
SKU	stock keeping unit
S/L	service level
SLT	supply lead time
SLTV	supply lead time variability
SRM	supplier relationship management
SS	safety stock
TAC	total acquisition costs
TOC	theory of constraints
TCO	total cost of ownership
TQM	total quality management
VOT	variable order time
VOQ	variable order quantity
WMS	warehouse management system
VMI	vendor managed inventory
WIP	work in progress
WLC	whole life costs

About this book

In writing this book, we have endeavoured not to include anything that if used, would be injurious or cause financial loss to the user. The user is strongly recommended before applying or using any of the contents, to check and verify their own company policy/requirements. No liability will be accepted by the authors for the use of any of the contents.

It can also happen in a lifetime of learning and meeting people, that the original source of an idea or information has been forgotten. If we have actually omitted in this book to give anyone credit they are due, we apologise and hope they will make contact so we can correct the omission in future editions.

About the authors

Stuart Emmett

My own journey to today, whilst an individual one, does not happen, thankfully without other peoples involvement. I smile when I remember so many helpful people. So, to anyone who has ever had contact with me, please be assured you will have contributed to my own learning, growing and developing.

After spending over 30 years in commercial private sector service industries, I entered the logistics and supply chain people development business, courtesy of my co-author David Granville. After nine years working closely with David, I then chose to become a freelance independent mentor/coach, trainer and consultant. This built on my past operational and strategic experience - gained in the UK and Nigeria - and my particular interest in the "people issues" of management processes.

Trading under the name of Learn and Change Limited, I enjoy working all over the UK and also on four other continents, principally in Africa and the Middle East, but also in the Far East and South America. Additional to undertaking training, I am also involved with one-to-one coaching/mentoring, consulting, writing, assessing and examining for professional institutes and university qualifications.

I can be contacted at stuart@learnandchange.com or by visiting www.learnandchange.com

David Granville

With a fascination for the practical application of statistics and an interest in supply chains, inventory management is a natural place to work. Following a number of years in line management, I moved into training and development and have spent 20 years working on assignments connected with Logistics and Supply Chain Management. My experience has involved working with manufacturers, retailers and logistics service providers, over a wide range of industries throughout the world.

I established the People Development Group in 1990 and have led its growth into becoming the leading UK supplier of training and development services in the supply chain sector. One of the first members of my team was Stuart. During my career, I have had the privilege of advising professional institutes and governments in the UK, Europe, South Africa and Asia on the development, design and implementation of professional qualifications using a competence-based approach.

Having spent many hours training inventory managers around the world their feedback has helped me hone the approach. My sincere thanks go to them.

Above all, I believe that people lie at the heart of business. Supply chain potential lies in the hearts and minds of your staff – unless they are developed the opportunities will not be harnessed.

I can be contacted at david.granville@pdgplc.com or www.pdgplc.com

1: Inventory and the Supply Chain

In this part of the book, we look at the role in inventory in the supply chain; and we start by looking at the reasons for holding stock, the types of stock and the key aspects to be covered by inventory managers. The centrality of inventory in supply chain management will then be examined, as well as how this relates to how the supply chain is managed and performs. Key aspects and Supply Chain Rules will further illustrate this connectivity. Following this we look at the importance of statistics, and explore standard deviation and poisson distributions and how these impact on stock policy and decision making. Finally, the aspects of service levels and stock levels are examined.

Inventory Management

Inventory management manages the product flow in a supply chain. The aim is to give the required service level of product availability to customers and to do this, at an acceptable cost. Movement and product flow are key concepts for Supply Chain Management and Inventory Management, however, when the product flow stops and we stock inventory, then in most cases we will incur cost.

So why then do we decide to hold stock? The following is a summary of the reasons why:

To decouple supply and demand: Warehouses actually sit between supply and demand where the following examples of stock may be found:
   E.g. supply of raw materials to be used in production.
   E.g. work in progress and semi-assembled items awaiting final assembly.
   E.g. finished goods stock waiting for orders from customers/users.

As safety/protection:
   E.g. to protect against supplier uncertainty.
   E.g. to cover for errors in demand forecasts.

In anticipation of demand:
   E.g. promotional or seasonal build up.
   E.g. bulk supply price discounts.

To provide service to customers (internal and external):
   E.g. cycle stocks of finished goods
   E.g. availability from safety stock

There could also be stock in transit either from suppliers and/or to customers. This length of time could be considerable if goods are undergoing a long sea journey. Whilst some organisations include transit stock as part of cycle stock, others separate it out, particularly if the travel duration is long.

A senior person in a large retailer once said that buyers stored their mistakes in the warehouse, thus emphasising that sometimes excess stock holding can result from wrong buying decisions. We would also add however, that wrong decision making is not only the fault of buyers; excess stock is also held in many organisations both because of unclear polices and poor understanding of inventory principles.

In financial accounting, stock appears on the company balance sheet as an asset. However, holding stock, as we shall see later, also carries costs which will appear in the financial profit and loss accounts. For a trading business, the turnover of inventory will also mean increased sales and profits, therefore the faster the inventory turns; the greater the profitability.

The reality however, for most organisations, is that they carry too much inventory and this extra surplus inventory will be significant; indeed as noted by Barrar and Relph (2000), evaluations of 20 companies in different business sectors "show between 10% and 98% of the inventory values were in overage (that is, in excess of planned levels). For most businesses this will not be a trivial amount and any actions that can reduce it will bring significant benefit."

Types of stock
The types of stock being held by companies will vary and will be one or more of the following types:

1) **Raw materials, parts and component stock:** For example, ready to be used in production. Here the cost of stock holding needs to be balanced against:
- Cost of interruptions to production.
- Purchasing power to avoid increases in prices (such as natural commodity price fluctuations, exchange rates and market price increases).
- Bulk discount pricing.
- Ability to work with suppliers, especially to achieve reliability of supply, most notably the lead-time.
- Ability to work with customers/users on forecasting orders, access to consumption data etc.

2) **Work in Progress (WiP) stocks of unfinished goods:**
There are various WiP stages and each adds value to a product as it passes through production. The cost of stock has to be balanced against:
- Production method used e.g. continuous, flow, batch.
- Penalties of lost production.
- Ability to work with suppliers e.g. for sub-assemblies and J.I.T.
- Ability to work with users on forecasting orders, access to consumption etc.

3) **Finished goods stocks** are those goods ready for sale, and stock levels held will vary by industry. The cost of stock will need to be balanced against the following:

- Customer requirements.
- Certainty of demand.
- Market competition.
- Ability to work with suppliers e.g. for cross docking and J.I.T delivery.
- Ability to work with customers on forecasting orders, access to consumption etc.

4) Consumable stocks are goods consumed other than directly in manufacturing and producing products, for example fuel, stationery and spare parts. Here the cost of stock will have to be balanced against:
- Reliability of supply.
- Bulk discount prices.
- Expectations of price rises.
- Ability to work with suppliers, e.g. for on demand reliable supply/J.I.T delivery.
- Ability to work with users on forecasting orders, access to consumption, demand levels, etc.

It should be noted that we will be using the terms stock and inventory interchangeably, and not in the sense of inventory as monetary value; and as a strategic word: as stock, as a quantity of units and an operational word. We will also be using, interchangeably, the varied words to express quantities, e.g. number of lines, items, stock keeping units (SKU's).

Key aspects
The key aspects to be considered by inventory managers are as follows:
- Determining the products to stock and the location where they are held.
- Maintaining the level of stock needed to satisfy the demand (by forecasting of demand).
- Maintaining the supply.
- Determining when to order (the timing).
- Determining how much to order (the quantity).

These key aspects involve activities such as demand forecasting, defining supply lead-times (SLT) and selecting replenishment methods. We will be examining all of these more indepth.

It should be appreciated that inventory management is more than just matching supply and demand; it is also a fundamental part of wider integrated systems and networks: the supply chain.

Inventory and the Supply Chain
The Supply Chain is the process which integrates, coordinates and controls the movement of goods, materials and information from a supplier through a series of customers to the final consumer. The essential point with a supply chain is that it

links all the activities between suppliers and customers to the consumer in a timely manner. Supply chains therefore involve the activities of buying/sourcing, making, moving, and selling. The supply chain "takes care of business" with activity being triggered by the initial customer/consumer demand signal. Nothing happens with supply until there is an order; it is the order that drives the whole process. Indeed, some people argue that the term supply chain could be called the demand chain.

So the Supply Chain bridges the gap between the fundamental core business aspects of Supply & Demand, as shown below:

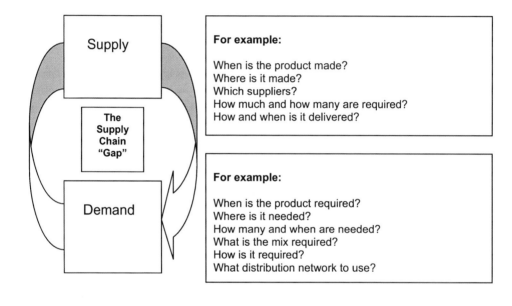

The philosophy of Supply Chain Management is to view all these processes as being related holistically so that they:
- Integrate, co-ordinate and control
- the movement of materials, inventory and information
- from suppliers through a company to meet all the customer(s) and the ultimate consumer requirements
- in a timely manner

A diagrammatic view of Supply Chain Management follows, where it can be seen that the flows of products and the flows of information are also represented by flows of ideas, order creation, and cash/orders:

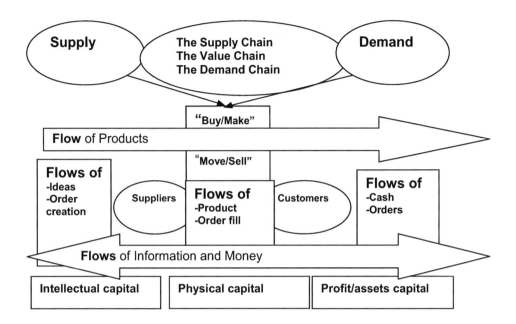

In the above diagram:
- The demand chain represents the creation of demand, for example, marketing and selling with product development.
- The supply chain represents fulfilment, for example, procurement and buying, production and making with distribution and moving.
- The value chain represents performance, for example, financial measures and capital.

The activities of Buying-Making-Moving and Selling take place in the operational functions of Purchasing, Production, Distribution and Marketing. If each of these functions were to work independently, then inventory stock levels are likely to increase not only internally, but also across all of the supply chains that feed in and out from a company.

Supply Chain Networks
Each company has not one supply chain, but many, as it deals with different suppliers and has different customers. For each individual finished product or line item, whilst some of the buying, making, moving and selling processes will be identical or very similar, the total supply chain for each product will be different and will involve often a complex network. This also goes, for example, far beyond the first supplier and includes the supplier's supplier, then that supplier's supplier and so on.

Different types of business and industry sectors will have different views of what the supply chain is about for them, and will therefore have different inventory polices; for example:

- Retailers are driven by customer demand creation requiring the stocking, availability and fulfilment of a wide variety of finished and consumable products. They will stock products for the minimum time possible and will use suppliers who have varied production options of make to stock, supply from stock and pack-to-order options.

- Oil companies are driven by production, so supporting production by the supply side is of utmost importance. Therefore there is often high stock holding by the oil companies on a "just in case" basis, as the cost of stopping production is of prime concern to the secondary costs of holding stocks needed to facilitate production.

- Car assemblers are more consumer demand driven, meaning closer integration of the supply and demand sides. They will use assemble to order production options using suppliers who have synchronised and scheduled make/assemble to order options and who can supply "just in time" and therefore low stock levels are held for the majority of required components and parts.

Supply chains differ, and with supply chain management, there are many different supply chains to manage. These supply chain networks will also contain companies from all the main following sectors:

- **Primary sector:** Raw materials from farming/fishing (food, beverages, and forestry), quarrying/mining (minerals, coals, metals) or drilling (oil, gas, water).

- **Secondary sector:** Conversion of raw materials into products; milling, smelting, extracting, refining into oils/chemicals/products and then maybe; machining, fabricating, moulding, assembly, mixing, processing, constructing into components, sub-assemblies, building construction, structures and furnitures, electronic, food, paper,metal, chemicals and plastic products.

- **Service or tertiary sector:** business, personal and entertainment services which involve the channels of distribution from suppliers to customers via direct, wholesale or retail channels. Services include packaging, physical distribution, hotels, catering, banking, insurance, finance, education, public sector, post, telecoms, retail, repairs etc.

Companies will therefore be connected, externally, with many supply chains that will interact through a series of simple to complex networks. Companies will therefore have many supply chains both internally and externally that interact through a series of simple to complex networks. These networks can be domestic, international or global in reach and will involve the flows of materials, information and money.

Flows of Materials, Information and Money

Flows are critically important to effective and efficient management of supply chains. Indeed, one senior manager said that holding stock in supply chains was an admission of defeat. This was said to emphasise that when the flow stops, usually a financial penalty is incurred, for example from storage charges, from inability to satisfy orders etc. It is only the flow of materials to customers which adds value; stop the flow and usually we will be adding cost (as we will explore later).

In organising the **material flows** from any national, international or global locations, the following will be required:
- Forecasting of the demand requirements.
- Sourcing and buying from vendors/suppliers. At some stage in the supply cycle there will be a manufacturer/producer involved. These may possibly be well down the supply chain when the supplier is an agent, a trader or a wholesaler or some other kind of middle person.
- Transport.
- Receiving, handling and warehousing.
- Stock holding.

These material flows are triggered by information, as information is needed for decision-making. Information is also used to:
- Implement other activities.
- Plan.
- Organise.
- Direct and co-ordinate.
- Control.

Information flows therefore link internal company activities and also link external suppliers and customers. Effective Information Communication Technology (ICT) will process orders, track and trace progress and provide timely and real time visibility. There are two information flows, the supply loop and the demand loop:

The supply cycle information loop covers the following:
- Forecasts.
- Buying.
- Purchase order and transactions.
- Stock information.

The demand or customer cycle information loop covers:
- Stock information.
- Replenishment and picking/order assembly.
- Transport and delivery.
- Invoicing.
- Payment.

The integration of the supply and demand cycles gives an integrated system.

It can also be seen that **money flows** are involved, as information integrates materials and money flows. The design of the supply chain will determine the following monetary aspects:

- Asset investment, for example, this is minimised by outsourcing.
- Inventory holding and carrying costs, for example, from decisions on stock holding policy.
- Debtors balances, for example, the customer order cycle times.
- Creditor balance, for example, from holding lower stock levels.
- Exchange rate variations from non domestic trade, for example by balancing the material flows.

Individual companies therefore need to work together to manage the flows. These flows are determined by demand; therefore demand "pulls" the product, in turn meaning flexible response is need from upstream to satisfy the downstream information-flows demand. Supplier bases may therefore have to be rationalised, as not all will be able to provide any new requirements for flexible, on-time, in-full deliveries (the requirement for a demand driven supply chain).

Demand amplifications

Demand can be amplified as it passes down the supply chain (the "Forrester effect"). In a four-player supply chain the following will typically occur with the stock levels:

Factory	<<>>	Distributor	<<>>	Wholesaler	<<>>	Retailer
250		245		205		100

Note: these figures represent stock levels, being indexed at 100 with the retailer. So the multiple, for example, at the factory end, is times 2.5.

This increase in stock and the "bullwhip" effect is explained by the following diagram, where it can be seen that each player is holding safety stock as a protection from both the uncertainty in supply and/or demand:

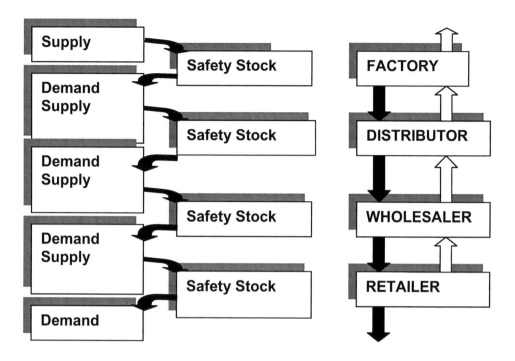

The only way to prevent such extra stock holding is by having all the four players integrate, coordinate and control together. For example, the factory, distributor and wholesaler have visibility of the retailers end demand and all work together collaboratively. This effect has been shown above in a single supply chain. Imagine the impacts on the common reality of multiple level supply chains and networks.

Case Study- Supply Chains and Forrester Effect

In this case, the information ripples backward through the delivery process to create havoc at the production end of the chain.

Megadrug is a well-established pharmaceutical company. It has a wide range of products distributed over the world. One of its newer products is a homeopathic drug, Homeocold, to stop colds from evolving into real nastiness. Megadrug supplies retail shops from various regional centres. In March last year, at the end of the winter season, orders from retailers unexpectedly started to pour in. The regional centres serviced the shops and placed orders at the plant for more Homeocold. Unfortunately, the production line at the plant had already been switched to another 'summer' drug, and it would take at least a week before Homeocold could be produced again.

As the regional centres stocked out, the retailers were frantically ordering more Homeocold. Megadrug's management team realised then that a media-triggered 'poisonous drugs' scare had resulted in millions of customers switching from traditional drugs to homeopathic alternatives. After a crisis meeting, they decided to switch production back to Homeocold in order to service the increasing backlog with the regional centres. Even at full production for one month, they would not be able to catch up; but one thing Megadrug could not afford was a reputation for unreliability with retailers and customers.

Weeks later, the regional centres finally started servicing the retailers again. To their surprise, they were greeted with relief at first, but, as the weeks went by, with embarrassment. Retailers started cancelling orders, faster and faster. The regional centres, watching piles of Homeocold accumulate in their warehouses, started screaming at the plant to stop producing and shipping Homeocold.

The plant director was pulling out his last remaining strands of hair. He was now asked to stop producing Homeocold and to catch up with the summer production that had got way behind schedule. The management team was too busy blaming each other to notice that Homeocold was still selling steadily more than usual and decided to delay production next year to get rid of the stocks at the regional centres. By increasing expectations and ignoring the obvious delays involved, the company faced a "Forrester effect". Minor market changes at the end of the supply chain accumulated to cause great havoc with production planning. Once again not reacting would have been safer than over-reacting.

Source: Michael Balle: Managing with Systems Thinking

Demand Replenishment in networks

Supply chain management involves multiple levels of supply chain involvement. Therefore managing inventory in a sequential and simple supply chain is different to that found when having to manage inventory across multiple level supply chains; for example within a distribution network, or across many different players. The following (overleaf) shows some of these differences:

Key Area	Simple supply chain	Multiple supply chain
Objective for inventory levels	Incremental view per DC/stock holding place	Total view across the supply chain
Demand forecasts	Independent at each level	Based on end customer
Lead times	Work on first level suppliers lead time and variability	Use all/ holistic lead times
Forrester effects	Ignored, "not my problem"	Measured and allowed for in replenishment planning
Visibility	To first level supplier and customer only	Holistic visibility
Customer service	Differentiation is not possible	Differentiation is possible
Cost implications	Incremental costs giving high holistic cost levels	Modelled for optimisation across the supply chain

Manage the flows

In the supply chain, the flows of goods and information will need coordinating to optimise inventory levels. Levels of inventory that are too high can be viewed as the main weak symptom of a supply chain, and a root cause that needs treatment. Additionally and as noted above, in supply chain management there are many different supply chains to manage, and these supply chains will usually contain companies in many different sectors; all of these companies in the network can have weak inventory.

As has been said, holding stock is an admission of defeat in supply chain management. Stock holding is anti-flow and can be analogous to water flowing: Water does not always flow evenly and at the same pace everywhere along a stream. Water sometimes gets trapped in deep pools, is blocked by rocks and other obstacles hidden below the surface. These rock and obstacles impede the smooth swift flows of the stream.

Here, the stream represents the flow of goods and information in the supply chain. The pools of water are the inventory holdings, and the rocks/obstacles represent the waste in the process from poor quality, re-ordered goods, returned goods etc. If a stream is to flow fast and clear, the rocks and obstacles have to be removed. To do this, the water (and inventory) level has to be lowered so that the rocks are exposed. Inventory can therefore be hiding more fundamental problems that are currently being hidden from view. As such inventory can be seen as the "root of all evil" in the supply chain. Indeed, it represents the consequence of how well the supply chain is managed.

Inventory is therefore the linking theme throughout the total Supply Chain. It enables product availability throughout the chain. The format of inventory will change from being raw material to sub-assemblies/work in progress and finally to finished goods (which are often held at multiple places in the supply chain). The format of inventory and where it is held is of common interest to all supply chain players and must therefore be jointly investigated and examined.

The way the supply chain is structured and managed is therefore critical, and some reported benefits of adopting a supply chain approach follow: it should be noted that different approaches give different results:

	No Supply Chain: Functional Silos	Internal Integrated Supply Chain	Plus, External Integration to the first level only
Inventory days of supply Indexed	100	78	62
Inventory carrying cost % sales	3.2%	2.1%	1.5%
On time in Full deliveries	80%	91%	95%
Profit % Sales	8%	11%	14%

It will be seen that with a supply chain approach, inventory costs fall, with profit and on-time in full deliveries increasing; the "best of both worlds" for the company undertaking the approach.

Additional benefits of supply chain management will only come when there is an examination of all costs/service levels together with all the players so as to obtain reduced lead-times and improved total costs/service for all parties in the network. This means, therefore, going beyond the first tier of suppliers and looking also at the supplier's supplier and so on. It represents more than data and process; it includes mutual interest, open relationships and sharing. The optimum and the "ideal" cost/service balance will only ever be found by working and collaborating with all players in the supply chain; a topic we shall come back to later.

Type I and Type II supply chains

Inventory is found throughout the supply chain, and we have briefly explored the many different forms of supply chains. The following simplified model for two types of supply chain presents an extreme view to stimulate debate and discussion about the types of supply chains that are found in practice. The reality and the practice will be found in the "grey" between the "black/white" extremes; also, some aspects can be mixed between the two types.

Attribute	Type I Supply Chain Production led Push More about supply	Type II Supply Chain Market led Pull More about demand
Main driver	Forecast driven. Growth from volume output and ROI. Financial performance profit driven. "Pump" push. From Supply to demand. Mass production.	Order driven. Growth from customer satisfaction. Customer focus, value driven. "Turn on the Tap" pull. From demand to supply. Mass market.
Products	Launched. Functional, standard, commodities. Low variety. Long product life cycle.	Transition. Innovative, design and build, fashion goods. High variety. Short product life cycles.
Inventory	"Turns." Stock holding. Just in case. Hold safety stock. Seen as an asset/protection.	"Spins." Little stock holding. Just in time. No safety stock. Seen as a liability.
Information	Demand information is sometimes passed back. Used mainly for "executing".	Demand information is mandatory. Used also for planning purposes.
Deliver from stock lead times	Immediate, fast in one or two days.	Immediate to long; slower and from days to weeks.
Make to order lead times	1-6 months as mainly making "standard" products for stock.	1-14 days.
Costs	Mainly in physical conversion/movements. Inventory costs in finished goods. Cost control very strong and any gained savings are retained.	Mainly in marketing. Inventory costs in raw materials/WiP. Revenue generation and any gained savings are shared.

The Supply Chain Rules

"The Supply Chain in 90 minutes" (Stuart Emmett 2005) has noted the following supply chain "rules". Whilst these cover the total supply chain, we have added some specific amplification on inventory matters. Once again the significance of inventory in the supply chain will be seen:

Supply Chain Rule number one: "Win the home games first".
- Many companies start in supply chain management by working only with the closest suppliers and customers. They should, however, first

ensure that all of their internal operations and activities are "integrated, co-ordinated and controlled". From an inventory perspective, this means that those inside a company who have to make decisions on, for example, inventory, will need to communicate and work cross-functionally with all relevant people and departments.

Supply Chain Rule number two: "The format of inventory and where it is held is of common interest to all supply chain players and must be to be jointly investigated and examined".

- The format of inventory being raw material, sub-assemblies/work in progress or finished goods. This is often held at multiple places in the supply chain and, is controlled (in theory), by many different players who are usually, working independently of each other. This results in too much inventory being held throughout the supply chain. All players need therefore to work together and jointly examine inventory formats and levels. This for example could enable an assemble to order production method from a former make to stock method ensuring that cheaper work in progress stocks are held instead of finished more expensive stocks.

Supply Chain Rule number three: "The optimum and the 'ideal' cost/service balance will only ever be found by working and collaborating fully with all players in the Supply Chain".

- Full benefits of supply chain management will only come when there is an examination of all costs/service levels together with all the players. This will result in reduced lead-times and improved total costs/service for all parties in the network. This means therefore, going beyond the first tier of suppliers and looking also at the supplier's supplier and so on. It represents more than data and process, it includes mutual interest, open relationships and sharing, for example on demand data to facilitate better inventory management.

Supply Chain Rule number four: "Time is cash, cash flow is critical and so are the goods and information flows; fixed reliable lead-times are more important than the length of the lead-time".

- The importance of lead-time in inventory is seen in the expression, "uncertainty is the mother of inventory." The length of lead-time is of secondary importance to the variability and uncertainness in the lead-time. Again, an examination of lead-time throughout the supply chain, involving different players and interests, is critically needed.

Supply Chain Rule number five: "The Customer is the business; it is their demand that drives the whole supply chain; finding out what Customers value and then delivering it, is critical".

- The customer is the reason for the business – so – continually working to serve the customer better is critical. The customer is the business, after all. But who is the customer? The traditional view is perhaps the one that has placed the order/pays the suppliers invoice, but by seeing the next person/process/operation in the chain as the customer means that there are many supplier/customer relationships in a single supply chain. If all of these "single" relationships were being viewed as supplier/ customer relationships, then the "whole" would be very different and the sharing of demand information creates more effective supply chains.

Supply Chain Rule number six: "It is only the movement to the customer that adds the ultimate value; smooth continuous flow movements are preferable."
- The movement to the customer, undertaken as quickly as possible whilst accounting for the associated cost levels, is really all that counts in adding value. Holding stock is therefore seem by some as being "an admission of defeat" as this stops the movement and adds storage and holding costs.

Supply Chain Rule number seven: "Trade-off by looking, holistically, with all the supply chain players".
- There are many possibilities and opportunities available to Integrate / Co-ordinate / Control across the supply chain(s) networks, starting by "winning the home games first" in and between the internal functions; followed by all of the external connections to the supply chain networks. Physical inventory holding is commonly traded for information.

Supply Chain Rule number eight: "Information flows lubricate the supply chain; using appropriate ICT is critical".
- Information is required at every stage of the supply chain and for all of the levels of supply chain planning. All parts of the supply chain rely on ICT in the planning, operational, administrative and management processes.

Inventory and Statistics

Inventory management involves the manipulation of historic data by statistical analysis to give objective information on which decisions can be made. It is not the purpose of this chapter to explain the rationale behind the statistics but to mention the statistics that are used, so that these may be verified and checked out fully if needed. Where computer systems undertake the calculations, it should be appreciated that by default the system may not always use the "correct" statistics. It is therefore important to have knowledge about how the different statistics can be applied.

Statistics involve questions of probability that an event will happen, so inventory management statistics is a classic application of the techniques. Customer demand follows different patterns of occurrence. An item that has a demand typically occurring in each time period is referred to as a fast moving item. In other words a fast moving item has a regular demand pattern. If we graph this pattern of demand with the level of demand on the horizontal axis and the frequency of occurrence on the vertical axis we obtain a graph, shown overleaf, with the approximate usage figures shown.

Normal Distribution
The above type of demand distribution is called the Normal Distribution.

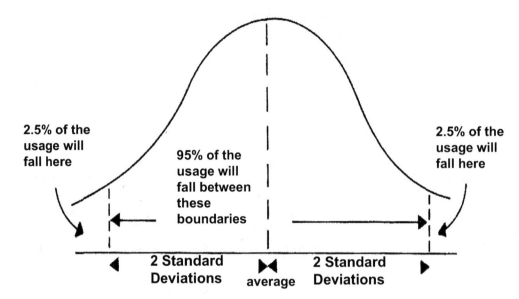

2.5% of the usage will fall here

95% of the usage will fall between these boundaries

2.5% of the usage will fall here

2 Standard Deviations   average   **2 Standard Deviations**

A normal distribution has some interesting characteristics:

*   Firstly, it is symmetrical with the same amount of demand above and below the average.

*   Secondly, as demands get further away from the average they occur less frequently. This means that very large or very small demands occur infrequently.

*   Thirdly, the curve does not cross the horizontal axis meaning that there is always a probability (albeit very small) that you could receive a demand that is bigger than anything you have ever seen before.

All normal distributions have this "bell-shaped" appearance. Some are tall, thin bells and others are short, fat ones. The shape is determined by two parameters, the height of the mean or average demand and the spread of the standard deviation. The standard deviation is a way of measuring the variability or volatility of the demand data.

Irrespective of the shape of the normal distribution it always follows a special relationship between these two defining parameters. In the diagram above, it is shown that if we add and subtract two standard deviations from the average demand then 95% of the demands that have occurred will be in this range. Let's take a simple example of an item with an average demand of 100 and a standard deviation of 10. If we add and subtract two standard deviations from the average demand it gives us a range of 80 (100 minus 2x10) and 120 (100 plus 2x10). 95% of all the demands would occur in this range.

If we added and subtracted just one standard deviation giving a range of 90 to 110 in our example, 68% of all the demands would occur within it. If we added and subtracted three standard deviations giving a range of 70 to 130 in our example 99% of all demand occurs within it. These relationships hold for any normal distribution.

Exploring standard deviation a little more
In any set of data an average can be calculated. If we subtract average demand from an actual demand we determine a "deviation". The deviations can either be positive or negative (occasionally an individual demand will be the same as the average). Consider the example below where we have 6 demands with an average of 70.

Variability of Demand
If all these deviations were added together the result would be zero. (This is what average means, the same amount above as below).

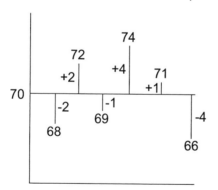

(+2) + (+4) + (+1) + (-2) + (-1) + (-4) = 0

This is not particularly helpful, so we need to find a way of overcoming the sign associated with the deviation. There are two methods to do this called, the standard deviation and mean absolute deviation.

Calculating the Standard deviation
This method squares each of the deviations to remove the minus signs.

In the example this would give the following:

Deviation	+2	+4	+1	-2	-1	-4
Squared Deviation	+4	+16	+1	+4	+1	+16

These squared deviations are then summed to give +42 and an average taken by dividing by the number of deviations 6 to give 42/6=7 (N.B. if the deviation is zero, it still counts). This figure of 7 is in squared demand units and is not easy to work with (it is sometimes referred to as Mean Squared Deviation). To return to the same demand units, the answer is square rooted to give the standard deviation. In the example this is 2.65.

The significance of the standard deviation as a measure of variability can be seen by looking at the following two sets of figures, which represent product demand over ten periods.

Firstly, the deviation is calculated by subtracting average demand from each actual demand. The deviations are then squared. An average of these squared deviations is found and then square rooted.

PRODUCT A			PRODUCT B		
Actual Value	Deviation	Deviation Squared	Actual Value	Deviation	Deviation Squared
69	0	0	100	31	961
70	+1	1	54	-15	225
73	+4	16	52	-17	289
65	-4	16	33	-36	1296
67	-2	4	78	9	81
70	+1	1	42	-27	729
65	-4	16	70	1	1
68	-1	1	75	6	36
71	+2	4	60	-9	81
72	+3	9	126	57	3249
690		68	690		6948

Average demand in both cases is 690/10=69

Standard Deviation is therefore, the square root of the average of the squared deviations, and therefore the Standard Deviation is:

$$\sqrt{\frac{68}{10}} = \sqrt{6.8} \text{ and } \sqrt{\frac{6948}{10}} = \sqrt{694.8}$$

= 2.607 and 26.36.

Standard deviation is therefore used to describe the spread of the numbers and the difference from the average, or mean and when translated into an inventory management system, the product with a smaller standard deviation has the smaller demand variability and will require a smaller buffer or safety stock.

Meanwhile for those who wish to see the method of calculation differently, SD is calculated as below:
1. Determine the mean (average) of the numbers.
2. Determine the differences between each number and the mean.
3. Square these differences.
4. Calculate the average of these squared differences.
5. Calculate the square root of the average = the standard deviation.

Mean absolute deviation
In this method, the sign of our deviation is ignored, each is taken as positive and an average found (in mathematical terms absolute means taking everything as positive).

Using the data for Product A, set out above, the calculation of the Mean Absolute Deviation (MAD) would be:

Actual Demand	Absolute Deviation	Mean and MAD
69	0	
70	1	
73	4	Mean = <u>69</u>
65	4	
67	2	MAD = 22/10
70	1	
65	4	= <u>2.2</u>
68	1	
71	2	
<u>72</u>	<u>3</u>	
<u>690</u>	<u>22</u>	

Note that the differences between the mean value of 69, and the individual demands are unsigned. It is the absolute, variation that is being measured, not its direction. It will be seen that the MAD has a smaller value than the standard deviation. This is always so.

The MAD can therefore be used to obtain an approximation to the Standard Deviation as follows:

MAD x 1.25 = Standard Deviation

i.e.   2.2 x 1.25 = 2.75 (2.607 was the actual Standard Deviation value).

Standard Error
In demand forecasting, forecast error is an important measurement. It is calculated by subtracting the forecast from the actual demand. Since the forecast is of

average demand you will note that there is a very close relationship between demand deviation and forecast error.

Demand deviation = Actual demand – Average demand
Forecast error = Actual demand – Forecast of average demand

Consequently it is possible to replace deviation in the calculations above with forecast error to calculate Standard Error, Mean Squared Error (MSE) and Mean Absolute Error (MAE). This measurement can be used to determine safety stock and we will explore this later on.

Concept of Service Level
Items with a regular demand pattern follow the normal distribution. As we have seen above it is important to consider not just average demand, but also the variability of demand when trying to manage inventory levels. However, demands that occur below the level of average demand will not pose the inventory manager problems, since if we provide sufficient stock to meet average demand anything occurring below it would be satisfied. The problem demands are those that are greater than the average. Consider the following diagram:

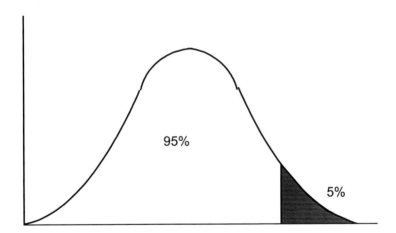

For example, in the diagram it is planned to meet 95% of the demand and 5% would not be met.

It is important to remember that we cannot plan to cover 100% of the curve because it does not cross the horizontal axis! In other words we must recognise that we cannot plan to be in stock 100% of the time. In practice this could happen because the demands that occur are below our expectations, but we can't plan for it. Consequently we have to choose some other level. In this example we have chosen 95%.

The question now becomes what level of demand does this 95% represent?

Fortunately, the normal distribution has been further analysed by statisticians and the following table determined; for example, 95% is 1.64 standard deviations.

Service Level	SD Factor		Service Level	SD Factor
50.00%	0.00		90.00%	1.28
55.00%	0.13		91.00%	1.34
60.00%	0.25		92.00%	1.41
65.00%	0.39		93.00%	1.48
70.00%	0.52		94.00%	1.55
75.00%	0.67		95.00%	1.64
80.00%	0.84		96.00%	1.75
81.00%	0.88		97.00%	1.88
82.00%	0.92		98.00%	2.05
83.00%	0.95		99.00%	2.33
84.00%	0.99		99.50%	2.58
85.00%	1.04		99.60%	2.65
86.00%	1.08		99.70%	2.75
87.00%	1.13		99.80%	2.88
88.00%	1.17		99.90%	3.09
89.00%	1.23		99.99%	3.72

To illustrate its use, let's return to our example of an item with average demand 100 and standard deviation of 10. We can determine the level of demand we need to provide cover by performing the following calculation:

Demand Level = Average demand + (Service level factor x Standard deviation)

Our aim to provide cover for 95% means that we must be able to cover: 100 + (1.64x10) = 116.4. The additional 16.4 above the average demand of 100 would be our safety stock.

It is important to note that this is only the start of safety stock and as we progress there will be other factors that need to be considered. The service level factor has been found from the table by finding 95% in the first column and then looking to the right of it to find 1.64.

This means that for this item, with an average demand of 100 and an SD of 10, there is a 95% chance that a demand will occur less than or equal to 116.4. There is a 5% chance that a demand will occur that is greater than 116.4.

If we change our 95% target to 99% our demand level changes to:
100 + (2.33 x 10) = 123.3. This means that there is a 1% chance of receiving a demand greater than 123.3. In this case safety stock would be 23.3.

The service level factor represents the probability of having a stock out. Another way of looking at this is that with a target of 95% we can expect that 5 time periods out of every 100 there will be stock out. Of course it does not tell us which 5 periods they will be, it could be the first 5, the last 5 or they could be spread about the 100 periods. This definition of service is different to the more usual inventory service level of availability.

Availability or fill rate is determined by dividing the amount of demand satisfied by the amount of demand requested. Using our 95% example above, if a demand of 117 occurred; it would be one of the 5% of occasions when we would expect a demand greater than 116.4. However, we would be able to satisfy 116.4 giving a fill rate of 116.4/117 or 99.5%; a bigger service level than our target 95%.
Using probability of stock out definitions, usually yield higher fill rates than the target figure.

The critical thing to recognise here is the effect on the amount of safety stock as the target service level increases.

Notice that if we move from 90% to 95%, the service level factor increases from 1.28 to 1.64; a 28% increase.

If we move from 95% to 99.99% (almost 100%) the same 5% increases the service level factor from 1.64 to 3.72 a huge 227% increase.

Increasing service levels therefore gives an exponential increase in the extra safety stock required. The relationship between the stock held and the service level is not a linear one, as for example, a 3% increase in stock does not equal a 3% increase in the extra stock required. This means that careful consideration should be given to the setting of the target service level, since once we progress beyond 95%, it will carry a big financial impact from the holding of extra safety stock.

Notice also, that the service level factor for 50% is 0. Clearly if we plan to meet average demand we will be able to satisfy any demand that occurs below it. Meanwhile, the relationship between service level and safety stock is shown graphically on the opposite page. The selection of the appropriate service level is an important management decision. Increasing the target could be an offensive tactic to try and win market share from a competitor. Alternatively, it could be used

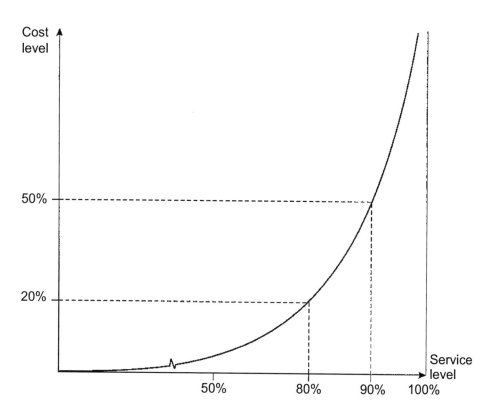

defensively to prevent a competitor from taking your market share. In practice though the target is often set using noise levels, for example, if you keep getting complaints about being out of stock, raise the target a little. Keep doing this until you receive no complaints and then you know you have perhaps gone a little too high?

Of course, the idea of setting say a 90% service level for stock availability is fraught with problems both for customers and for sales/marketing departments. All they rightly expect is 100% service and levels below this will mean little to them. There comes a point when the extra sales secured from the higher service level are more than offset by the extra stock costs so reducing profitability. The key aspect here however, is to explore other tactics to ensure customers will always get their demand requirement satisfied.

For example, suppose we satisfy 90% from stock but then place the other 10% on back order providing an accurate delivery date. In many cases this might be acceptable and thus it would influence how the level is set in the first place, what the extra costs are for maintaining higher levels stock and also how the supply chain is being operated.

In many companies the majority of profit will come from a relatively small number of lines; the 80/20 rule again. For the profitable lines we might set a higher target level, whilst for the less profitable lines we might reduce it. Therefore, safety stock levels can be set to minimise the value that may be on back order and therefore minimise the cost to the company. Whilst lost sales are extremely difficult to analyse, some companies do have the view that it is better to let a competitor have such sales, as this prevents the high cost of stocking for relatively low profit lines.

Slow demand items and Poisson distribution

The normal demand distribution applies for fast moving items only. The other type of items is slow moving. These items follow a distribution called the Poisson distribution. The Poisson distribution was derived by the French mathematician Poisson in 1837, and the first application was the description of the number of deaths caused by horse kicking in the Prussian army.

Slow demand items are defined as those where the demand pattern has a high proportion of zero demand time periods. For example, spare parts for a machine will have many periods of zero demand with the occasional period when 1 or 2 are required. In most cases the average demand for such items is usually small.

In constructing a histogram for slow demand items it can be seen that applying the normal distribution as a basis for designing a control system is unacceptable.

The approach for this type of item, therefore, is to use an alternative known as the 'Poisson Distribution', which describes the basic pattern of variation of demand of slow moving items.

An example of a slow demand item would be: 0 1 0 0 0 0 2 0 0 1 0

Assuming that this pattern represents the demand for an item over ten periods - say weeks - the average demand is 4/10 = 0.4 per week. Clearly it is not possible to use 0.4 items. The actual usage would be integer values (1, 2, 3, and very occasionally 4).

The variance (the standard deviation squared) is 0.44 - is very close to the mean. Put another way, the Standard Deviation will be close to the square root of the mean.

The Law of Poisson Distribution

The law of the Poisson distribution enables calculation of the probability that a given number of events will occur provided the average number (e.g. usage per week) is known, and is constant over time.

Questions	Answers
Do all items with a low average demand conform to the Poisson distribution (i.e. that the Standard Deviation is close to the square root of the mean?	No. e.g. Demand over ten periods = 0, 0, 0, 0, 10, 0,0,0,0,0 　Total = 　　10 　Av - 　　　1 　Std Deviation = 3 　Variance 　= 9 This demand would be termed 'LUMPY' as well as slow-moving.
If slow-moving 'lumpy' items fall outside the range of the Poisson and the Normal distributions – how are they managed?	Typically such items are associated with one user. They can best be managed by being aware of them, and by trying to identify the timing of the need. They can then be made or purchased in anticipation of the need.
What sorts of items have Poisson demand characteristics?	High value consumer products, engineering spares, vehicle spares, many retail products at stock level.
Is it mainly the higher value items that would be managed in this way?	Yes. A two-bin replenishment process could manage low value slow movers, with each replenishment covering 3-6 months of demand.
At what level of demand does the need for using the Poisson distribution become less related?	Once the level of demand is above one unit per time period, e.g. 2-3 per period would make the Normal distribution more appropriate.

The Poisson tables (in the appendix) show the probability of an event, e.g. a product being requested. Given that the average period demand is known to be 1.5 per week, then the tables indicate the probability of various weekly demands.

Here is the part of the Poisson table relating to an average demand of 1.5 per period.

M =	1.5
r = 0	1.000
r = 1	0.7769
r = 2	0.4422
r = 3	0.1912
r = 4	0.0656
r = 5	0.0186
r = 6	0.0045
r = 7	0.0009
r = 8	0.0002

M =   the average demand per period; in inventory demand this would typically be a day, week, or a month.

r =   random events, e.g. r = 3 is read as meaning the probability of 3 or more events occurring, given that the average number of events per period is 1.5

The value of 0.1912 is equivalent to 19.12%. As you move down the table you will see that the probability gets smaller.

The first value r = 0 is 1.000. This is read as "the probability of 0 or more is a certainty". This is because, in probability theory, certainly is described as having a probability of 1.0.

You will see that the first entry of every column in the table is 1.0. By definition, the tables do not allow negative (less than zero) values. Each line on the table shows the probability of (N) or more. How can this be used to show the probability of individual values?

The probability of any of the values shown is calculated as follows:

- To find the probability of zero demand \ (H)   =   0
- The probability of 0 or more   =   1.000
- The probability of (H + 1), 1 or more   =   0.7769
- Therefore, the probability of 0 being demand is   =   0.2231

The probability of (H) = $\left\{ \begin{array}{l} \text{Probability of} \\ \text{H or more} \end{array} - \begin{array}{l} \text{Probability of (H+1)} \\ \text{or more} \end{array} \right\}$

From the Poisson table it will be seen that final demand figure quoted is 8. Beyond that number, the probability is considered not measurable.

The above calculations can also be expressed in terms of the number of weeks of each demand occurring during the total time period for which the average was established.

In the example above let us assume that the average demand was based on a 52 week time period.

The expected number of weeks when the demand will be:

0 is 1.000 - 0.7769 = 0.2231 or 22.31% or 12 weeks
1 is 0.7769 - 0.4422 = 0.3347 or 33.47% or 17 weeks
2 is 0.4422 - 0.1912 = 0.2510 or 25.10% or 13 weeks
3 is 0.1912 - 0.0656 = 0.1256 or 12.56% or 7 weeks

The calculation can be extended until all 52 weeks are covered.

The same technique can also be used in determining the probability of the total demand over a specified lead-time given an average demand.

Lead-time 4 weeks.

Average Demand over the Lead-time 0.3 per week.
What is the probability of the total demand over the lead-time exceeding:

1.   3
2.   4

From the Poisson Table for an average of 1.2 per time period.

1.   Probability of demand exceeding 3 is equal to the probability of demand
       of 4 or more = 0.0338 or 3.38%.

2.   Probability of demand exceeding 4 is equal to the probability of demand
       of 5 or more = 0.0077 or 0.77%.

The above examples are the basis upon which control systems are established for slow demand items with a recognised Poisson Distribution pattern.

Control system for slow moving items
The control system used for slow demand items is similar to that of the Periodic Review System for fast moving items in that a maximum stock level is established together with an Imprest Ordering System based on the principle of one issued, one ordered.

To establish the maximum stock level the following information is required:

1.   Average Demand per time period.
2.   Supply Lead-time.
3.   Target Service Level.

These together with the use of the Poisson Tables will establish:
*   The maximum stock level.
*   The related service level.
*   The related percentage probability of a stock out.

Example:
Average demand per period 0.4
Supply lead-time periods 4.0
Target service level 95%
Average demand over the lead-time 0.4 x 4.0 = 1.6

Step 1
Establish from the Poisson Tables the probability of the range of demands. For a demand over the lead-time of 1.6 provides the following:

Demand Over The Lead	Probability	
0	0.2019	= 1 - 0.7981
1	0.3230	= 0.7981 - 0.4751 etc.
2	0.2585	
3	0.1378	
4	0.0551	
5	0.0177	
6	0.0047	
7 or more	0.0010	

Example:

Average lead-time demand = 1.6

The probability of 3 items being demanded is:

                Probability of 3 or more = 0.2166 (21.66%)
Less   Probability of 4 or more = 0.0788 (7.88%)
=   Probability of demand   = 0.1378 (13.78%)
                for three items

Step 2
Calculate the number of times of being out of stock over the lead-time for various levels of maximum stock.

Note: the important assumption here that when an item is taken from stock, a replacement is ordered. If two items are taken from stock, a replacement order for two will be raised.

This model is designed to set a reorder point, which will give the required level of service during the replenishment cycle. The higher the reorder point, the lower the probability of running out during the replenishment cycle.

The calculation proceeds as follows. Select a reorder point, and then calculate the probability of various demands exceeding that reorder point. Thus if 2 is selected on the reorder point you must calculate the probability that it will be exceeded by 1, 2, 3 and so on.

This is how to set out the evaluation.

$(3 - 2)$ x probability of 3 (see table above)

=	(3 - 2) x .1378	=	.1378
+	(4 - 2) x .0551	=	.1102
+	(5 - 2) x .0177	=	.0531
+	(6 - 2) x .0047	=	.0188
+	(7 - 2) x .0010	=	.0050
	Average stockout	=	.3249

Step 3
With a reorder point of 3, repeat the calculation as follows:

=	$(4 - 3)$ x .0551	=	.0551	(Probability of 4)
+	$(5 - 3)$ x .0177	=	.0354	
+	$(6 - 3)$ x .0047	=	.0141	
+	$(7 - 3)$ x .0010	=	.0040	
	Average stockout	=	.1086	

Step 4
Calculate the service level given by each reorder point as follows:

$$Service\ Level = 1 - \frac{Average\ Stockout}{Average\ Lead\text{-}time\ Demand} \times 100$$

With a reorder point of 2:

$$Service\ Level = 1 - \frac{0.3249}{1.6} \times 100$$

Service level = 79.69%

With a reorder point of 3 the calculation is:

$$Service\ Level = 1 - \frac{0.1086}{1.6} \times 100$$

Service Level = 93.2%

The Summary table looks like this:

Reorder Point	% Service Level
2	79.69
3	93.21
4	98.12
5	99.58
6	99.94

Questions	Answers
Would this be an EOQ calculated slow moving item?	Since they are often high value, these items are replenished on a "use-one, buy-one" basis.
Given that some stock is used before the reorder point is reached, as an EOQ is not being used to what level would the stock be restored?	This would depend on the average period demand. In the example above, the average period demand is 0.4. This would be rounded up to 1. Therefore, for any required level of service – determined by the reorder point – 1 more would be added to give an 'order up to level'.
What would be the 'order up to level' if the average period demand was 1.1?	Two would be added to the reorder point, which gave the required service level.
What assumption is made about lead times with this type of model?	Lead times are assumed to be fixed – and in many cases this may be 6-12 weeks.
Do the reorder points for these items need to be revised?	Yes. Because the average demand, and the average lead time can change over time. Therefore, the reorder point, for high value items should be reviewed 3-4 times per year.
Once a replenishment cycle has been started – by stock falling to or below the reorder point, how are future demands during lead time handled?	By restoring the stock on hand plus the stock on order to the specified level about the reorder point.

The table below shows how stock flows out of the system, and is replaced on a 'use-one, buy-one' basis.

Assume a reorder point of 4 is set for an item of average period demand of 0.4, and a lead-time of 4 periods, giving a lead-time demand of 1.6. On top of this a further 1 unit is added. Therefore, assuming there has been no demand for 5 periods the stock on hand will be 5, with no outstanding replenishment orders. The next few weeks might look like this:

	Opening Stock	Usage	Closing Stock	Order placed + on hand	Stock Rec'd
Week 25	5	0	5	-	-
Week 26	5	2	3	2	-
Week 27	3	0	3	2	-
Week 28	3	1	2	3	-
Week 29	2	0	2	3	-
Week 30	2	2	2 (2-2+2)	3	2
Week 31	2	0	2	3	-
Week 32	2	1	2 (2-1+1)	3	1
Week 33	2	0	2	3	-
Week 34	2	1	3 (2-1+2)	2	2

The average closing stock is **26/10** = 2.6

Not all slow-moving demand items can be managed in the way described so far. Whilst the average period demand may appear to lie within the level where Poisson can be used, the pattern of demand may prevent its use.

An example might be:

0, 0, 0, 75, 0, 0, 25, 0, 0, 150

=	Total demand	= 250
	Average demand	= 250/10 = 25
	Variance	= 2250
	Standard deviation	= 47.4 (square roof of variance)

A simple measure to decide whether a pattern of demand can be managed using the Poisson distribution is to compare the variance with the mean. In this instance, the variance is much greater than the mean. So although most of the periods have zero demands (one of the main criteria for designating an item as slow-moving), this cannot be managed in this way.

The design of a control system for such items is almost impossible. It is necessary to establish if the demands are:

- Totally random.
- Are time correlated.
- Related to specific customer ordering patterns.

The decision on how much to hold in stock usually depends on the level of desired service and the level of investment cost that is considered acceptable.

The processes described for managing slow-moving stock are undoubtedly difficult to understand. It is however very important for many companies because it provides a structure for dealing with some very expensive parts of the inventory, whether in a vehicle repair shop, an engineering spares store, or in a warehouse/ retail environment.

2: Inventory Key Concepts

In this part of the book we look fully into the Key Concepts in inventory and examine the following:

- Demand analysis, including product classifications, dependent and independent demand, demand profiling, ABC analysis.

- Demand forecasting, including forecasting processes and method with characteristics and approaches. Finally, forecast errors, tracking signals and seasonal forecasts are examined.

- Lead-time; as this is often misunderstood, we concentrate on a full explanation and show its criticality in inventory management and how lead time should be examined and improved.

- Cost and benefits looks at methods of valuing the impact on financial analysis such as revenue, balance sheets, share capital, cash flow and return on investment.

Key Component - Demand analysis

Product Classification

Product is received from a supplier into stores and warehouses and at some later time (maybe within hours or within years), it is then despatched to meet a demand from a customer/user that may be located internally or externally.

The product being supplied will have resulted from the company inventory ordering policy. These will involve the "when to order" and the "how much to order" replenishment decisions. The product being despatched will be dependant upon the demand patterns arising from the customer orders. In turn, the despatch of the order to customers will give rise to replenishment and the supply cycle starts once again.

Analysis of demand is therefore important as it is the demand that "kick starts" the whole supply chain process. Many organisations therefore place emphasis on demand, and create demand driven supply networks (complete with its own acronym, DDSN). With many intermediate points between demand and supply where data can be monitored and analysed, the resulting information is used for decisions on making, stocking and allocating products.

In the DDSN model, demand visibility can be the real time insight into what is happening with consumers (for example on the shelf in retail stores) and this, combined with wider demand intelligence such as forecasting, will identify what is needed and when.

Such demand visibility is afforded by appropriate use of ICT in the supply chain, right from the place of use/consumption to the modelling of where stocks are needed, to placing supplier orders and transit monitoring up to receipts. This end-to-end visibility has demand as the starting point, but it is clearly also related to supply; they are inter-dependent processes.

Central to the management of inventory is the issue of risk. Each product will have a different risk profile depending upon its market, profile and value. There are two sources of risk: supplier reliability and forecast error. Forecast error represents the demand side risk and supplier reliability represents the supply side risk. These two risk sources are multiplied by the lead-time of supply. The longer this supply lead-time; the greater the risk that things can go wrong.

Strategic plans derived from the companies objectives will link to the marketing and service strategies that will drive the targets required for availability. As we noted earlier, the setting of availability targets is a key management activity.

The combination of availability target with the sources and multipliers of risk, dictate the level of inventory investment of each line item. In turn this investment profile then dictates the ordering pattern from the supplier.

Since the purpose of holding stock is to satisfy future demand, it is important to understand the characteristics of the demand behaviour. To undertake this correctly, every individual line/product/ stock keeping unit (SKU) will need to be examined. This will also help to determine product requirements from a stockholding point of view.

Independent and Dependant demand

Demand is found in two basic forms:

1. Independent or random demand is that which is independent of all other products; e.g. tyre manufacturer with tyres needed for puncture repairs. It is the classic consumer driven demand for "end use" products or services and therefore is more random with uncertainty being found. This does not have a consistent pattern and may have high or low volumes. It uses re-order point/level (ROP/ROL) systems for inventory management/ replenishment. These systems will be fully examined in Chapter 3.

2. Dependant or predicative demand is that derived from consumer demand which produces "end use" products or services: e.g. tyre manufacturer for new cars; this being driven by the derived requirement for new cars and is planned for by the car assembler based on their view of the independent demand from consumers. Dependant demand is therefore found commonly in manufacturing or kitting environments where a plan (such as a Master Production Schedule) has been already established based on a forecast.

With dependant demand, this means that the previous event has to happen first and that subsequent events will then depend on the ones preceding them. Dependant demand is more consistent, with there being some degree of certainty about orders. It is therefore more certain for the upstream suppliers, enabling some degree of anticipation, for example the tyre manufacturer obtains from the car assemblers their forward planning on production. It uses requirement/ resource planning systems (RP). These systems will be looked at in Chapter 3.3

Comparisons of dependant and independant demand

Feature	Dependant demand	Independent demand
Replenishment method	MRP /MRPII/DRP	ROP/ROL
Orientation	Product components	All individual parts/items
Demand patterns	Lumpy and discrete patterns	More continuous patterns
Order signal	Time phased	ROP/ROL
Time perspective	Future production /sales	Historic demand often will greatly help to predict the future
Forecasts	Forecast is on the final end items only	Forecast on all items
Safety Stock	Safety stock is carried for the end items	Safety stock is carried

Demand profiling

As first steps, then the following profiles are looked for in demand analysis, where group one to four will apply to every item/line/SKU whereas group five applies in specific instances only:

Group 1: pattern of demand

*   Stable demand is represented by an average demand that remains constant from period to period. Whilst there may be peaks and troughs of demand the average remains more or less the same. It is possible to have stable demand items that have a high level of volatility, sometimes referred to as lumpy demand or a low level of volatility.

*   Trend demand is displayed where average demand can be either upwards/ positive/rising, for example following a successful promotion where demand per period is increasing, or can be downwards / negative / falling, for example at the end of a products life cycle where demand per period is decreasing (see diagram overleaf).

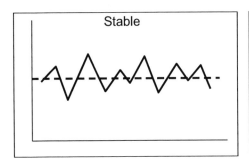

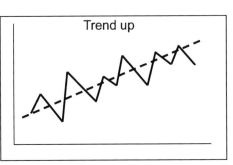

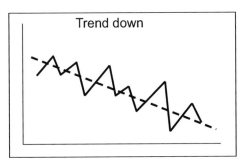

Group two: movement of demand

- High movement has a relatively consistent high volume.
- Slow movement is relatively consistent but with low volume.

Group three: value of product/item

- High or low product value.

Group four: frequency of demand

- Frequency of demand can follow a normal distribution curve for the most fast to medium products. With slow moving products that have many zero demands, a poisson distribution maybe needed; this deals with low probability events.

Group five: other aspects that may be involved in demand analysis are as follows:

- Seasonality is where the pattern of average demand is repeated over time; this can be annually, like holiday periods such as Christmas, other once per year celebrations like lemons for the English pancake eating day, monthly following consumers pay time, and weekly, as with one main day for food shopping. This is called step seasonality. The peak periods tend to be quite short. Alternatively we have an evolving seasonal pattern where demand gradually increases as we move into the peak season and then gradually declines as we move out of the season. UK examples of this might be sales of ice cream as we enter summer and sales of snow chains for cars as winter begins.

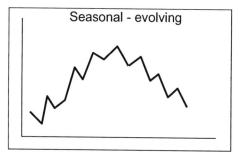

Seasonal - evolving

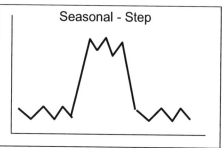

Seasonal - Step

- Promotions typically will give a sharp increase in demand. This is then followed by a sharp decrease in demand, as re-orders are delayed until the promotional items have been used/consumed. Similar types of promotions often display a similar type of profile, which can then be used to manage them.

- Product life cycle; for example new products being launched and promoted need higher levels of stock than those declining and diminishing products. The product life cycle can also be profiled to help with management.

- Obsolescence; this is where there is no demand over a long period, typically over one year. This may be due to technical changes, spoilage or defects, although it can be because the item is no longer required. In this latter event, this of course should ideally have been pre-notified so that stock levels could have been reduced. Whilst some long time stock holding may be necessary for some zero demand items, for example with critical spares, often no real examination is undertaken on all the obsolete lines; they are therefore not declared as being dead stock.

There is also often a natural reluctance to admit items need disposal, for many it seems to represent "failure" as perhaps the items should never have been ordered in the first place? This reluctance may also be due to the perceived lack of future availability to service any future "rogue" demand or may be due to writing off the money that has been spent. The best approach however, is to undertake as policy, a continuous review of the entire obsolete inventory and arrange for scheduled write offs in small amounts on a regular basis.

Finally, demand must also, critically, be related to the service levels (the availability from the stock holding). For example, on the amount of stock being held to give availability, where say a 70 per cent stock cover may be held for slow moving and less critical items, and 95 per cent for fast moving and critical line items.

Any given product can be categorised against each of the above and as an example, for a UK based fast moving grocery product range:

- Stable / Seasonal demand: the staple items like milk, bread, petfood are stable / seasonal lines are Jiffy lemons for Pancake Day and tinned soups in winter.

- Fast/ slow demand: the staple items / baked beans with taco sauce flavouring.

- High value/ Low value: baked beans with taco sauce/ budget priced items and the staple items that will be most likely be very competitively priced to attract shoppers into the store.

- Product life cycle – launching: "fashion products" like alcopops of the mid 1990s and the smaller-sized mobile phones in the 2000s.

- Product life cycle - diminishing: "mild" beer and the older larger mobile phones.

- Low service level/ high service level: beans with taco sauce/ the staple items.

It can be seen here that the staple items like baked beans, bread, milk, pet food are the fast movers, having stable demand requiring high service levels but with a low value. Meanwhile slow movers are more random but have a higher value and lower service level. However, these distinctions on the slow movers are not absolute as each "unique" and different product will have different patterns and can also be viewed differently by different companies; for example high value items may have a high profit margin and mean that high stock levels are required so as to ensure both high availability and profitability.

A critical point here is that each company will have its own specific demand categorisations and for example, where inventory controls may be managed as part of Materials Management or Purchasing & Supply management, then the following categories may be found (taken specifically from oil production but also used by other organisations):

The point to be appreciated with Demand Analysis is that to be effective, each company must undertake their own demand analysis.

Category	Description	Demand characteristics
Maintenance repair and operating or overhaul (MRO) items:	Spares etc and daily used consumables(such as office supplies)	Slow moving mainly with a few fast moving items, mainly independent demand. Some dependant demand for scheduled maintenance e.g. shutdowns.
Maintenance items	Non-time critical and dependant demand.	
Repair items (for breakdowns)	Time critical and independent demand.	
Operating items	Non-time critical and independent demand.	
Project materials	Specific items e.g. for a new manufacturing plant	One off usually phased in with building / construction schedules. Dependent demand.
"Insurance " items	Critical spares and items that are held in case of a need where the costs of non-availability are high e.g. chemicals for a LNG plant	Used only in exceptional cases. Watch for obsolescence. Independent demand.
Surplus	Have no foreseeable use	Use as substitutes, move to salvage/"scrap"
Programme materials	Support normal work programmes e.g. drilling sequence in oil exploration	Planned and predictable. Dependant demand
Direct charge	Acquired for specific and immediate use and charged directly to revenue account	Ad hoc, maybe call offs from suppliers

ABC Analysis

If there are lots of individual items that need managing it is sensible to target management time to those items that are important. A useful analysis to enable the identification of important items is to analyse the products in terms of high/ low movers using ABC Analysis. This involves the classic Pareto analysis named after the Italian economist who, in 1906, reckoned that 80 % of the wealth lay in the hands of 20 % of the population. So, the other name for this type of analysis is the 80/20 rule, where a high incidence in one set of variables equates to a smaller incidence in a corresponding set of variables.

The best way to demonstrate this is by the following simple exercise:

Question:
Conduct an ABC Analysis on the following demand volume information.
300, 40, 25, 15, 8, 5, 4, 3, 2, 225, 30, 15, 10, 150, 6, 5, 25, 4, 3, 125

Answer:
By ranking in high to low demand order, in the following table, we can make the calculations as shown:

Volume High to Low	Cumulative Volume	% of Cumulative Volume	No of Items	% of Items	
300	300	30	1	5	
225	525	52.5	2	10	**A**
150	675	67.5	3	15	**items**
125	800	80	4	20	
40	840	84	5	25	
30	870	87	6	30	**B**
25	895	89.5	7	35	**items**
25	920	92	8	40	
15	935	93.5	9	45	
15	950	95	10	50	
10	960	96.0	11	55	
8	968	96.8	12	60	
6	974	97.4	13	65	
5	979	97.9	14	70	**C**
5	984	98.4	15	75	**items**
4	988	98.8	16	80	
4	992	99.2	17	85	
3	995	99.5	18	90	
3	998	99.8	19	95	
2	1000	100	20	100	

It will be seen that this simple exercise comes out classically at 80/20. In reality there would be much more volume demand information, but the calculations would be same. However, where the lines would be drawn between "A" and "B" and "C" items is arbitrary and is a matter of judgement.

Indeed, it could be possible to make the break down, into say around 10 items categories, such as AAA, AA and A items (very fast, fast, slower fast), 3 x B items etc. When graphed, the following relationship is found; in this example the ABC analysis shows that:

A - 20% of items represent 80% of profit, sales or usage.
B - Next 30% represents a further 15% of profit, sales or usage.
C - Next 50% of items represent only 5% of profit, sales or usage.

ABC Analysis

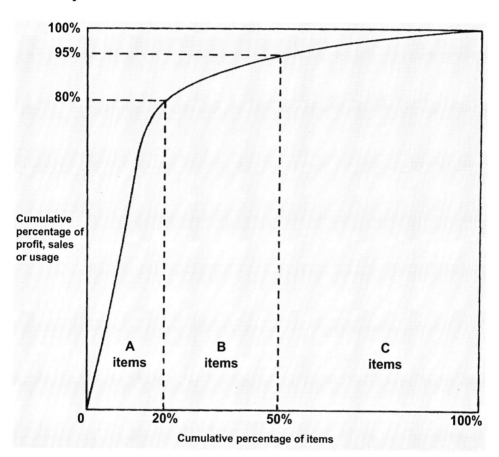

Sometimes it is useful to trace the curve from the bottom left to look for points where the slope of the curve significantly changes. These are called break points. The first break point happens where 20% of the items provide 80% of the demand. As progress is made along the curve it can become harder to spot the break points.

Whatever method of categorising is done the principle is the same; that a high percentage of, for example, volume movement, is found from a small number of lines – the A items above (the fast movers), and the converse, that the slow movers (the C items above), will account for a high number of lines for a low percentage of volume movement.

To summarise then:
- A items: high movers = high volume, few lines
- B items: medium movers = medium volume, medium lines
- C items: low movers = low volume, many lines

ABC Analysis is usually undertaken in two formats. The first one is based on demand/ sales/ usage. The second uses demand value, which is derived by multiplying the demand volume by the cost of the item; these figures provide the basis for the first column and then the rest of the table is completed in a similar way to that shown above.

When the results of the two analyses are compared it is likely that different items will appear as A items in each list. In those organisations such as retailing, where there is a requirement to ensure items are stocked to give both a high volume of sales and also a high value of sales; the results can be merged to form a joint list.

Meanwhile additional categories can be used, as shown below for MRO items (taken from a case study latter in the book).

- A Fast moving

- B Moving

- C Slow moving

- D Very slow moving

- E Slowest moving

- F Non moving, in a defined time frame, but which still need to be stocked

- G Highly critical and / or insurance materials that must be held in stock

- H Dead or obsolete awaiting signature or verification

- I Buried which are the materials awaiting final disposition

- J Unknown

Key Component - Demand Forecasting
When demand levels are not known exactly, as with independent demand, then forecasting proactively aims to give the best estimate of future demand and to predict changes. With fast moving consumer goods (FMCG), forecasting is a key aspect in replenishment. Forecasting also aims, reactively, to minimise errors in previous forecasts (i.e. the difference between the forecast and what actually happened).

A simple view of forecasting is provided as follows:

Forecasting rules
Forecasting is easier when:
- Product is old and established
- Product is a consumer product (end demand)
- Demand is stable
- Time period is short

Forecasting is harder when:
- Product is new and starting
- Product is a part/ assembly of a consumer product
- Demand is erratic
- Time period is long

It can be recalled that the purpose of holding inventory is to be able to satisfy future consumer demand. In situations where the consumer order cycle time is shorter than the time it takes the supplier to capture the order, make and deliver the goods, it will be necessary for the supplier for the supplier to hold stock. In such situations forecasting is needed to determine when a demand will occur so that appropriate actions can be taken.

Opinions on forecasting are as diverse as views on any scientific subject. Some may question the validity of an activity that is aimed at predicting an uncertain future. However, it should be recognised that substantial progress has been made in the forecasting area over the last few decades aided by a dramatic increase in computing power. There are also a large number of phenomena whose outcomes can be easily predicted.

Forecasting is a process and like any process, if it is not understood and managed, then it will not produce the expected outputs. We will therefore look at the following:

* The forecasting process and how it combines with other business activity
* Different forecast methods that can be utilised
* Characteristics of the forecasting task
* An approach for forecasting
* The decomposition of demand data into its component parts
* Measuring forecast error and performance
* Forecasting using time series analysis
* Seasonal forecasting
* Using profiles in forecasting

Forecast Process

A forecast alone may not always be directly useful to management. An organisation must know how to use the forecast effectively and exploit its information.

It is important to distinguish between uncontrollable external events and controllable internal events. The external events are linked to developments in the economy, and actions from governments, customers, suppliers and competitors; these are the events that forecasting help to predict. The internal events happen as a result of decisions in marketing, manufacturing and other functions and success comes from being able to combine both the decision-making and forecasting. This integration is the domain of planning.

This realisation is particularly important in the area of demand forecasting. The external factors that could impact demand are:

- **Economy:** trend and cycle of economy, consumer expectations and confidence, prices and characteristics of competing products.

- **Customers:** the number of customers, characteristics of customer incomes, cash and level of debt, existing levels of stocks and rate of usage, product preferences.

- **Competitors:** level of advertising and sales effort, prices, distribution capability and level of availability, product features and launch of new products, production levels, inventories and capacity availability.

- **Distributors:** efficiency of channel usage, level of inventories, competitive effectiveness.

All of the above are largely uncontrollable. On the other side there are the internal factors, most of which are controllable:

- **Company marketing activity:** level of advertising and sales effort, prices, distribution capability and level of availability, product features and launch of new products.

- **Company production activity:** capacity levels, current inputs and labour employed, inventories, production methods and costs, new products scheduled.

- **Company financial activity:** cash position, level of receivables, credit policy competition for funds, position in the reporting calendar.

- **Company leadership:** company goals for profit, return on capital employed, market share.

In common use of the word, forecasting can use subjective or objective methods. It is important to appreciate the differences here as in inventory management we should be dealing with objective facts; forecasting in inventory management is concerned with the manipulation of data in a scientific and an objective way.

Subjective methods may be educated guesses, "crystal ball gazing" or "blue skying". Additionally, the forecasting of customers demand can come from varied subjective sources such as a marketer's special "feel" or from competitor activity that has just "appeared" and needs reacting to etc. This is not to say that such subjective methods have no value, they clearly may have when they are undertaken by experienced people, for example with a brand new product launch. However if the promotion of such products is not correctly considered and not planned and coordinated correctly between internal departments (for example, retail stores, buyers, marketing, distribution, inventory control) and the external suppliers, then the resulting incorrect forecasting of demand will cause ripples and Forrester effects in the supply chain and result eventually in un-sold stocks.

Objective methods however, involve a mathematical statistical analysis of past demand to predict the future. From the inventory management view of forecasting, this is exactly what forecasting is: the analysis of historical and actual demand patterns.

Demand Forecasting will therefore be easier when product is:
* old and established.
* the product is a consumer product where the end demand is more visible.
* when the demand is stable.
* the time period is short.

Demand forecasting will be more difficult when the product is:
* new and launching.
* the product is a part/ assembly of a consumer product and may therefore suffer from "Forrester effects".
* when the demand is erratic, for example due to new competitor activity that is taking away sales or due to short term weather pattern changes.
* when the time period is far into the future, as forecasts further out have higher errors than forecasts for tomorrow.

Sales and Operating Process

Recognising the role of forecasting in an organisational planning context is as important as calculating the forecast itself. An example of this is how forecasting fits within a sales and operating planning process (S&OP). This is a process that enables the organisation to create one plan with one set of numbers and a one forecast. It is usually performed on a regular cycle, such as monthly.

Sales and Operating Process

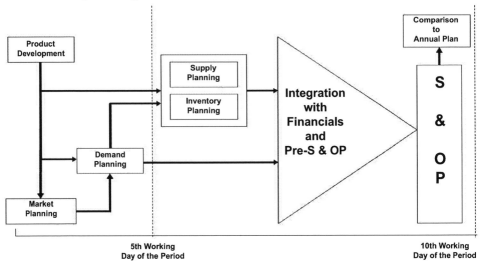

The S&OP process starts with the product development team specifying any new products or modifications to existing ones. This product development should operate to a strict guideline timetable to ensure that launch dates are set with due regard to production and material supply lead-times. Information from here is then fed into both the demand and supply reviews.

The demand review is the forum that establishes the unconstrained forecast of demand. By unconstrained we mean that it determines what the demand could be if there was no constraints on supply. This demand review is a crucial part of the forecast process and we will examine it in more detail later.

Output from the demand review is then fed into the supply and inventory review. This review considers the forecast demand and determines how much will need to be manufactured and when to meet it. Any building of inventory, for maintenance or holiday shutdowns, will also be incorporated. This is then matched with the available capacity.

Any issues that emerge from the reviews will be presented to the pre-SOP for resolution. For example, if there is insufficient capacity decisions will need to be made to acquire it from elsewhere or to constrain demand by perhaps allocating stock to customers. During the pre-SOP the financial implications are also considered and comparisons are made against the company plan to check whether or not the goals will be achieved. The pre-SOP then presents its plans to the full SOP for ratification. The SOP is usually chaired by a senior manager and its decisions provide the authority for materials to be purchased and products to be made.

The S&OP process is a disciplined process that follows a strict timetable for when activity needs to be completed to allow the next stage of the process to be performed on time. When it operates well it removes the noise and uncertainty from operations and ensures that everyone in the organisation is working to the same plan.

So forecasting is an integral part of the S&OP process but unless we recognise its role and the accompanying objectives its importance is likely to be diminished.

The Demand Review in S&OP
Let's examine the demand review in more detail:

Demand Review

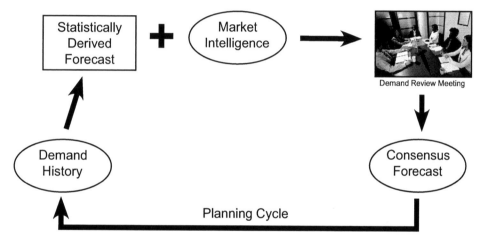

The first step of the review is to gather the base demand data that will be used. It is important to be clear about what the data represents. Although we often call it demand usually it represents something entirely different. It might be orders from the immediate customer who then supplies the consumer. It could be shipments to the next stage in the supply chain. It might even be just sales, representing the quantity that we could satisfy.

This "demand" data will likely contain some inconsistencies caused by disruptions in the supply pattern or special events. For example, if the item is out of stock its possible that orders would not be accepted and hence the recorded demand would appear to be less. It is important therefore that we cleanse this data so that it only includes information that represents acceptable or typical demand. This is often done by setting system filters to exclude the periods of demand that are not typical.

The cleansed data can then be inputted into the forecasting system to produce a baseline forecast. The baseline forecast seeks to fit a mathematical equation to the historic demand pattern so that it can be extrapolated into the future. In essence it is saying that the future will look like the past, assuming you will continue to do the same things in the future. This is an important point, since if the historical situation will not be repeated in the future, an alternative forecasting method must be used.

The baseline forecast can then be presented to the demand review group who will discuss whether or not additional activity will need to be accounted for. The baseline forecast provides the science; the demand review provides the judgment. The judgmental aspect is usually much more subjective based opinion, rather than, hard data. At this review meeting, additional internal and external factors will be discussed. Internal factors include promotional activity and price changes. These are things that we have control over and if used correctly can shift or create demand. Also external factors, such as competitor activity will need to be considered.

This demand review meeting should produce a consensus forecast having taking into account the statistical baseline, internal and external factors. This forecast will be documented at SKU level along with the assumptions and any reasons for changes since the last meeting. It is important to document the assumptions made. It is much more useful to challenge assumptions than the size of specific forecasts. If they are not documented, people will not remember why they altered the baseline forecast. Similarly there should be specific reasons for changing forecasts period to period and the changes must therefore be identified and recorded. As a consequence of the judgmental nature of the demand review, it is often useful to monitor the forecast accuracy of both the baseline and consensus forecast. It is not unusual for the baseline to be more accurate!

Forecasting Methods
Forecasting methods can be classified in many ways. This diagram shows one way.
1) Qualitative methods

Forecasting Methods

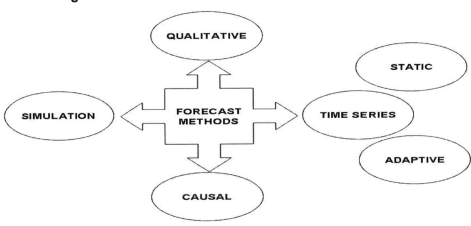

These methods are subjective methods based on intuition, judgment, and opinion, past experience or best guesses of experts. In general, qualitative forecasting methods are often used for long-range forecasts, especially when external factors may play an important role. They are also of use when historical data are very limited or nonexistent. They are used for forecasting new products and also for adjusting quantitative forecasts. Whenever there is reason to suspect that the future will not be like the past, a prediction derived qualitatively is preferable to quantitative forecasts. They are the most common type of forecasting method for the long term strategic planning process. Qualitative forecasts are made using information such as telephone surveys of customer attitudes, consumer panels, test marketing, expert opinion and panels.

2) Causal methods

These methods analyse the effects of outside influences and use these to forecast. They are based upon the computational projection of numerical relationships of external patterns. Regression analysis is one of the causal methods and involves investigating the statistical correlation between the demand and the market indicator concerned, such as inflation rate, and attempting to use any correlations found in a predictive sense. The simplest form of this, is to plot demand against the indicator concerned, and provided reasonable correlation exists, to use a least squares fit to draw the regression line. The expected change in demand resulting from a given change in the economic indicator is obtained from the slope of the regression line.

3) Time Series Methods

These methods involve looking at the pattern of the past demand and extending this into the future; predicting the future using the past. A fundamental assumption that is used is that the future is related to the past in some way. This assumption does not require tomorrow to be just like today; it only requires stable relationships. Even in today's rapidly changing world fundamental relationships usually hold at least in the short term.

There are several different time series methods that we will explore in detail later on.

Time series methods have two categorisations: static and adaptive. In an adaptive system estimates of level of demand, trend of demand and seasonality are made every time a new demand is observed. In a static system the level of trend and seasonality remain constant for several periods before they are recalculated.

4) Simulation methods

Simulation forecasting methods attempt to replicate the consumer choices that give rise to demand to arrive at a forecast. Using simulation you can combine time series and causal methods to answer such questions as these:

• What will the impact of a price increase be?

- What will the impact of a competitor entering the market be?

The result produced by the simulation will only be as good as the underlying algorithm.

Whilst there can be applications for all the methods in inventory management the principle method used is time series and we will concentrate on this one. In situations where relevant historic demand is not available, such as, new product launches other methods will need to be used.

Forecasting Characteristics

The choice of a forecasting methodology is only one component of a comprehensive approach to demand management. Each method will produce a different result and so it will often be hard to decide which one to use. Ultimately we are looking to reduce the forecast error and hence this will be a key criterion in selection.

- It is worth noting at this stage some key characteristics of forecasts. Firstly, the further out we forecast the more inaccurate we will be. This means the forecast for next week will be more accurate than the forecast for the same week next year.

- Secondly, the greater the detail we forecast in the more inaccurate it will be. The forecast for all SKU's combined together (called an aggregate forecast) will be more accurate than the forecast for each individual SKU. Combining these two characteristics together means that if we need to forecast a long way into the future we should try and do it in as little detail as possible. For example, we may have to forecast 24 months ahead to ensure that we have sufficient factory capacity. In doing so, we do not need individual SKU forecasts, it is likely that product family or even total volume for all SKU's would be sufficient.

- The third characteristic is that forecasts will always be wrong. No matter how much time and effort is applied this will always be the case. It is essential therefore to not only produce a single figure forecast, but to accompany it with an estimate of the error. For example, stating the forecast of demand is 100 per month, but from past experience we know that it will be between 80 and 120. This is much more helpful than giving the single figure of 100.

Forecasting Approach

Before we explore different techniques in detail and the calculations that underpin them, it is worth mentioning that the overall approach used in forecasting is far more important, than the results obtained from a particular calculation. Thoroughly understanding the whole picture of managing demand, and how different levers can be applied to reduce the error, will prove much more beneficial than being able to perform a specific calculation. Calculations are means to an end, but they are not an end by themselves.

There are six steps that help to perform effective forecasting operations:
1.   Forecasting objective.
2.   Link forecasting with other planning activities.
3.   Identify factors that impact demand.
4.   Consider different customer segments.
5.   Select appropriate techniques.
6.   Measure forecast performance.

1) The first step is to clarify the **objective of the forecast** to be created. The objective of every forecast is to support decisions that are based on the forecast, so it is important these are identified. The example used above to determine the amount of capacity needed in a factory, suggested that an aggregate forecast may be better than an SKU level forecast. The moral: understand what you are trying to achieve, before diving in to produce a forecast.

2) The forecast should be **linked to all planning activities** that will use the forecast or influence demand. As a variety of functions are affected by the outcomes of the planning process, it is important that all of them are integrated into the forecasting process. The S&OP process detailed above highlighted the forecast as just one component of the overall planning system. It was surrounded by other decisions, that when looked at together, produce an integrated plan.

3) The **factors that influence a forecast** must be identified next. A proper analysis of these factors is central to developing an appropriate forecasting technique. The main factors influencing forecasts are demand, supply and product related phenomena. On the demand side we must identify trend and seasonality. In supply we must determine lead-times and supply sources. If an item is to be sourced overseas and will be transported by sea lead-times could be long requiring that we use a technique to accommodate this. We need to understand product characteristics, such as substitutability and degree of proliferation. For example, if as a retailer, we are out of stock of one SKU, will customers buy an alternative one, such as a bigger or smaller size? Is the alternative one of ours or one of a competitor?

4) To understand and identify **customer segments**, customers may be grouped by service requirements, demand volumes, order frequency, demand volatility and seasonality. These help to identify which methods should be used in forecasting. For example, we may have customers who are retailers or wholesalers. We could consider demand for all customers or for each group separately and then combine them together. However, if each group displays different demand patterns, it may be better to separate the forecasts.

5) Select the **appropriate forecasting technique** to match with the identified requirements. Forecasting techniques are tools; therefore select the right tool for the job.

6) Finally clear **performance measures** need to be established. Simply producing a one-number forecast is not as useful, as we need to accompany it with a suggestion of the degree of error. Knowing with a high degree of certainty that a forecast will be between an upper and lower limit enables robust plans to be produced and good management decisions to be made.

With the above factors in mind, we can explore forecasting techniques in more detail.

Demand Composition

The demand that we see is known as observed demand. Observed demand is made up of two components: a systematic one and a random one.

The systematic one can be forecasted. It usually consists of an underlying average demand to which we add any trend that is present and then any seasonal build-up or reduction that is necessary. In essence this gives us a view of what average demand is going to be. All of the statistical forecasting methods are attempting to forecast this systematic component or the average demand.

This is particularly important because many people believe that we are attempting to forecast the peaks and troughs in the demand pattern. This is not the case, since predicting such turning points is extremely difficult, if not impossible. If you could do it, then you wouldn't be reading this text!

The random component is added to the systematic component and reflects the volatility of the demand pattern. You cannot (and should not) forecast the random component. You can forecast its estimated size and variability, which provides a measure of forecast error. Randomness also means you cannot forecast this component's direction. Of course we use this information to determine the safety stock that we require to protect against the peaks and troughs.

Observed Demand

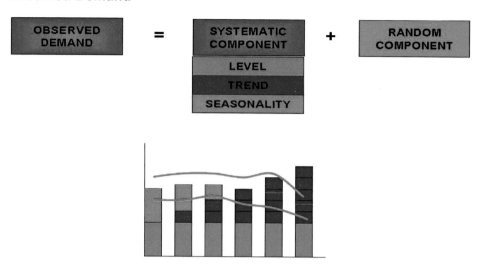

The diagram helps to show the build up. The light blue represents the base level of demand. The dark blue represents the trend gradually increasing. The red represents the seasonal component, adding extra demand in the early periods but reducing it in the later periods. Finally, the green line represents the random component creating fluctuations between a maximum and minimum level.

The objective of forecasting is to screen out the random component so that an estimate of the systematic component can be derived.

Sometimes of the variations that are found in a time series, can be due to a difference in the number of days in each time period. Some organisations use a cycle of a 4 week, 4 week, and 5 week periods. Of course it could appear that there is a seasonal cycle in the 3 period unless an adjustment is made. Similarly if the time period is represented by calendar month, this can have a large effect as there can be as much as a 10% difference in the number of days. In such cases, it is a good idea to adjust the data to allow the identification of the systematic components mentioned above. The adjustment can be made using this formula:

$$\text{Demand Period X} = \text{Observed Demand} \times \frac{\text{No. of Days Average Period}}{\text{No. of Days Period X}}$$

Suppose we have observed demand of 100 in a time period and that there are 28 days in this period compared to 30 on average. We can adjust the demand using the formula to be:

$$\text{Demand} = 100 \times \frac{30}{28}$$

Demand = 107

Measuring Forecast Error

The objective of the forecasting process is to reduce the forecast error. As we have seen it will not be possible to reduce it to zero because of the random component contained within the data. However, our aim should be to reduce the error, until we reach a consistent level of error. This will indicate that we have been successful at filtering out the noise in the demand information. Measuring and understanding forecast error. is an important element in the forecasting process. Two things are required to calculate the forecast error:

1) **The actual demand** that occurs in the time period that is under consideration. This means of course that we cannot calculate the error until after the actual demand has occurred. The error is therefore a delayed or lag measurement.

2) **The forecast** relating to the time period.
This poses the question of which forecast should be used. For example, during January we may produce forecasts of demand for each month for the rest of the year. As we move into February we use the actual demand in January to recalibrate our forecasts. This means that potentially the forecast for October could be different each time we recalculate it.

Most organisations use the forecast that was last calculated, but there is no reason why another one could not be used. If, as a manufacturer you had to commit to material purchases two months before the actual demand happens, you may choose the forecast calculated at this time, as the basis of the error measurement.

Forecast error can then be calculated as:
Forecast Error = Actual Demand – Forecast

Consider the example below:

Period	Demand	Forecast
1	58	60
2	62	58
3	60	62
4	64	66
5	57	55
6	61	64
7	59	58
8	64	60
9	57	62
10	62	60

The figure in the forecast column represents the forecast that corresponds to the time period specified in the first column.

Using the formula above the error for the first period can be calculated as follows:

Forecast Error = Actual Demand – Forecast

Forecast Error = 58 – 54 = 4

The remaining errors can be determined in a similar way.

Period	Demand	Forecast	Error
1	58	60	-2
2	62	58	4
3	60	62	-2
4	64	66	-2
5	57	55	2
6	61	64	-3
7	59	58	1
8	64	60	4
9	57	62	-5
10	62	60	2

Notice that some of the errors are positive and others are negative. This is the pattern you would expect to see. If we are forecasting correctly sometimes we will expect to over forecast, in which case the error will be negative, and sometimes we will under forecast giving a positive error.

If the errors are all negative or all positive this would indicate that the forecast could be made better and that perhaps there are characteristics in the demand pattern that have not been identified, such as a trend.

The second thing to notice is that the errors range from -5 to +4, which for example in cloth sizes, is quite a range. However, the size in any period does not give us any indication about the effectiveness of the forecast. This is because a large error could be caused by an actual demand that is at either extreme of the demand pattern.

If in period 11 we obtained a forecast error of 15 it would alert us to the fact that something might have changed in the demand pattern. Consequently, we need to undertake further calculations to help us improve the forecast process.

There are several measures that can be used:

1) Mean Error (ME)
This is calculated by summing all the errors and dividing by the number of errors.

Period	Demand	Forecast	Error
1	58	60	-2
2	62	58	4
3	60	62	-2
4	64	66	-2
5	57	55	2
6	61	64	-3
7	59	58	1
8	64	60	4
9	57	62	-5
10	62	60	2
		Total	-1
		Mean	-0.10

The ME is likely to be small since large positive errors will be offset by large negative errors. As a performance measure it is not particularly helpful, indeed it is possible to have a zero ME with a very bad forecasting method. The ME will only tell you if there is consistent over- or under-forecasting in which case ME would get bigger negatively or positively respectively.

Bias

The bias is calculated from the cumulative sum of the errors. We take the error from period 1 and add the error from period 2 and then period 3.

Period	Demand	Forecast	Error	Bias
1	58	60	-2	-2
2	62	58	4	2
3	60	62	-2	0
4	64	66	-2	-2
5	57	55	2	0
6	61	64	-3	-3
7	59	58	1	-2
8	64	60	4	2
9	57	62	-5	-3
10	62	60	2	-1

If the error is truly random the bias will fluctuate around zero. In our case you will see that it switches between positive and negative. If the bias gets bigger in either direction it is again an indication of over- or under-forecasting.

Probably the first sin of forecasting is to over- or under-forecast. It is so easy to spot with the measures detailed above that early warning signals are always present to help you avoid it.

2) Mean Absolute Error (MAE)

This is a similar calculation to the MAD we covered in an earlier section. Using the errors calculated we take the absolute values of each one. Remember that absolute means that the all the errors are taken as positive.

Period	Demand	Forecast	Error	Bias	Absolute Error
1	58	60	-2	-2	2
2	62	58	4	2	4
3	60	62	-2	0	2
4	64	66	-2	-2	2
5	57	55	2	0	2
6	61	64	-3	-3	3
7	59	58	1	-2	1
8	64	60	4	2	4
9	57	62	-5	-3	5
10	62	60	2	-1	2

The MAE is then calculated by averaging the absolute errors. For example in period 2 the absolute error of 2 from period 1 is added to 4 from period 2 and the total is divided by 2 (2 errors from period 1 and 2) to give an MAE of 3.

Period	Demand	Forecast	Error	Bias	Absolute Error	MAE
1	58	60	-2	-2	2	2.00
2	62	58	4	2	4	3.00
3	60	62	-2	0	2	2.67
4	64	66	-2	-2	2	2.50
5	57	55	2	0	2	2.40
6	61	64	-3	-3	3	2.50
7	59	58	1	-2	1	2.29
8	64	60	4	2	4	2.50
9	57	62	-5	-3	5	2.78
10	62	60	2	-1	2	2.70

3) Mean Squared Error (MSE)

As an alternative to using the absolute values of the errors we can square the errors and then average them.

(see table overleaf)

Period	Demand	Forecast	Error	Squared Errors	MSE
1	58	60	-2	4	4.00
2	62	58	4	16	10.00
3	60	62	-2	4	8.00
4	64	66	-2	4	7.00
5	57	55	2	4	6.40
6	61	64	-3	9	6.83
7	59	58	1	1	6.00
8	64	60	4	16	7.25
9	57	62	-5	25	9.22
10	62	60	2	4	8.70

The MSE is easier to handle mathematically and in computer programming so it is often used and later on you will see it forms the basis of the safety stock calculation. However, it can be intuitively difficult to interpret because it is presented in square units. This often makes the numbers large and difficult to understand. The MAE on the other hand is in the same units as the demand data. In both cases notice that the wide swings in the errors have been smoothed out giving a much more consistent pattern.

4) Standard Error (SE)
The SE overcomes the squared unit problem of the MSE by square rooting the MSE to get back to the original units.

Period	Demand	Forecast	Error	Squared Errors	MSE	SE
1	58	60	-2	4	4.00	2.00
2	62	58	4	16	10.00	3.16
3	60	62	-2	4	8.00	2.83
4	64	66	-2	4	7.00	2.65
5	57	55	2	4	6.40	2.53
6	61	64	-3	9	6.83	2.61
7	59	58	1	1	6.00	2.45
8	64	60	4	16	7.25	2.69
9	57	62	-5	25	9.22	3.04
10	62	60	2	4	8.70	2.95

Sometimes the SE is referred to as the root mean squared error (RMSE) for obvious reasons. These standard errors are important because of the structure of the normal distribution. If the demand data follows a normal distribution then the forecast errors will also follow one with a mean of zero and standard deviation equal to the SE. Remember we can also approximate the SE by multiplying the MAE by 1.25.

The ME, MAE, MSE and SE are all impacted by the relative size of the demand data. This means that whilst being useful to measure the error of a specific item they are not suitable to compare the error on one item to another.

5) Mean Percentage Error (MPE)
The MPE takes the forecast error and divides it by the actual demand to present it as a percentage error.

In period 1 the error is -2 and dividing by the demand of 58 gives a percentage error of -3.45%.

The comments we made in relation to the ME hold here as well. Usually the MPE is not used since large negative and positive PEs cancel each other out. The more usual method is to use the MAPE.

Period	Demand	Forecast	Error	Percent Error
1	58	60	-2	-3.45%
2	62	58	4	6.45%
3	60	62	-2	-3.33%
4	64	66	-2	-3.13%
5	57	55	2	3.51%
6	61	64	-3	-4.92%
7	59	58	1	1.69%
8	64	60	4	6.25%
9	57	62	-5	-8.77%
10	62	60	2	3.23%
		Total	-1	-2.47%
		Mean	-0.10	-0.62%

6) Mean Absolute Percentage Error (MAPE)
The basis of this calculation is similar to the MAE. Instead of using the actual error values we take the absolute value and calculate the absolute percentage error. For period 1 this becomes +3.45%.

(see table overleaf)

Period	Demand	Forecast	Error	Percent Error	Absolute PE	MAPE
1	58	60	-2	-3.45%	3.45%	3.45%
2	62	58	4	6.45%	6.45%	4.95%
3	60	62	-2	-3.33%	3.33%	4.41%
4	64	66	-2	-3.13%	3.13%	4.09%
5	57	55	2	3.51%	3.51%	3.97%
6	61	64	-3	-4.92%	4.92%	4.13%
7	59	58	1	1.69%	1.69%	3.78%
8	64	60	4	6.25%	6.25%	4.09%
9	57	62	-5	-8.77%	8.77%	4.61%
10	62	60	2	3.23%	3.23%	4.47%

Knowing that the MAPE of a method is 4% means a great deal more than knowing the MSE is 10. MAPE is often used to compare the performance of the forecast from one item to another. In addition we would expect the MAPE of an "A" item to be smaller than the MAPE of a "C" item.

It should be noted that if the demand data contains zeros, the PE cannot be calculated.

In summary:
- The first measure to examine is the bias to check for under or over forecasting.
- The SE can then be used to evaluate the relative accuracy of different forecasting methods for an individual item.
- The MAPE can be used to compare the forecasting performance on one item to another.

Tracking Signals

Before we leave forecast error measurements, some forecasting systems utilise something called a tracking signal. Since quantitative methods of forecasting assume a continuation of some historical pattern into the future, it is often useful to develop some measure that can be used to determine when the basic pattern has changed. A tracking signal is the most common such measure.

One frequently used tracking signal involves taking the bias and dividing it by the MAE. When the tracking signals then goes outside predetermined limits, it indicates that a new model should be considered. In the example below, the limits are -6 to +6. Tracking signals are particularly useful to detect trends when they have not been identified.

Period	Demand	Forecast	Error	Bias	Absolute Error	MAE	Tracking Signal
1	58	60	-2	-2	2	2.00	-1.00
2	62	58	4	2	4	3.00	0.67
3	60	62	-2	0	2	2.67	0.00
4	64	66	-2	-2	2	2.50	-0.80
5	57	55	2	0	2	2.40	0.00
6	61	64	-3	-3	3	2.50	-1.20
7	59	58	1	-2	1	2.29	-0.88
8	64	60	4	2	4	2.50	0.80
9	57	62	-5	-3	5	2.78	-1.08
10	62	60	2	-1	2	2.70	-0.37

The tracking signal is very much like the process control charts you may have seen in manufacturing. So long as the process measurement stays between an upper and lower limit the process is said to be under control. As soon as it goes beyond a limit it triggers remedial action.

Periods of Measurement

The measures of forecast error detailed above measure the goodness of fit of the model used to historical data. It is possible in the initial phase to use elaborate fitting models to obtain what at first hand looks like an excellent fit. In our example of just ten periods we could attempt to fit sophisticated models (outside of our scope here) to try an obtain forecasts that are very close to the actual demand. This is of course with the benefit of hindsight! If the forecast is close to the actual demand the error will be nearly zero and hence the measures of MSE, SE and MAPE will all be close to zero.

As we progress in examining different forecasting techniques you will notice that the accuracy depends, on the selection of particular parameters in the starting phase. For example, with moving averages the number of periods we utilise, or with exponential smoothing the decision of what demand to use for the first smoothed average, the selection of the smoothing constant etc.

These problems can be overcome by breaking the demand data down into an initialisation set and test or holding set. The initialisation set is used to estimate any parameters and to initialise the method. The initialisation period allows the model to settle down and work out the effect of the initial figures. Forecasts are then made for the remaining test or holding data. Since the test data are not used in model fitting, the forecasts produced are genuine and do not use the actual observations for these periods. The accuracy measurements are then computed for the test data only and not the initialisation data.

Time Series Forecasts

The common time series methods used for forecasting are:
*   Simple averages.

- Weighted averages.
- Moving averages (simple and trend).
- Exponential smoothing.

To illustrate the calculations that follow we will utilise a common set of data as follows:

Period	Demand
1	58
2	62
3	60
4	64
5	57
6	61
7	59
8	64
9	57
10	62

If we draw a graph of this data we see the following:

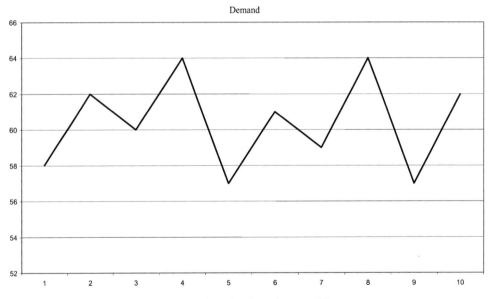

Demand

It will be apparent from this graph that the item is a stable one.

1) Simple Averages

This method of predicting future demands is attractive due to the simplicity of calculation.

An example of the method can be seen from using the first six periods of data;

Period	1	2	3	4	5	6
Demand	58	62	60	64	57	61

Average demand = (58+62+60+64+57+61) / 6

Average demand = 362/6 = 60.33

With no apparent increasing or decreasing trend, it would be reasonable to assume that an estimate of 60.33 for the next period would be acceptable. It should be remembered that the range of the variations are not relevant for this type of item, providing there is a generally constant average. The forecast of 60.33 would be the forecast for 1 period ahead, 2 periods ahead and so on until further information became available to recalculate.

The calculations for the remaining periods are shown in the table below. Notice that the forecast produced in each period is for the following periods. For example the forecast produced in period 1 refers to the demand for period 2.

Period	Demand	Forecast
1	58	58.00
2	62	60.00
3	60	60.00
4	64	61.00
5	57	60.20
6	61	60.33
7	59	60.14
8	64	60.63
9	57	60.22
10	62	60.40

If we graph the forecast alongside the demand pattern we see the following:

(see graph overleaf)

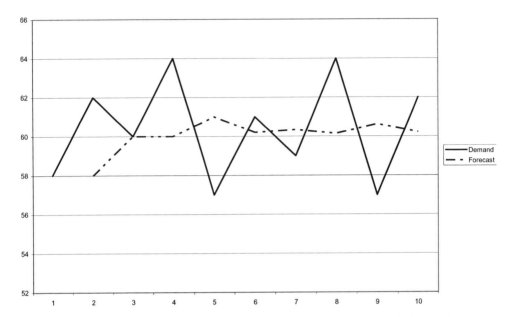

Notice how the forecast line tracks through the middle of the actual demand smoothing out the randomness.

This can only be used, therefore, for stable demand items. In selecting items for using this technique the problem of how many past demands to include will always be present. The more individual demands included in the series, the less emphasis placed upon the random fluctuation. The less individual demands included, the greater the chance the pattern has changed and the less reliable the estimate.

2) Weighted Average

This method is used where the demand pattern might indicate a change and increased emphasis needs to be placed on the more recent demands as being indicative of the future pattern.

An example of this method can be seen from the following:

Period	Demand	Weight	Demand x Weight	Forecast
1	58	1	58	58.00
2	62	2	124	60.67
3	60	3	180	60.33
4	64	4	256	61.80

The weighting applied usually follows the pattern illustrated. The highest weight is assigned to the most recent period demand and then you work backwards, deducting one for each period. If we had decided to perform the calculation over three periods, the weighting against 64 would have been 3, against 60 it would be 2 and against 62 it would be 1.

Having allocated the weights we multiply each period demand by the weight. The forecast is then calculated by the totalling the weighted demands and dividing by the sum of the weights.

Forecast = (58+124+180+256)/(1+2+3+4)

Forecast = 618/10 = 61.80

The table for all the calculations appears:

Period	Demand	Weight	Demand x Weight	Forecast
1	58	1	58	58.00
2	62	2	124	60.67
3	60	3	180	60.33
4	64	4	256	61.80
5	57	5	285	60.20
6	61	6	366	60.43
7	59	7	413	60.07
8	64	8	512	60.94
9	57	9	513	60.16
10	62	10	620	60.49

Once again, the problem of how many past demands to select exists. The more that are included, the less emphasis will be placed upon the random fluctuations.

The forecast for period 11 would be 60.49, for period 12 it would also be 60.49 and so on until a new demand occurs to allow recalculation.

It can also be seen that when a trend exists, the forecast lags behind. To illustrate this, consider a weighted average for period demands of 3, 5, 7, and 9. The weighted average is 7 so the forecast for the next period would be 7, which is clearly lagging behind the 11 that we would expect.

3) Moving Averages – simple

This method is very common in manual inventory systems. To illustrate its use it is again necessary to select a number of periods over which to perform the calculation, e.g. a four period moving average or a five period moving average.

Consider the example for a four period moving average:

Period	Demand	Dropped Demand	Total	Moving Average
1	58			
2	62			
3	60			
4	64		244	61.00

Starting with the first four periods of demand, the moving average is calculated by summing the demand for the four periods to give 244 and dividing by the number of periods, 4 in this case.

This forecast of 61.00 would be for 1, 2, 3 or more periods ahead until a new demand occurs to enable recalculation.

When period five data becomes available we then have the following:

Period	Demand	Dropped Demand	Total	Moving Average
1	58			
2	62			
3	60			
4	64		244	61.00
5	57	58	243	60.75

The new demand for period 5 is 57. The "moving" average now moves down to cover periods 2, 3, 4 and 5. The dropped demand is the demand, which is dropped from the calculation, which is from period 1, 58 in this case.

The new forecast of 60.75 is for 1, 2 or more periods ahead until once again, a new demand occurs to enable recalculation. The process continues by adding in the latest demand and dropping the oldest demand.

Period	Demand	Dropped Demand	Total	Moving Average
1	58			
2	62			
3	60			
4	64		244	61.00
5	57	58	243	60.75
6	61	62	242	60.50
7	59	60	241	60.25
8	64	64	241	60.25
9	57	57	241	60.25
10	62	61	242	60.50

In the previous example, the calculations were based on a four period moving average. The selection of the number of periods is arbitrary and will give differing results. For example, if we had chosen a five period moving average for the data we would have got:

Period	Demand	Dropped Demand	Total	Moving Average
1	58			
2	62			
3	60			
4	64			
5	57		301	60.20
6	61	58	304	60.80
7	59	62	301	60.20
8	64	60	305	61.00
9	57	64	298	59.60
10	62	57	303	60.60

The larger the number of periods used, the slower the response will be to changes in demand. The smaller the number of periods used, the quicker the responses to changes in demand.

4) Moving average – trend

The drawback of the simple moving average is that there is no allowance for a trend. To overcome this problem additional calculations are necessary. They include the following:

- a weighting applied to each of the number of periods selected, at each period review.
- a calculated weighted total.
- a calculation of the trend.
- a calculation of the trend correction.
- a calculation of the trend corrected moving average.
- a calculation of the forecasted demand for one or more periods ahead.

Using the above data from the 4 period simple moving average examples we have:

Period	Demand	Dropped Demand	Total	Moving Average
1	58			
2	62			
3	60			
4	64		244	61.00

Step 1
Apply a weighting factor to each period. The weight applied must total zero and the difference between two consecutive weights must be one. For a four period average, the weights are −1.5, -0.5, 0.5, 1.5. Whereas for a five period average, they would be −2, -1, 0, +1, +2.

This gives:

58 x (-1.5)	=	- 87.00
62 x (-0.5)	=	- 31.00
60 x (+0.5)	=	+ 30.00
64 x (+1.5)	=	+ 96.00

Step 2
Sum the totals above

$$-87.00 - 31.00 + 30.00 + 96.00 = 8.00$$

The fact the total is positive indicates the presence of an upward trend. If it were negative, a downward trend would be present.

Step 3
Calculate the trend using the weighted total and the formula

$$\text{Trend} = \frac{12 \times \text{Weighted Total}}{\text{Number of Periods} \times (\text{Number of Periods}^2 - 1)}$$

$$\text{Trend} = \frac{12 \times 8.00}{4 \times (4^2 - 1)}$$

$$\text{Trend} = 1.60$$

Note: 12 is a constant in the formula, which will not change for different period calculations.

Once again, the positive indicates an upward trend. A negative figure would have indicated a downward trend.

Step 4
Calculate the trend correction factor using the formula:

$$\text{Trend Correction} = \text{Trend} \times \frac{(\text{Number of Periods} - 1)}{2}$$

$$\text{Trend Correction} = 1.60 \times \frac{(4 - 1)}{2}$$

Trend Correction = 2.40

Step 5
Calculate the trend corrected moving average (TCMA) using the simple moving average and trend correction.

Trend Corrected Moving Average = Simple Moving Average + Trend Correction

Trend Corrected Moving Average = 61.00 + 2.40 = 63.40

Step 6
Calculate the forecast for one or more periods ahead using:

Forecast = TCMA + (Number of Periods Ahead x Trend).

For one period ahead this gives: 63.40 + (1 x 1.6) = 65.00

For two periods ahead it would be: 63.40 + (2 x 1.6) = 66.60

The calculations are now complete and look like the following:

Period	Demand	Weighted Total	Trend	Trend Correction	TCMA	Forecast
1	58					
2	62					
3	60					
4	64	8.00	1.60	2.40	63.40	65.00

Using the remaining data, we would obtain the following comparative results.

Period	Demand	Weighted Total	Trend	Trend Correction	TCMA	Forecast
1	58					
2	62					
3	60					
4	64	8.00	1.60	2.40	63.40	65.00
5	57	-5.50	-1.10	-1.65	59.10	58.00
6	61	-2.00	-0.40	-0.60	59.90	59.50
7	59	-5.50	-1.10	-1.65	58.60	57.50
8	64	9.50	1.90	2.85	63.10	65.00
9	57	-3.50	-0.70	-1.05	59.20	58.50
10	62	1.00	0.20	0.30	60.80	61.00

In this process the forecast for the next period ahead is carried out each time of review, in order to follow the movement in demand.

To forecast more than one period ahead, the calculated trend for the current period is multiplied by the number of periods ahead and added to the trend corrected moving average. However, it will be seen from the samples below that the results of the calculation from period to period can vary considerably.

Forecast of demand in period 10 made in earlier period:

Forecast Made in period	TCMA	Trend	No. of periods ahead	Forecast for period 10
4	63.40	1.60	6	73.00
5	59.10	-1.10	5	53.60
6	59.90	-0.40	4	58.30
7	58.60	-1.10	3	55.30
8	63.10	1.90	2	66.90
9	59.20	-0.70	1	58.50

For those that feel uncomfortable with mathematical formula it might help to see the use of the above calculations with data that displays a perfect trend, such as 3, 5, 7, 9...The results are shown below.

Period	Demand	Weighted Total	Trend	Trend Correction	TCMA	Forecast
1	3					
2	5					
3	7					
4	9	10.00	2.00	3.00	9.00	11.00
5	11	10.00	2.00	3.00	11.00	13.00
6	13	10.00	2.00	3.00	13.00	15.00
7	15	10.00	2.00	3.00	15.00	17.00
8	17	10.00	2.00	3.00	17.00	19.00
9	19	10.00	2.00	3.00	19.00	21.00
10	21	10.00	2.00	3.00	21.00	23.00

Notice how the forecast is exactly what would be expected and the trend is identified as being 2.

5) Exponential Smoothing

This method of short term forecasting is the most commonly used in inventory systems. It is another form of smoothed averaging which has the following benefits:

- All historical data can be retained with the calculation.
- Weighting factors are applied to the data, which recognise the significance of the most recent data.
- A smoothing constant is applied to the data, which can vary the weightings.
- Ease of calculation and limited data storage requirements.

The basis of the calculation is straightforward and is based upon the following principle: the new forecast is equal to the old forecast plus a percentage of the forecast error.

This type of forecast is again suitable for a stable demand item so intuitively the basis of the calculation seems sensible. The question becomes what percentage should be used? Clearly it must be between 0 and 100; the actual value chosen will be discussed later.

The percentage used is incorporated into a smoothing constant and reflecting the possible range, it cannot be larger than 1.0 and must be greater than 0. As the smoothing constant gets larger, it increases the emphasis placed on the more recent data. This emphasis is shown below:

- Value of constant 0.01; smoothed average depends 5.85% on the last six periods demand.

- Value of constant 0.10; smoothed average depends 46.85% on the last six periods demand.

- Value of constant 0.20; smoothed average depends 75.78% on the last six periods demand.

- Value of constant 0.50; smoothed average depends 98.45% on the last six periods demand.

It will be seen from this data, that there is a similar effect to varying the number of periods demand as in that used in moving averages. In fact, there is a direct relationship, which for the four examples of smoothing constant above, would be the equivalent to 199, 19, 9, and 3 periods of moving average respectively. In practice, in most inventory systems, the smoothing constants are set at between 0.10 and 0.30.

The basis of exponential smoothing can be summarised as follows:

New Forecast = Old Forecast + α x Forecast Error (where α is the smoothing constant.)

Since the forecast error is equal to the actual demand minus the forecast, the new forecast is in effect the old forecast, plus a proportion of the difference between the old forecast and the most recent actual data. This new forecast is taken as the forecast for subsequent periods. It is recomputed each period, so that the demand forecast for future periods will change each period.

Using our data the basic calculation as follows:

SC	0.1	
Period	Demand	Forecast
1	58	58

To begin, we have chosen to use a smoothing constant of 0.1. As the period 1 demand occurs of 58, we only have this to base a future forecast upon. The usual convention is to use this first demand as the forecast for the next period.

When the second period demand occurs the situation becomes:

SC	0.1	
Period	Demand	Forecast
1	58	58.00
2	62	58.40

The forecast is calculated:

$58 + 0.1 \times (62 - 58) = 58 + 0.4 = 58.4$

As the next period actual demand becomes available the calculation is repeated:

SC	0.1	
Period	Demand	Forecast
1	58	58.00
2	62	58.40
3	60	58.56

Every time a new actual demand becomes available the calculation can be refreshed showing the overall picture.

SC	0.1	
Period	Demand	Forecast
1	58	58.00
2	62	58.40
3	60	58.56
4	64	59.10
5	57	58.89
6	61	59.10
7	59	59.09
8	64	59.58
9	57	59.33
10	62	59.59

As a check, the new forecast should always be between the old forecast and the new actual demand.

If we vary the smoothing constant we will get different forecasts:

Period	Demand	Forecast 0.1	Forecast 0.3	Forecast 0.5
1	58	58.00	58.00	58.00
2	62	58.40	59.20	60.00
3	60	58.56	59.44	60.00
4	64	59.10	60.81	62.00
5	57	58.89	59.67	59.50
6	61	59.10	60.07	60.25
7	59	59.09	59.75	59.63
8	64	59.58	61.02	61.81
9	57	59.33	59.82	59.41
10	62	59.59	60.47	60.70

Graphing these results shows how as the smoothing constant increases the forecast reacts to the more recent data reducing the smoothing effect.

(see graph overleaf)

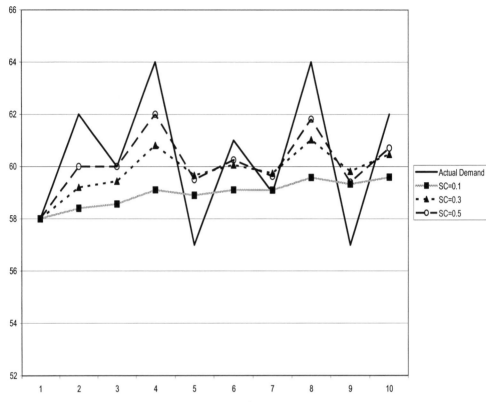

The question now becomes which smoothing constant we should use. If we recall our objective of reducing forecast error, we would therefore look to select a constant so that it minimises the SE. If we consider our calculations for a smoothing constant of 0.1 and we add in our error calculations we get the following:

SC	0.1					
Period	Demand	Forecast 0.1	Error	Squared error	MSE	SE
1	58	58.00				
2	62	58.40	4.00	16.00	16.00	4.00
3	60	58.56	1.60	2.56	9.28	3.05
4	64	59.10	5.44	29.59	16.05	4.01
5	57	58.89	-2.10	4.43	13.15	3.63
6	61	59.10	2.11	4.44	11.40	3.38
7	59	59.09	-0.10	0.01	9.50	3.08
8	64	59.58	4.91	24.07	11.59	3.40
9	57	59.33	-2.58	6.68	10.97	3.31
10	62	59.59	2.67	7.15	10.55	3.25

The SE we obtain is 3.25. If we change the smoothing constant to 0.2 the SE becomes 3.17 and for 0.3 the SE is 3.23. Consequently, we know that a constant of 0.2 is better than 0.1 or 0.3. Using for example, the "solver" facility in Microsoft Excel, we can find the value of the constant that minimises the SE. Doing this gives a constant of 0.1919 and a SE of 3.17. A computerised forecasting system would perform these calculations automatically and select the best constant.

It is also possible, to build additional calculations into the process, to create an adaptive forecasting system that changes the smoothing constant each time the forecast is reviewed.

Exponential Smoothing with Trend

Simple exponential smoothing has a drawback in that it has no predictions for the presence of a trend.

Demand patterns with a trend will require additional calculations to those used in simple exponential smoothing. Exponential smoothing with trend is sometimes called double exponential smoothing or Holt's exponential smoothing, after its founder.

As the name suggests two smoothing constants are used. One to smooth the demand pattern (usually referred to as a) and one to smooth the trend (usually referred to as b).

Using our data with a smoothing constant of $\alpha = 0.1$ and $\beta = 0.2$ we have:

| | | Alpha | Beta | |
| | | 0.1 | 0.2 | |
Period	Demand	Smoothed Demand	Smoothed Trend	Forecast
1	58	58.00	0.00	58
2	62	58.40	0.08	58.48

As in the simple exponential smoothing, we need to have starting values for the smoothed demand and also for the trend. In the absence of any other information, the usual choice is to use the first actual demand and zero for the trend. The three steps of the calculation are as follows:

Step 1
Calculate the smoothed demand using the formula:

Smoothed Demand = α x New Actual Demand + (1 - α) x (Old Smoothed Demand + Old Trend)

For period 2 the calculation is:

Smoothed Demand = 0.1 x 62 + 0.9 (58 + 0)

Smoothed Demand = 58.40

Step 2
Calculate the smoothed trend using the formula:

Smoothed Trend = β x (New Smoothed Demand - Old Smoothed Demand) + (1 - β) x Old Trend

For period 2 this gives:

Smoothed Trend = 0.2 x (58.40 - 58.00) + 0.8 x 0

SmoothedTrend = 0.08

Step 3
Calculate the forecast using:

Forecast = New Smoothed Demand + Number Periods Ahead x New Trend

For period 2 this is gives a forecast for one period ahead of:

Forecast = 58.40 + 1 x 0.08

Forecast = 58.48

The remaining calculations for the other periods give:

| | | Alpha | Beta | |
| | | 0.1 | 0.2 | |
Period	Demand	Smoothed Demand	Smoothed Trend	Forecast
1	58	58.00	0.00	58
2	62	58.40	0.08	58.48
3	60	58.63	0.11	58.74
4	64	59.27	0.22	59.48
5	57	59.24	0.17	59.40
6	61	59.56	0.20	59.76
7	59	59.68	0.18	59.87
8	64	60.28	0.27	60.54
9	57	60.19	0.19	60.38
10	62	60.55	0.23	60.77

The selection of the smoothing constant is significant.

Where the data does not have an obvious trend, there can be considerable risk in applying trend correction. The selection of trend items as against stable items is important.

There are available a number of developments based upon the basic exponential smoothing process which provide for increasing the accuracy of forecasting. As much more complex calculations are required, these are generally used only in computerised inventory systems.

The use of an adaptive constant i.e. changing the smoothing constant at each review, where appropriate, to obtain the best correlation, is a further method of obtaining increasing accuracy in forecasts using this method.

Seasonal Forecasting

So far we have seen how we can forecast both the level of the average demand and the trend. Sometimes the demand data will display a seasonal pattern either in an evolving or step pattern. In such circumstances it is important to allow for this seasonality in the forecast calculations.

Exponential smoothing can be extended to triple smoothing, or Winters' Model (named after the founder), by using three smoothing constants for the demand, trend and seasonality. This method assumes however, that as well as being seasonal, the demand also has an in built trend, which is not always the case.

An alternative method, is to deseasonalise the data using seasonal indices and then to apply an appropriate forecasting technique.

To illustrate the approach, we need to use a different set of data that contains some seasonality. Listed below is an item with 3 years of demand data.

Period	Year 1	Year 2	Year 3
1	1924	2268	1950
2	1652	1434	1610
3	1446	1454	1500
4	931	1195	890
5	1300	864	1100
6	879	861	850
7	839	989	900
8	1269	949	1150
9	1542	1223	1450
10	1884	1610	1670
11	2034	1937	1970
12	1507	1254	1350

In order to identify seasonality, it is important to examine several years of history, ideally at least three. It is also useful, to graph the data to check for the pattern.

This could be done by graphing all three years in one line, but this makes spotting the pattern more difficult.

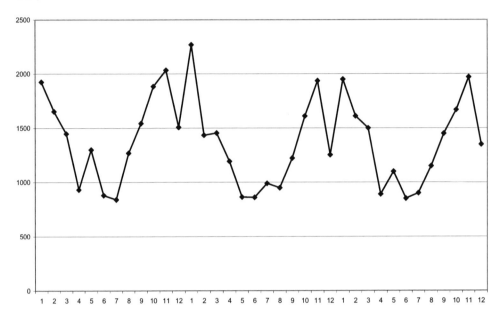

It is preferable to overlay the three years onto each other to make the seasonal easier to detect.

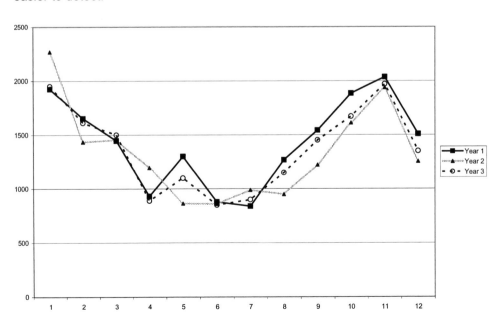

From this graph, we can clearly see that there is some degree of seasonality present. The determination of the seasonal indices proceeds as follows.

Firstly, we total the demands for each period across the 3 years.

For period 1 the total is derived by adding 1924, 2268 and 1950.

Period	Year 1	Year 2	Year 3	Total
1	1924	2268	1950	6142
2	1652	1434	1610	4696
3	1446	1454	1500	4400
4	931	1195	890	3016
5	1300	864	1100	3264
6	879	861	850	2590
7	839	989	900	2728
8	1269	949	1150	3368
9	1542	1223	1450	4215
10	1884	1610	1670	5164
11	2034	1937	1970	5941
12	1507	1254	1350	4111

The column of totals is summed and divided by the number of periods to obtain period average.

Period	Year 1	Year 2	Year 3	Total
1	1924	2268	1950	6142
2	1652	1434	1610	4696
3	1446	1454	1500	4400
4	931	1195	890	3016
5	1300	864	1100	3264
6	879	861	850	2590
7	839	989	900	2728
8	1269	949	1150	3368
9	1542	1223	1450	4215
10	1884	1610	1670	5164
11	2034	1937	1970	5941
12	1507	1254	1350	4111
			Total	49635
			Average	4136.25

The indice for the period 1 is then calculated by using the following:

(see formula overleaf)

$$\text{Period Indice} = \frac{\text{Period Total}}{\text{Average}}$$

$$\text{Period Indice} = \frac{6142}{4136.25}$$

Period indice = 1.48

This indicates that Period 1 is 148% of an average period. The remaining calculations are:

Period	Year 1	Year 2	Year 3	Total	Indice
1	1924	2268	1950	6142	1.48
2	1652	1434	1610	4696	1.14
3	1446	1454	1500	4400	1.06
4	931	1195	890	3016	0.73
5	1300	864	1100	3264	0.79
6	879	861	850	2590	0.63
7	839	989	900	2728	0.66
8	1269	949	1150	3368	0.81
9	1542	1223	1450	4215	1.02
10	1884	1610	1670	5164	1.25
11	2034	1937	1970	5941	1.44
12	1507	1254	1350	4111	0.99
			Total	49635	
			Average	4136.25	

Notice that some periods have an indice below 1 and some have an indice greater than 1. We can use these indices to deseasonalise the data by dividing each demand by its indice.

Year	Period	Demand	Indice	Deseasonalised Demand
1	1	1924	1.48	1295.69
	2	1652	1.14	1455.09
	3	1446	1.06	1359.32
	4	931	0.73	1276.81
	5	1300	0.79	1647.40
	6	879	0.63	1403.77
	7	839	0.66	1272.11
	8	1269	0.81	1558.46
	9	1542	1.02	1513.19
	10	1884	1.25	1509.04
	11	2034	1.44	1416.11
	12	1507	0.99	1516.26
2	1	2268	1.48	1527.36
	2	1434	1.14	1263.07
	3	1454	1.06	1366.84
	4	1195	0.73	1638.87
	5	864	0.79	1094.89
	6	861	0.63	1375.02
	7	989	0.66	1499.54
	8	949	0.81	1165.47
	9	1223	1.02	1200.15
	10	1610	1.25	1289.57
	11	1937	1.44	1348.58
	12	1254	0.99	1261.70
3	1	1950	1.48	1313.20
	2	1610	1.14	1418.09
	3	1500	1.06	1410.09
	4	890	0.73	1220.58
	5	1100	0.79	1393.96
	6	850	0.63	1357.46
	7	900	0.66	1364.60
	8	1150	0.81	1412.32
	9	1450	1.02	1422.91
	10	1670	1.25	1337.63
	11	1970	1.44	1371.56
	12	1350	0.99	1358.29

If we graph this deaseasonalised demand we see the following:

Deseasonalised
Demand

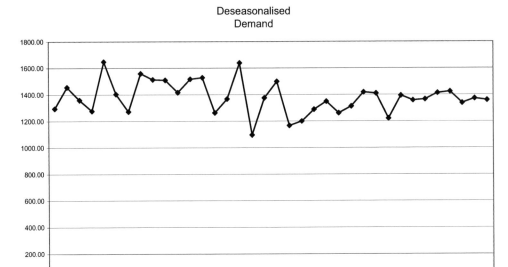

Notice how the seasonal pattern has been removed.

We can now apply one of our forecasting techniques to this Deseasonalised demand. For illustrative purposes we have used simple exponential smoothing with a constant of 0.1.

Year	Period	Demand	Indice	Deseasonalised Demand	Smoothed Demand
1	1	1924	1.48	1295.69	1295.69
	2	1652	1.14	1455.09	1311.63
	3	1446	1.06	1359.32	1316.40
	4	931	0.73	1276.81	1312.44
	5	1300	0.79	1647.40	1345.94
	6	879	0.63	1403.77	1351.72
	7	839	0.66	1272.11	1343.76
	8	1269	0.81	1558.46	1365.23
	9	1542	1.02	1513.19	1380.03
	10	1884	1.25	1509.04	1392.93
	11	2034	1.44	1416.11	1395.25
	12	1507	0.99	1516.26	1407.35
2	1	2268	1.48	1527.36	1419.35
	2	1434	1.14	1263.07	1403.72
	3	1454	1.06	1366.84	1400.03
	4	1195	0.73	1638.87	1423.92
	5	864	0.79	1094.89	1391.01
	6	861	0.63	1375.02	1389.41
	7	989	0.66	1499.54	1400.43
	8	949	0.81	1165.47	1376.93
	9	1223	1.02	1200.15	1359.25
	10	1610	1.25	1289.57	1352.29
	11	1937	1.44	1348.58	1351.91
	12	1254	0.99	1261.70	1342.89
3	1	1950	1.48	1313.20	1339.92
	2	1610	1.14	1418.09	1347.74
	3	1500	1.06	1410.09	1353.98
	4	890	0.73	1220.58	1340.64
	5	1100	0.79	1393.96	1345.97
	6	850	0.63	1357.46	1347.12
	7	900	0.66	1364.60	1348.87
	8	1150	0.81	1412.32	1355.21
	9	1450	1.02	1422.91	1361.98
	10	1670	1.25	1337.63	1359.55
	11	1970	1.44	1371.56	1360.75
	12	1350	0.99	1358.29	1360.50

This provides us with a forecast of 1360.50. We can apply the seasonal indices to this to obtain a forecast for each period of Year 4.

The forecast in period 1 is calculated by multiplying the smoothed average 1360.5 by the indice 1.48.

Period	Smoothed Demand	Seasonal Indice	Adjusted Forecast
1	1360.50	1.48	2020.24
2	1360.50	1.14	1544.61
3	1360.50	1.06	1447.25
4	1360.50	0.73	992.03
5	1360.50	0.79	1073.60
6	1360.50	0.63	851.91
7	1360.50	0.66	897.30
8	1360.50	0.81	1107.81
9	1360.50	1.02	1386.40
10	1360.50	1.25	1698.55
11	1360.50	1.44	1954.12
12	1360.50	0.99	1352.20

Using Profiles in Forecasting

The use of seasonal indices is an application of using a profile in forecasting. The creation of an indice for each period builds a seasonal profile. It may be that an organisation has several seasonal profiles and that items are categorised by the profile type.

In addition to seasonality there are other uses for profiling.

The first is the aggregation and desegregations of forecasts. To illustrate the concept suppose that we have three items that represent different sizes of one product type. The demand pattern for each is displayed opposite:

Period	Item A	Item B	Item C
1	30	100	190
2	40	120	220
3	25	80	180
4	45	110	210
5	50	90	200
6	35	125	240
7	25	85	170
8	40	95	190
9	35	135	220
10	55	120	170
11	25	100	220
12	35	95	190
Total	440	1255	2400
Average	36.67	104.58	200.00
	10.74%	30.65%	58.61%

An organisation may need to produce a forecast of demand for each item. Of course, it could apply the methods covered above to each individual item to produce a forecast. If we used simple exponential smoothing, with a smoothing constant of 0.1 (since each item displays a stable demand pattern) , the forecast for the next period would be 34.82 for item A, 99.50 for item B and 217 for item C.

Period	Item A	Item B	Item C
1	30.00	100.00	190.00
2	31.00	102.00	193.00
3	30.40	80.00	180.00
4	31.86	83.00	183.00
5	33.67	90.00	200.00
6	33.81	93.50	204.00
7	32.93	85.00	170.00
8	33.63	86.00	172.00
9	33.77	135.00	220.00
10	35.89	133.50	215.00
11	34.80	100.00	220.00
12	34.82	99.50	217.00

Alternatively, rather than produce a forecast for each individual item, we could add the demand for all three items together and produce a forecast for the total demand.

Period	Item A	Item B	Item C	Total	Forecast
1	30	100	190	320	320
2	40	120	220	380	326
3	25	80	180	285	285
4	45	110	210	365	293
5	50	90	200	340	340
6	35	125	240	400	346
7	25	85	170	280	280
8	40	95	190	325	284.5
9	35	135	220	390	390
10	55	120	170	345	385.5
11	25	100	220	345	345
12	35	95	190	320	342.5

This suggests that the forecast for the total volume will be 342.5. Historically, we know that item A has accounted for 10.74% of total demand (440/4095), item B 30.65% and item C 58.61%. We can then apply these percentages to the overall forecast to obtain an individual item forecast.

Total forecast		342.5
Item A	10.74%	36.80
Item B	30.65%	104.97
Item C	58.61%	200.73

Often this type of forecasting can produce more accurate results, particularly when product substitution is involved. For example, if we are out of stock of item A, a customer will purchase item B or C instead. Since we are forecasting in less detail, accuracy is likely to increase, and of course it is less work.

This type of aggregation is often undertaken on product profile, going from SKU, to product family, to total product. It can also be undertaken geographically from delivery point, to central warehouse, to region and finally global volume. Of course, it is also possible to combine both product and geographical aggregation. Many forecasting systems now undertake all these permutations automatically and select the forecast which yields the smallest forecast error.

The second application of profiles applies to event management, such as promotional activity or new product launches. Often these types of events pose real forecasting problems for the forecaster because there is limited or no historical data to utilise.

Often promotions display a repeatable pattern of activity for a particular type of promotion. For example a buy one, get one free (BOGOF) promotion might display the following pattern.

Week	% of average sales
1	100
2	100
3	100
4	100
5	120
6	140
7	140
8	120
9	50
10	60
11	70
12	100

Here we see the promotion starting in week 5 and continuing for 4 weeks. In week 5 we see an extra 20% of sales, increasing to an extra 40% of average sales in weeks 6 and 7 and a further 20% increase in the last week of the promotion in week 8. After the promotion we see in week 9, that normal sales decline because consumers have brought forward their purchasing, resulting in a decline in sales until it returns to normal in week 12.

By analysing the outcome of different promotions we can build promotional profiles, which when applied, make the overall forecasting process simpler and much more accurate. For new products, product life curves are built that represent sales as a percentage of the first period. An example might be:

Period	% of Period 1
1	
2	120%
3	130%
4	150%
5	170%
6	200%

If we then produce a forecast for period 1, probably by using a qualitative method, we then have a forecast for subsequent periods. When period 1 actual demand is known we can update the forecast for the other periods. Using this method many organisations have found that there forecasting of new products becomes much more accurate.

Demand links to other activities

Finally in this section looking at the Key Aspect of Demand, the following case study shows in one company, how the patterns of demand affect the physical warehouse operations:

Case Study: Entertainment UK, Demand and Warehousing

Entertainment UK is the UK's largest wholesale distributor of home entertainment products, supplying many of Britain's best known retailers with nearly a quarter of the UK music and video industry's entire output. With the ability to unite the interests of suppliers and retailers, it makes it attractive, simple and profitable for them to do business together.

Founded in 1966 as Record Merchandisers Limited, the company achieved rapid growth to become the largest wholesale distributor in the UK. Following Record Merchandisers' Limited rebirth as Entertainment UK in 1988, the company has concentrated on building the systems to become entirely responsive to the commercial and operational needs of individual customers and suppliers.

Specialises
Entertainment UK is a wholly owned subsidiary of the Woolworth's Group plc which specialises in delivering a range of entertainment, home and family products, through its retail, distribution and publishing arms. Entertainment UK's clients include Tesco, Woolworth's, MVC, Safeway, Comet, Waitrose and Makro. Last year its turnover was over £750 million and, with business growing at about 10 per cent a year, Entertainment UK has installed an integrated materials handling system at its new distribution centre. The £114 million system, which has been designed and installed by Vanderlande Industries, uses a mix of picking techniques and automated handling systems to deliver exceptional 99.9 per cent order accuracy.

The project is part of Entertainment UK's development of a new 200,000 sq ft distribution centre in Greenford, Middlesex that will work alongside three existing facilities in the London area. To handle the rapid growth in Entertainment UK's business the new system has been designed to provide a flexible expansion path to accommodate a throughput of up to 120 million items a year by 2003, while supporting an increase in the number of sku's from the current level of 25,000.

The entertainment industry is unusual in having a very large number of both suppliers and products, with the most popular 10 per cent of titles accounting for more than 95 per cent of throughput. This 10 per cent is, however, extremely dynamic, with around 200 changes each week, and new items ('chart toppers') frequently coming in with an exceptionally pronounced volume spike. "The broad mix of products and throughputs made this a very challenging project," commented Alan Faulding, development manager at Entertainment UK. "Inventory is a major part of our costs, so order accuracy, product protection and the accuracy of our stock management are all critical factors in our business improvement."

Reliable
The solution, developed jointly by Vanderlande Industries and Mr. Faulding's team at Entertainment UK, provides reliable, efficient movement and tracking of product from receipt, through appropriate storage and picking systems, to sortation and dispatch. Of the eight companies originally approached, Vanderlande's proposal was slightly more capital intensive but was able to provide substantially greater operational benefits and a preferred operating philosophy. To meet the business requirements efficiently, Vanderlande used automated conveyor systems to integrate storage and picking operations that are optimised for four different levels of throughput. Super-fast items are held in a four-crane high-bay then order picked off pallets in full-tray quantities. Fast and medium movers are batch picked (using a pick to light system) from totes held in a miniload system.

Slow moving items are picked from flow racking or shelving. Product from these three areas is held in the miniload system and sorted for dispatch in a two hour wave. Very slow moving items are order picked directly into cartons. The eight miniload cranes are thought to be the first in Europe to be fitted with four individual handling devices, allowing up to four totes to be stored or retrieved in each pass. Each Tilt Tray Sorter is fed by fully automatic high speed induction units incorporating a combination of state of the art inline labelling and security tagging machines.

Gentle
The tilt-tray sortation system has been optimised for gentle handling of small single items and incorporates sophisticated flow control to ensure that even small products are accurately placed. "We were impressed by the overall quality of the Vanderlande organisation and the rigour they applied to ensure the system delivers the best possible performance," says Mr. Folding. "It was commissioned within the agreed budget and timescales and is proving very accurate."

Source: Distribution Business

Key Component - Lead-time

Lead-time is a critical component in making inventory decisions but is commonly miss-understood or ignored. Understanding demand is an essential first step in inventory management and the time spent in determining the underlying characteristics of demand behaviour will seldom be wasted. However, once this analysis is complete, attention can be switched to the other side of the balance, the supply.

Our ability to be able to balance supply and demand will ultimately determine how much inventory will be required to act as a buffering mechanism. The key aspect about supply is the lead-time. Unfortunately, the term lead-time is interpreted to mean quite different things by different people. We will begin therefore in explaining exactly what we mean by lead-time and how it contributes to inventory management.

For many organisations, supply will necessitate acquiring products from another organisation, typically referred to as a supplier. For others, particularly manufacturing companies, the supplier might be a different part of their own organisation. In either case, the supplier can be asked how long it will take for the buyer/customer/user to receive the goods, after the order has been received by the supplier. The response is used as the supplier lead-time.

It is important to understand that the starting point for the supplier lead-time is the time that the supplier receives the order. The exact ending point will depend on the policy of the supplier. If the customer purchases the product to include delivery, then the end point will be when product arrives at the customer's warehouse.

Supplier lead-time

Sometimes, the customer will buy the product ex-works, in which case the supplier lead-time will end when the product is available at the supplier for despatch.

Of course, it will immediately be apparent that the mode of transport selected will have a defining effect on the length of the lead-time. So will the location of the supplier in relation to the customer. If customer and supplier are separated by long distances and sea transport is used, then the final transit leg of the lead-time will be quite long. In the event of international transport, it is probable that customs clearance will also be involved, which can also add extra time into the calculation.

Impact of order processing

Supplier lead-time is not however the full picture. Before the supplier receives the order the customer must place it. These days most orders are placed using some form of electronic transmission, such as the Internet, EDI, fax or phone, and in these circumstances time between the customers placing the order and the supplier receiving it is in effect zero. However for those organisations that sends orders by post, there will be delays before the supplier receives them. Additionally, for other organisations, there may be some time involved in getting approval to place an order.

Before an order can be placed a decision has to be made to order product. Often as decisions are made, orders will be raised and transmitted to the supplier immediately, thus minimising this time. However, this time may be considerable when a procurement tendering process is used with tender boards meeting infrequently. Also, if decisions are made through the week to place orders, but then all orders are placed on the Friday, a further delay will occur.

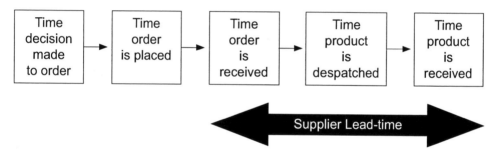

Impact of Receipt operations

At the other end of the supplier lead-time there can also be further time added. When the customer receives the product they may perform inspections and quality checks, these will also add time. It may also be that product is received and put away but delays occur in entering the receipt into the system, meanwhile, the product will be shown as not being available.

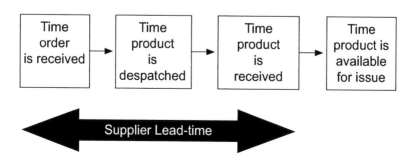

The Supply Lead-time

The total of all the above times, from when the decision is made to order until the product is available for issue represents the supply lead-time. It is this supply lead-time that is important in inventory management and it is used, as we shall see later, as a key component in the replenishment decision of when and how much to order.

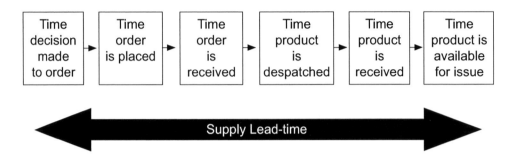

The supply lead-time is the major multiplier of inventory risk and hence it is very important that its make up is fully understood. Too often customers take the lead-time provided by suppliers as given and don't attempt to challenge it or indeed to understand how it has been derived. This can be dangerous as the following story illustrates.

When working with one client that had 300,000 SKU's and very demanding inventory availability targets, we identified that supply lead-times were both long and unreliable. This gave birth to a project to work with suppliers to improve the situation. During the discussions with one supplier, they were asked if it would be possible to reduce the current 20 week supplier lead-time. The supplier responded that it would be and asked what they would like it to be. The client tentatively suggested 18 weeks which received a positive response. Somewhat surprised by the quickness of the response, the supplier was then asked, what they could provide. The supplier stated that they could achieve 2 weeks. This begged the question as to why 20 weeks was being used when 2 weeks could be achieved. The supplier stated that they had never been able to understand why the customer gave them 20 weeks notice, because all they did with the order was to place it in a drawer for 18 weeks before processing it!

Together they explored how the situation had been created and discovered that when the initial relationship had been set up, the customer's buyer had dealt with the supplier's sales manager. For the supplier this was a new account and a significant one. Hence the initial order was larger than they could supply from stock. A lead-time of 20 weeks had therefore been quoted to allow sufficient time for the supplier to manufacture the order and deliver the goods. However, no one had then thought to ask what the lead-time would subsequently be when it was planned for the supplier to satisfy the replenishment orders from stock. If they had asked they would have been told 2 weeks! For several years our client had been using a longer lead-time than necessary and consequently was carrying more stock than was needed with the obvious financial penalty. Whilst this true story may seem unbelievable, it does demonstrate many issues that can arise when lead-times are defined in an arbitrary fashion.

Frequently, when inventory problems exist, people believe it is because forecasts are inaccurate. In our experience, it is more likely to be the result of lead-times being wrongly or inaccurately defined. Consequently analysing lead-times can be fertile improvement territory!

Analysing Lead-times

Since we manage inventory on an item by item basis, the analysis of lead-times must be done for individual items. The first step involves identifying the stages that comprise the overall lead-time. Whilst this may sound simple to do in practice, it will be much harder because people usually will not have thought about things in this way before.

Using our lead-time diagrams from above, we can identify the main stages as:
- Time decision is made to place the order.
- Time the order is placed.
- Time the supplier receives the order.
- Time the supplier despatches the order.
- Time the supplier delivers the order.
- Time the customer makes the product available for issue.

For each stage we can then build up a picture of the times involved for several orders of the same product. It could be that historical information is unavailable, in which case the analysis will have to be established for future orders.

Gradually it will be possible to build up a spreadsheet containing the data for each product code.

Order Number	Decide to order	Place Order	Receive Order	Despatch Order	Delivered Complete	Available for issue
1	14/03/06	14/03/06	15/03/06	29/03/06	07/04/06	08/04/06
2	20/03/06	21/03/06	22/03/06	10/04/06	27/04/06	30/04/06
3	25/03/06	25/03/06	27/03/06	17/04/06	15/05/06	15/05/06

Lead-time Stage Analysis

From this data we can analyse each stage in more detail. Each stage is likely to display the characteristics of the normal distribution.

Lead-time Stage Analysis

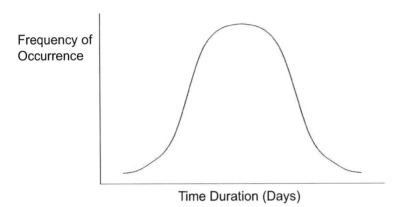

Frequency of Occurrence

Time Duration (Days)

Hopefully the shape of the curve will be tall and thin, indicating that most of the orders are hitting the stated average and that the standard deviation of the time is small.

If it is discovered that a stage contains a lengthy duration, or that there is considerable variability indicated by a high SD, it may be sensible to analyse the stage further and break it down into greater detail. For example, the stage from supplier despatch to customer receipt could be split further into:

- Time supplier despatched order.
- Time order is loaded onto ship at port.
- Time order arrives at destination port.
- Time order is cleared customs.
- Time order arrives at customer warehouse.

Each of these stages can then be analysed to find the likely problem area. If we seek to understand each stage in the process it should enable us to challenge the activities being undertaken and to look for ways to improve the situation.

As well as examining each stage in detail, we can of course build the normal distribution for the overall supply lead-time with its accompanying average lead-time and standard deviation. Later on we will see how this is used in the inventory calculations.

Although we mentioned above, the relative geographical location between customer and supplier, and the mode of transport both impact the overall lead-time, it is worth emphasising this again. Inventory decisions should not be made in isolation of the procurement sourcing and the logistics transport decisions. Selection of transport mode should not happen without consideration of the inventory impact.

Finally, it is also worth highlighting that the lead-time we provide to our customers, does not impact our inventory levels. It is only the supply lead-time that impacts our inventory. Of course, the lead-time to our customer impacts their inventory level and hence they will be keen to ensure it is both minimised and is reliable.

Before we depart the lead-time section there is one other aspect of time which impacts our planning horizons and in particular the forecast horizon.

Planning Horizon

The supply lead-time is the main determinant of the horizon over which we need to plan. For example, if we obtain our items straight from a supplier and the associated supply lead-time is 10 weeks, then it will mean that we have to produce forecasts for the item that extend into the future by 10 weeks.

The situation becomes more complicated when we manufacture the product ourselves. In such a case there will be a manufacturing lead-time that is preceded by a raw material supply lead-time. The planning horizon in this case is at least the length of the sum of the manufacturing and material supply times.

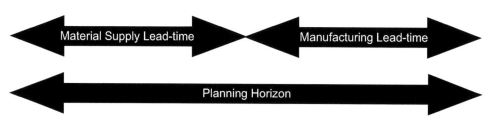

You will recall from the forecasting section that one of the characteristics of forecasts is that they become more inaccurate the further out we forecast. In other words the longer the planning horizon, then the more inaccurate the forecast. Hence seeking to reduce lead-times not only delivers a direct impact on stock levels, but it contributes to an improvement in forecast accuracy and hence also in a reduction of safety stock.

Lead-time Summary

We trust by now you will have appreciated that lead-time is a critical component in making inventory decisions. The following over-simplified example will serve to illustrate the importance of lead-time:

If demand is 70 items per week, and supply LT is 2 weeks:
Then the quantity to order to cover the demand during the supply lead-time (called the lead-time demand), is 140 items.

But if the supply LT is variable by +/- one week, then, the maximum order is 210 items and the minimum order is 70 items. But we may "play it safe" and order 210 items.

This is not the best decision but maybe an understandable one for those who are left to base replenishment decisions on protecting against personal "noise" factors when past stock outs have occurred. In such cases, then clearly inventory management is also not understood or involved both strategically and operationally in the business.

One of the main issues therefore to be resolved with lead-time therefore is not its length, but the uncertainty and variability that can occur. Consider another simple example:

Supply Lead-time (SLT) is halved from 12 to 6 weeks but the supply lead-time variability (SLTV) stays the same at 4 weeks

	Current SLT			**New SLT**		
	SLTV	SLT	SLTV	SLTV	SLT	SLTV
	-4	12	+ 4	-4	6	+4
Total LT	= 8 to 16 weeks			= 2 to 10 weeks		
	(Index 100 to 200)			(Index 100 to 500)		

So, if SLTV stays the same and only SLT is reduced, then there is actually a higher disruption factor.

As we have explored above, lead-time covers many aspects. The following is a comprehensive view of lead-time.

Lead Time	Action	By
Pre order Planning	User	Customer
Procurement	Order placing	Customer to supplier
Supplier	Order despatching	supplier
Production	Making to order	supplier
Warehouse	Supplying from stock	supplier
Transit	Transporting	supplier
Receivers	Receiving	customer
Payment	Paying	Customer to supplier

To repeat, the Supply Lead-time used in inventory calculations is not the same as the above supplier lead-time. The supply lead-time is the total time taken for deciding to order to the time it is available for issue. It is therefore made up of many parts both "internally" within the business and "externally," with the supplier lead-time; these "parts" are shown opposite.

Lead time	Lead Time Stage	Steps, by date
Pre Order Planning	User Need	Analysing status to determining need to order
	User Requisition	Need to order to date of order requisition
Procurement	Order preparation	Order requisition to order release date
	Order confirmation	Order release to date of confirmation
Supplier * see also the production and warehouse lead times	All the stages here are in the production and warehouse lead times	Confirmation to order despatched date
Production (e.g. made to order)	Order processing	Date of order receipt to date order accepted/ confirmed
	Preparation	Order accepted to date manufacture starts
	Manufacture (Queue time, set up, machine /operator time/inspect/put away times)	Start of manufacture to date it finishes
	Pack/Load (to the Warehouse or to Transit LT)	Finished manufacture to date order despatched
Warehouse (e.g. available ex stock	In stock	Date goods arrived to date of order receipt
	Order Processing	Order receipt to date order is accepted or confirmed
	Picking	Date order accepted to date order is available/ picked
	Pack/Load (to Warehouse or to Transit LT)	Order available to date order despatched
Transit		Date despatched to date order received
Receiving		Date order received to date available for issue/use
Payment	Credit	Date invoice received or of other "trigger," to date payment received
	Payment processing	Date payment received to date cash available for use

These lead-times need to be examined using real examples to ensure that all appropriate stages and steps are included. There may even be some additional stages, with for example on imports, the customs clearance lead-time.

After each stage has been quantified, each stage will then need analysing to ask, can we do things better? By understanding the processes first, then rationalising them, lead-time can be dramatically reduced. Often such reductions in lead-time will actually come from improvements to the information flows in the supply chain.

Reducing Lead-times

As already noted the main issue to be resolved with lead-time is not only the length of it but the uncertainty and variability that can occur. Nevertheless, examining lead-time reductions can be beneficial, as shown in the following examples; it will be noted that these go across all aspects of the supply chain, again emphasising the importance of lead-time and its connections to inventory.

Overall

- By simply measuring lead-time as a one-off exercise, this focused management attention on the problem which has lead to a culture which does not tolerate delays. By having a graph on the wall, this has stimulated continuous improvement activities which lead to further improvement.

- A cross-training programme to show inter-and intra-connections.

- A simple office re-organisation and sensible use of readily available IT systems reduced the time taken to conduct contract review for new orders by 80%.

- The scheduling frequency was halved from a monthly planning process to a fortnightly planning process. This reduced lead-times instantly by two weeks (in conjunction with other activities, which reduced the resulting workload).

Procurement

- Scrapped the use of "economic batch sizes" for purchased items and replaced it with a Pareto approach, which reduced shortages by a factor of 10 and did not increase raw material stocks at all.

- A supplier scheduling system which gave suppliers a 6 month planning horizon which reduced supplier shortages by 50%, and the lead-times waiting for the short items.

- A method of highlighting when supplier quotations had reached the end of their life. This meant never running out of order cover and always having an available supply. This had the added advantage of being able to negotiate contract renewals at a pace that helped in the negotiation, because of not being under pressure to do a "quick deal to get the supplies in yesterday".

- Strategic supplier alliances and supplier schedules in a hitherto spot buying situation, which reduced purchase costs by 40% and supplier on-time delivery by 25%.

- Measuring the accuracy of the system's forecasts.

Production

- Trebling of batch sizes on slow moving items and halved batch sizes on the fast moving items by decree, reducing set-ups by half, stock by 20% whilst simultaneously increasing output by 10%.

- Re-scheduling of arrears and removed associated Work in Process, which reduced Work in Process by 30% and lead-times by a similar amount.

- Scrapped a policy of building sub-assemblies because they were quick to assemble as lead-time analysis said we did not need to stock sub-assemblies.

- Reduced set-up times from approximately one hour to minutes by organising tooling racks so that tools were easy to find, and buying a few extra tools to avoid tool sharing (which inevitably meant that they became lost).

- Removed all sub-assemblies from Bills of material, and reduced shop floor paperwork by 50%.

- Stopped issuing materials to the shop floor until productivity started to reduce. Then increasing the rate of issuing again to regain previous productivity. Work in Process Lead-times reduced by 39% and so did Work in Process.

- Introducing a simple spreadsheet-based rough-cut capacity planning process which reduced lead-times by 20% and increased on-time delivery from 40% on-time to 80% on-time in 8 weeks.

- Improved the accuracy of lead-times in an MRP system which was overstated which gave less need to forecast demand.

Warehouse

- Reduced the space available for a quality quarantine area and date marked arrivals in the area, with a named individual who was responsible for scrapping, reworking or raising concessions for the items within 24 hours.

- Improved stock accuracy from about 60% correct to 95% correct by simple continuous stock checking and improving procedures, which reduced component shortages by half.

- Replaced computer-based stock recording systems with simple Kanban controls, which reduced shortages by 30%.

- Implemented a simple spreadsheet-based forecasting tool and a process to review recommendations, which increased first time pick rates by 20%.

Case Study: Lead-times at B&Q

Steve Willett, director of supply chain at B&Q, came to the firm last July from the US, where he worked for aerospace and engineering firm Allied Signal. There, he was on the other side of the fence feeling the pressure that Wal-Mart puts on its suppliers. But he has come away with a profound admiration for the quality of supply chain management in the US and a burning ambition to mimic it in the UK. "We want to be a world-class supply chain that is talked about as a leader in the field," he says.

"Effective delivery performance by the supplier has to become a minimum requirement for doing business with B&Q. The norm of delivery is far better in the US than in the UK, but the supermarkets here have effectively driven up the performance of their suppliers and we are going to do the same for the DIY industry."

B&Q's wider strategy of slashing the retail prices of goods through savings has led to growth of between 25 per cent and 30 per cent a year for the past few years. However, it has also meant that savings are being constantly sought from the supply chain. Since September, Willett has put different supply chain projects in place, with Easter at the front of his mind.

"The Easter trading pattern is very significant because it is so concentrated and there is no time to recover," he says. On some seasonal lines, such as garden furniture, there is a 15-month lead-time, but on others, such as peat, the constraint is how many lorries the company can get on the ferries from Ireland. At Easter, the line between store and warehouse often becomes a little blurred, with 40-foot containers sometimes sitting in the car parks to maximise the selling space inside the stores.

Project work
The supply chain projects, which have examined almost every aspect of the firm's supply process, have looked at:
- How handling can be minimised, so that stock can be taken from the delivery lorries to be stored on pallets in the 300 stores;

- Ensuring that space is given to the best-selling lines, so that they maintain a constant presence on the shelves;

- e-replenishment mechanisms;

- Ensuring that the five regional consolidation centres that handle stock from abroad are incorporated into the delivery from the four distribution centres;

- Ensuring that new procedures are put into place, with 30 implementation managers working in the stores;

- Supplier development

Willett says this last one is not as sinister as it sounds: "We are not expecting overnight revolutions and saying to suppliers, 'perform or else'. It's a matter of working with them to set targets and help them to get there. Supply chain management is one of the company's biggest internal costs and, if we are to deliver savings to the customer, we have to become more efficient. There will be suppliers that will be too slow and unable to get there as we ratchet the bar down, and I have no doubt we will lose some along the way. But, with that said, we want to achieve a fairly stable supplier base and work with suppliers in partnerships."

Mark-Paul Homberger, B&Q's vendor performance manager, predicts that some household names will be de-listed from the firm's supplier base. B&Q has instituted a system of green, amber and red status for suppliers, where green signifies a fine relationship, amber that there will be no new business and red that they should sort themselves out or face being de-listed. "We have to ensure availability to the customer and if suppliers can't get their act together on lead-times, we are absolutely serious that we will source elsewhere," explains Homberger.

B&Q is going the same way as supermarket giants Tesco and Sainsbury's (owner of rival DIY chain Home base), he suggests. "Our vendor-buying agreements will include agreed service levels and, crucially, lead-times," he says. "When things fall apart at the seams, we need to know what the action plan is to recover. Often with domestic suppliers, poor performance can be attributed to the fact that they won't invest the capital, but we want to emphasise that it is really in the supplier's interest to give us a better deal."

Source: Supply Management 20 April 2000

Key Component - Cost and Benefits

The aim of inventory management is to achieve the required level of availability at an acceptable cost. Achieving the desired balance between these two opposing requirements is not an easy task.

If the balance favours availability, the sales team and our customers are likely to be pleased, but the accountants will doubtless raise concerns about the increased financial investment. If the balance favours the cost side, the accountants will be happy, but the sales team is likely to be unhappy as sales are lost due to the poor availability.

The task of achieving balance will be even more difficult when the product characteristics of the item constrain the shelf life or allow product substitution to occur with a competing product. In such circumstances the consequences of "getting it wrong" can be financially very damaging.

For example in 2001, the cost for CISCO USA was a $2.1billion write-off and whilst the CISCO experience may be unusual in its scale, it does provide demonstration of how difficult it is to achieve balance between cost and availability in practice. It will therefore be helpful to understand how each side of the balance works in more detail; however a short "word of warning" first on traditional accounting practices.

Inventory and Traditional Accounting practices

The generally accepted accounting principles do create the foundation for all organisations to report financial data in the same way and such principles having a long history, for example, back to the early days of industrialisation. Such a history has meant that accounting rules have not always kept up with current business practices.

Whilst this has been recognised and has resulted in some new accounting methods, (for example Activity Based Costing), profit/ loss and balance sheets statements do still reflect traditional historic accounting practices and do not reflect current global supply chain practises.

Some of the differences between supply chain management and accounting have been noted as follows:

(Based on source: Tom Craig ttp://www.ltdmgmt.com/mag/index.html)

	Supply Chains	Accounting
Process	Horizontal flows across different organisations and functions.	Vertical transactions within one "silo" in an organisation.
Focus	External with suppliers and contractors and customers/consumers.	Internal looking and within organisational boundaries.
Time	Ongoing flows of products and information. For example, inventory turnover and lead times performances impact the financial figures, but are not reported in company accounts	Period reporting causes disconnects. For example, inventory is reported on the balance sheet annually but the warehouse holding costs appear monthly in the cost accounts
Perspective	Dynamic and changing. Forward looking.	Static and historical. Backward looking.

In view of these differences, it is important that inventory management ensure they understand how financial accounting practices work, as these will most certainly have an impact on the organisational decision-making.

Inventory Costs
The treatment of inventory in the financial accounts of a company is different to other cost areas. Of course the financial management will be undertaken by experts in this area. However, it is important for an inventory manager to understand how inventory appears on the balance sheet and how it impacts the profit and loss account, cash flow and the return on capital employed.

So far we have seen that there are typically three sorts of inventory that can be present in a company: raw materials, work in progress and finished goods. The nature and mix of the inventory will depend on the operating environment of the individual organisation. In particular, there will be significant differences between manufacturing and distribution companies. As a consequence of these differences the accounting treatment of inventory can vary.

Valuing Inventory
If a financial value is to be assigned to inventory some assumptions must be made about the inventory physically on hand. There are several methods that can be used:

1) First-In, First-Out (FIFO)
This valuation method assumes that the first goods that are purchased will be the first ones to be despatched irrespective of the timing of the sale. This method is the one that usually resembles the physical flow most closely.

2) Last-In, First-Out (LIFO)
This method assumes that the items that have been recently purchased will be the ones that are sold first, regardless of when the actual sales take place. Frequently, the items that are purchased most recently cost more than those acquired a while ago. This method is best used to match current costs with current revenues.

3) Average Cost Method
This method tries to overcome the issues of FIFO and LIFO by calculating an average cost for items. It is calculated by working out the total cost of all goods available for sale and dividing it by the total quantity of goods being held. Of course this method assigns the same cost to all items which is usually not the case.

4) Actual Cost Method
This method assumes that the actual cost of each item can be tracked. It requires powerful computer systems and is usually reserved for operations that are involved with make-to-order product strategies.

5) Standard Cost Method
This method is often used in manufacturing to give a standard value to an item for a specified period of time. It takes into account the actual cost and any foreseen changes that will occur during the period under review.

The choice of the one to use will depend on the circumstances of the company. Often the accounting conventions specified by fiscal authorities in the country of operation, will dictate which method is used for financial reporting purposes. The method that has been used is often stated in the financial reports.

We can now explore how inventory impacts each of the financial statements. To illustrate the impact we will use an example of running a small convenience store.

Inventory Impact on Revenue, Cost and Profit

Revenue is the total sales in financial terms that our organisation makes. So, for example, if a convenience store sold 50,000 items at an average of $2 per item, then it receives $100,000 in cash over one year. Our total revenue would be $100,000.

Cost is the total cost in financial terms, which is attributable to that years trading. For example, the costs in our store for 1 year may be as follows:

Lighting/Heating/Water	$2,000
Telephones/Faxes	$1,000
Staff salaries	$30,000
Cost of goods	$50,000 *
Total Cost	$83,000

* We bought each item for $1 dollar and sold 50,000 during the year. This gives a cost of goods sold of $50,000.

Profit can then be obtained from the following calculation:
Revenue – Cost = Profit

So for our business we can see that the Profit can be calculated as:
$100,000 - $83,000 = $17,000 Profit

In reality ,the profit here would be referred to as operating profit. There would still be interest to pay on any money borrowed for the business, for example from a bank. Once this charge has been removed, the final figure given is the contribution. There would also be a tax on this figure that is dependant on which country you were operating in.

For annual company accounts, this process can be seen within the "Profit and Loss" statement. This example shows a profit being realised. However, if the costs were more than the revenue our profit would be negative, demonstrating a loss; hence the term "Profit and Loss".

Company strategy can influence many variables that are seen on the profit and loss account. Price, for example, if increased whilst unit sales stay the same, will drive up revenue. If a discounting strategy is adopted, numbers of units sold may increase but revenue may drop for the business. Additionally, one of the biggest drivers of revenue is the overall customer service package on offer. The supply chain activities contribute to the make up of the cost of goods sold (COGS). The following diagram shows how this process takes place and identifies the competitive variables and the supply chain variables that influence the profit and loss (revenue and cost):

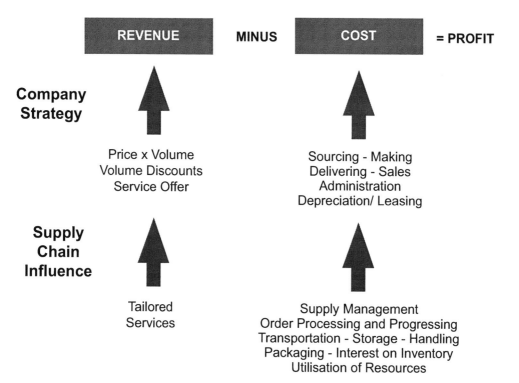

The profit and loss account covers a given period of time, usually one year. Providing the sale of the item and the purchase of the materials to make it, occur in the same period, both the revenue and cost will occur in the profit and loss statement. When however material is purchased in one time period and then is used in a later period and adjustment has to be made to the profit to allow for the increase in stock levels.

Inventory Impact on the Balance Sheet
The balance sheet of the company shows the financial worth of the company at a specific point in time.

In addition to revenue and cost as drivers of profit/loss, there are other factors to be taken into account, which have a critical impact on corporate financial performance.

These are:
*   Fixed assets
*   Current assets
*   Liabilities

1) Fixed Assets
By using our convenience store analogy, if the shop building were owned outright, its value would be listed on the balance sheet. Also the equipment that was owned, for example the store computer, would have its value listed as a fixed asset on the balance sheet.

2) Current Assets
In the analogy, debtors could be customers who hold an account with the store and pay their account balances one month in arrears. Debtors are current assets and the store would wish to turn them into cash as soon as possible.

Stock is also a current asset so all the products that are on shelves or in the stock room will have a value and will appear on the balance sheet.

Also if there is cash in the bank this will be recorded as a current asset.

3) Current Liabilities
These are third parties that are owed money (creditors). Examples here are suppliers that have not yet been paid for the goods they have delivered or a bank overdraft.

4) Long term liabilities
For example, the mortgage on the store.

Share capital or Shareholders funds
These terms refer to those who initially put money into the business or have since invested in the business and are owed money or a return on that money. It also refers to reserves and retained profit - the profit kept from previous years to reinvest in the business.

As the assets must equal the liabilities or "Balance" this statement is referred to as the Balance Sheet. Again the supply chain impact can be seen in the following diagram (opposite):

ASSETS

FIXED ASSETS

Property, plant and equipment

Own or lease distribution facilities, equipment?

Storage, transportation and systems choices?

CURRENT ASSETS

Cash - Liquidity
Inventory - Stock

LIABILITIES

CURRENT LIABILITIES

Trade creditors
Overdraft

SHAREHOLDERS' FUNDS

Share Capital Reserves
Return to Shareholders?

LONG TERM LIABILITIES

Return on total investment

It is important to see how a revenue and cost statement and balance sheet can work over a period of time. The convenience store analogy is further considered in the spreadsheet overleaf.

$2 Selling price of 1 unit
$1 Cost to purchase 1 unit

Revenue and Cost Statement

Revenue and Cost Statement	Year 1	Year 2	Year 3	Year 4	Year 5
Number of Units sold	50 000	50 000	50 000	50 000	50 000
Number of Units bought	75 000	75 000	75 000	75 000	75 000
Revenue	$100 000	$100 000	$100 000	$100 000	$100 000
Cost of Goods Sold	$50 000	$50 000	$50 000	$50 000	$50 000
Write Off Obselete Stock					$125 000
Operating profit	$50 000	$50 000	$50 000	$50 000	-$75 000

Balance Sheet

Balance Sheet	Year 1	Year 2	Year 3	Year 4	Year 5
Current Assets - Stock	$25 000	$50 000	$75 000	$100 000	$125 000

Take from Profit
$125 000

New Total
$0

If 75,000 units are purchased in Year 1 at a cost of $1 and 50,000 are sold at $2 then from the equation (revenue – cost = profit) the initial profit figure would be $50,000. From the spreadsheet, this can be seen continuing over 5 years. Notice how the stock that hasn't been sold builds on the balance sheet. Every year the store has not sold 25,000 units, and so has $25,000 on its balance sheet as assets.

The key point here is that, although for the first four years profits have been good (every year is $50,000), the unsold stock has been cumulatively building up on the balance sheet. By year 5 it has been decided that this stock is now obsolete and must be written off the balance sheet. Moving the figure from the balance sheet and taking it away from the profit on the revenue and cost statement does this. The stock on the balance sheet will then return to zero and the revenue and cost statement shows a large loss in Year 5 of $75,000!

Although this model is simplified, it can be seen occurring in industries that involve very short lifecycles in their products, e.g. clothing fashion retailing and technology products. These organisations often have issues with large obsolete inventories on their balance sheets that they are unwilling to write off, as it will severely damage the year-end profit figures. Some organisations will continue to pay for the storage of obsolete product, rather than absorb the loss against their profits; they delay the inevitable!

Inventory Impact on Cash Flow

Cash flow or 'funds flow' is concerned with the amount of cash available in the business at any one time. This is a very important part of operating a business. For example, a business may make a good profit but if it doesn't have cash available to pay the monthly interest to the bank or to pay suppliers, then it will fail. If the convenience store analogy is considered it is possible to examine two funds flow situations:

Scenario A
- Every week the store takes $2000 dollars in the till in sales from customers.
- At the start of every week the supplier delivers goods and receives a cash payment of $1000.
- The store then still has $1000 to invest in the business or use elsewhere.

Scenario B
- Every week the store takes $2000 dollars in the till in sales from customers.
- At the start of every quarter of the year the supplier delivers goods and receives a cash payment of $13,000 up front.
- The store needs to borrow money from the bank to pay for the stock, which it then pays back during the next quarter's trading while paying interest to the bank.
- The store has no spare cash available to invest elsewhere.

Even though sales through the store and the volumes received from the supplier are the same in both scenarios, the first example has a much better cash flow than the second. Scenario A has a better cash flow, as orders placed with supplier are smaller and more frequent. Other ways of improving cash flow are:
- Leasing both facilities and in-company transport equipment. By doing this capital is released in the same way as the stock example above.
- Reducing debtors; if people who owe money to the business are reduced or paid faster, cash flow is improved.
- By lengthening the time to pay creditors (e.g. suppliers), cash flow is improved. This can been seen in organisations that give terms and conditions to suppliers that their payment terms are no longer 30 days but are now 60 days from receipt of invoice.

This is summarised in the following diagram:

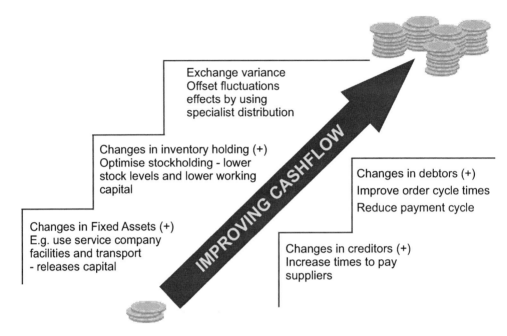

Inventory Impact on Return on Investment

The next step is to look at methods that are used to monitor how a business is performing or to be able to give a "Health Check".

Most organisations aim to give the best return possible to their shareholders. However, the majority aim to do this in order to retain their investors' money in the business, so they can continue operating and even attract new investors who can lend them money to grow or expand their businesses. The key attraction is to give an investor a larger return than if the investor had simply put the money in the bank for a nominal interest payment.

A future investor may want to know how much money they will see on a $100 investment in the company in a year's time. Another way of looking at it, is what return the investor would get on the capital employed ($1) in the business over one year.

The capital employed can be used in financial measures. For example, profit divided by the capital employed will give a common measure of the return on capital employed (ROCE). If, for example, the investor puts $1 into a business; the business makes a profit of $25,000, and has capital employed of $100,000, the ROCE will be 1:4 or 25%. If bank interest is 10% then the investor will get a good return. The process can be seen diagrammatically:

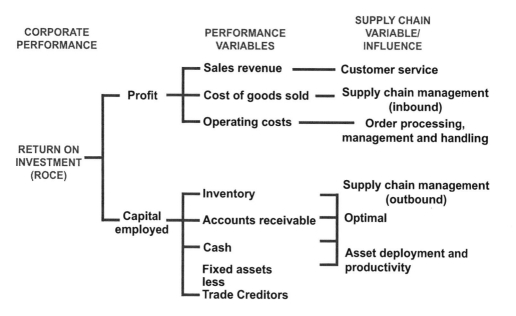

It is clear that in order to improve corporate financial performance the profit needs to be larger. By improving customer service within the supply chain, sales can be helped to grow. By managing the supplier product costs (COGS) and keeping operating costs down, the profit can be increased. There is also an argument for leasing company vehicles, equipment and facilities as this will reduce the capital employed and increase the ROCE. Similarly, by reducing debtors and lengthening times to pay creditors, the overall capital employed will go down. Within companies, the statements "get things moving and moving fast" and "sweat your assets" come from this philosophy.

The ROCE can also be referred to as return on investment (ROI). Other measures investigated are profit margin (profit/sales) and capital turnover (sales/capital employed). As shown below, when multiplied, they equal ROCE:

$$\frac{\text{PROFIT}}{\text{SALES}} \quad X \quad \frac{\text{SALES}}{\text{CAPITAL EMPLOYED}} \quad = \quad \frac{\text{PROFIT}}{\text{CAPITAL EMPLOYED}}$$

We know that the supply chain has an indirect impact on sales as improved service tends to lead to better sales. From the equation above we can see therefore that the supply chain has an indirect impact on profit and hence profit margin.

However, the supply chain has a direct impact on capital employed and therefore, capital turnover or asset turnover. The supply chain has therefore, a very powerful multiplicative impact on margin. If capital employed is reduced by 50% then our ROI will double.

Inventory Turnover Ratio

Since inventory is an asset, we can separate it out from the other assets to give us an inventory turnover ratio. There are two ratios that can be used.

Inventory Turnover Ratio 1 = Sales / Inventory Value

This measurement can easily be calculated from the information contained in the financial reports, since both sales (in profit and loss account) and inventory (in balance sheet) are stated. Consequently this ratio is often used by financial analysts as a means to assess how a company is managing its supply chain.

This inventory turnover ratio is an important measure because it indicates how quickly inventory is moved through an organisation. Sometimes an alternative calculation is used by replacing sales with the cost of goods sold (COGS).

Inventory Turnover Ratio 2 = Cost of Goods Sold / Inventory Value

This can be a preferable measure since it reflects actual costs incurred from purchasing the inventory. Sales may not directly relate to the cost of goods sold because of pricing policies. However, it is not always possible to determine COGS from the financial reports of an organisation.

Hidden Financial Impact of Inventory

Thus far we have indicated how inventory directly impacts the financial performance of a company. There is, however, a further impact which is often not as obvious.

The fact that we are holding inventory means that we must have a facility to hold it in. Usually this will be some form of warehouse. The costs of operating this warehouse will appear in the profit and loss account. If the building and equipment are owned, then they will appear as an asset on the balance sheet. Additionally, we may have costs associated with insuring the stock and disposal costs for destroying any damaged and obsolete items. Allowances may also have to be made for shrinkage and theft. All these will appear in the profit and loss account as a cost.

Furthermore, in order to manage our inventory, we will need computer systems and office facilities. We will also need to employ people to acquire and manage the stock.

Although inventory does not directly relate to transport cost there is a close relationship, for example, it may be preferable to incur higher transport costs by ordering goods in smaller quantities more often, so that we minimise the level of inventory that is being held.

Inventory Benefits

It is very easy to concentrate attention on the financial impact of inventory and in most organisations there will be direct action to seek to reduce inventory levels. However, it should be remembered that we hold inventory for a purpose; to provide product availability in order to secure sales and hence revenue.

Earlier we have discussed how the level of stock cover increases exponentially, as the availability target increases above 95%. We also highlighted how inventory could be used in an offensive strategy, to win market share and as a defensive strategy, to prevent the loss of share.

For many companies they would not be able to secure sales without holding inventory. Some people would therefore describe inventory as a necessary evil.

Clearly our goal should be to optimise the level of inventory to support the level of sales. This of course must be a business decision and not just one assigned to inventory managers and the ability to achieve this optimisation will be hindered or assisted by a number of key factors, as follows:

- The first is the ability to create visibility, to enable us to understand the variations that are happening within the supply chain. This requires us to develop and open up the flow of information, and will depend upon the levels of collaboration and trust between organisations in sharing what may be quite sensitive commercial information.

- A great deal is made of partnerships in the supply chain, however it should be noted that with the differing objectives of the different companies involved in a supply chain, this often means the reality of a true partnership is perhaps a long way off for many supply chain players. Collaborations however, with shared values and aims are possible, and there are many cases active today. This topic has been more fully explored in the book *"The Relationship Driven Supply Chain, creating a culture of collaboration throughout the chain"* by Stuart Emmett and Barry Crocker (2006).

- Sharing the retailers Point of Sale (POS) data with all collaborative members of a supply chain will ensure that all members are planning on the same set of numbers.

- The need for accurate forecasting is an obvious misnomer as all forecasting will, to a greater and lesser extent, have errors and be inaccurate. Only confirmed orders are truly accurate. Hence, there is a need to measure forecasting accuracy comparing actual with forecast. The aim here is to try and use the most accurate and focused data, within the shortest time period possible.

- The general direction of the supply chain is, wherever possible, to move to a Just-in-Time (J.I.T) replenishment method, which responds to customers replenishment requirements. Some suppliers and manufacturers may use a Vendor Managed Inventory (VMI) replenishment method; here it is the supplier who decides how much and when replenishment is required (VMI and other methods of managing the supply chain and inventory are examined later in the book).

Inventory policies

An important part of the inventory manager's role is the setting of inventory policies.

POLICIES

Stocking level and inventory turns
Order frequency and quantity
Safety stock and customer service
Surplus and excess definition
Inventory accuracy and adjustments
Organisational development, education, training

PLANNING

Dependent versus independent demand
Inventory allocation
Order quantity
Safety stock
Forecast

CONTROL

Issues and receipts
Adjustments
Transfers
Cycle counting
Identification

These policies are the rules that will dictate:
- When orders are placed on suppliers.
- How much those orders will be for.

The policies will also influence the accuracy of inventory records and hence the accuracy of the information used to make decisions. Policies will be needed for dealing with excess and damaged stock. Together the policies lay the foundation for inventory performance and the consequent service and investment balance.

Inventory planning involves the determination of future demand so that inventory can be put in place to support it. This will involve the positioning and allocation of inventory in the network. Safety stock levels and order quantities will also need to be planned.

The control elements of the job involve controlling the receipts and issues of inventory. When necessary, transfers and adjustments will need to be made. To ensure the accuracy of inventory records, inventory will need to be counted and reconciled.

The decisions about where to locate inventory, in what format and quantity, are clearly important in deciding the overall ability of an organisation to supply their customers cost effectively.

At the customer end, the decisions will focus upon availability and service requirements, whilst at the supply end the decisions focus on replenishment quantities and production batch sizes.

All these questions require answers that will impact upon the key decisions of:
- How much inventory will I carry?
- When do I replenish my inventory?
- How much inventory do I order?
- How long will it take to replenish?

Between the suppliers and the customers, the answers to these questions will enable the company to set a series of rules that will run the inventory decision-making within the supply chain.

The holding of inventory can have benefits in sales and marketing as the level of availability can drive sales upwards. Good, reliable customer service is a powerful competitive weapon and inventory availability is a key component of this customer proposition. Inventory levels can also secure benefits in manufacturing where holding stock can lead to improved yields and reduced downtime.

Inventory management needs to recognise it cannot work in isolation within the materials, logistics or the overall supply chain systems. It can have a significant effect, through the inventory policies it employs, on many of the inter-related activities of the organisation.

Inventory in the longer term in organisations

Inventory management is largely looked upon as a day-to-day operation concerned with meeting specified short-term targets. However, it does have a major role to play in the short, medium and long-term developments of an organisation and should be an integral part of the business planning cycle covering the strategic, planning, and operational and control requirements; these are now explored.

1) Strategic Requirements

The need to be aware of the expected development of the business in terms of future production, suppliers, customers and volumes, is essential to enable inventory management to make recommendations, measure the impact and plan the necessary actions to meet the long-term requirements.

Decisions on what product lines to stock, where to stock them and the form of the distribution network, to achieve the continuing optimisation of investment cost and service level is an on-going process in which inventory management needs to be involved.

2) Planning Requirements

Most inventory planning cycles follow the business planning cycle based on a one-year time frame.

Expected changes in such factors as seasonality, volumes, supplier lead-times, required service levels, product and operational costs, can have a big impact on inventory requirements. Such information, within the medium-term time frame, needs to be available to inventory management with sufficient lead-time to establish and implement any changes to the processes and/or control of the inventory system.

3) Operational Requirements

These refer specifically to those elements that create, in the short-term, constraints or opportunities within the inventory process. They are generally concerned with specific actions taken, or which need to be taken, to meet changes in the level of activities not previously identified within the medium term planning cycle.

4) Control Requirements

In most inventory systems, the parameters and controls that determine the key triggers that result in the levels of inventory held on a line-by-line basis, are not always capable of being responsive quickly enough to meet unexpected short-term variations and deviations.

At this stage inventory management may see fit to intervene.

It is essential that inventory management, at such times, have available sufficient data and information, in a usable form, to apply alternative decision-making processes to maintain the inventory system effectiveness.

In doing so the consistency of decision-making is a major objective in achieving the alternative course of action.

The key message is that inventory management must be geared towards achieving the target level of inventory at the right target time and place.

3: Inventory Replenishment Methods and Systems

In this chapter we are concerned with the two fundamental decisions that must be made: when to order and how much to order. We begin by explaining the basic mechanics of any inventory system. Next we look in detail at the available methods and systems that can be used:

- Fixed order quantity (also known as variable order time, reorder level or continuous review) method.

- Variable order quantity (also known as fixed order time cycle, reorder point or periodic review) method.

- Requirements planning methods.

Basic Mechanics of Inventory Systems

Many people practice inventory management in their daily routine without ever realising it. One such area that illustrates this is how we purchase petrol when driving a car.

When the fuel gauge is registering full, we pay little attention to the level of stock and there is little concern about running out. As the level of stock falls, the fuel gauge gradually descends until at a certain level the light comes on or there is an audible warning. This is a warning of **when to order**, as unless we think about placing an order, we will run out of stock.

In determining this point we have to think about two things:

Firstly, supply - obviously if the location of the petrol station is known and we also know that it is open, there is less uncertainty and we may be prepared to run the level of fuel stock quite low. If however, we do not know the area we may be inclined to call at the first fuel station we find, effectively placing our order early to protect against the uncertainty.

The second factor to consider is demand - if we are driving fast, then more petrol will be used as our consumption figures are higher. If we have travelled this way before, then we can in effect forecast how much fuel will be used before we reach the fuel station.

Taking both the supply and demand conditions into account, we formulate a plan. If things go according to plan, then we will reach the fuel station and refuel without any mishaps.

On reaching the fuel station we then have to make the second inventory decision, deciding **how much to order**. Some who travel only locally, doing few kilometres, may put a fixed quantity in each time, perhaps using a certain sum of money or a certain volume; this is a fixed order quantity (FOQ) system. Others who travel longer distances may fill the fuel tank up, needing a variable order each time; this is a variable order quantity (VOQ) system.

Some people may believe that the level of uncertainty is too great and hence increase their safety stock by carrying a spare can of fuel.

This cycle of activity is repeated over and over again without much thought. If, however, circumstances change, we have to question whether the parameters are still relevant or make adjustments. It is a simple but effective inventory system.

The Stock Time curve
Within the inventory system the cycle of activity can be represented by a stock time curve. This curve is the foundation of inventory management. From it we can understand:

- The characteristics of the stock time curve.
- The components of inventory.
- The average stockholding stock investment.

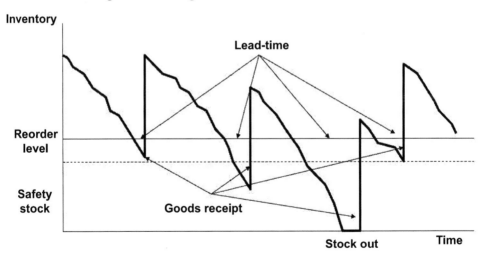

The stock time curve identifies:
- The pattern of stock carried resulting from the supply and demand activity (the complete curve).

- The time of receipt of supplies and the quantity received.

- The point in time or stock level when orders should be placed (reorder point and reorder level).

- The stock held against uncertainty in supply and demand (Safety stock).

- The point in time when a stock-out occurs (Stock out).

- The time between ordering and receipt (Lead-time).

A stock time curve is like a fingerprint. It is unique to that item and it is unlikely that any two items will behave in the same way. It is for these reasons that inventory must be managed on an item-by-item basis.

The two basic stock components
The Stock Time Curve illustrates the two basic components of inventory as being:

- Replenishment or cycle stock
- Safety or buffer stock

1) Replenishment or Cycle Stock
This is the stock that comes from the ordering policies. The level of cycle stock is determined by the quantity and frequency (the how much and when).

2) Safety or Buffer Stock
This is the stock that is held as a "cushion" against uncertainty in supply and/or demand. It is the prime source of stock availability to satisfy customer demand and as a consequence the safety stock determines the service level.

Other stock components
In addition, further components of stock can be found in many companies and have special requirements that we will not address directly.

1) Anticipation stock
This is the stock procured in advance of known requirements e.g. scheduled planned requirements, product launch, promotions, seasonal demands, purchases to take advantage of market exploitation. It is essentially demand-orientated.

2) Movement stock
This is stock which is in transit between suppliers and customers and can be separately identified.

3) Speculative stock
This is stock bought for investment purposes, e.g. raw material bought forward. It is essentially supply-orientated.

Stock investment
To establish the level of stock investment it is necessary to understand the basis upon which this is calculated. It will, of course, be determined by the policies,

methods and techniques used in the management and control of inventory. The first of the contributors to stock investment is that which results from the ordering policies related to quantity and frequency i.e. the replenishment or cycle stock.

The basis of the calculation is the order quantity. However, the level of stock resulting from the receipt of an order will vary between the maximum at the time of receipt and the minimum, which is zero.

It is necessary, therefore, to express the stock investment as an average condition, as the following diagram shows:

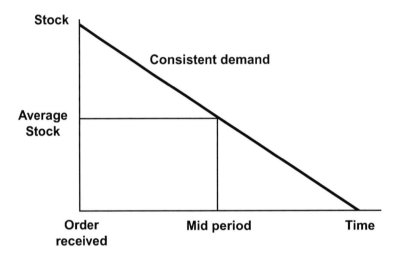

If we assume the order quantity that is initially received is 3,000 and covers the total demand for one year, then the average stock Q/2 or 3000/2 = 1500.

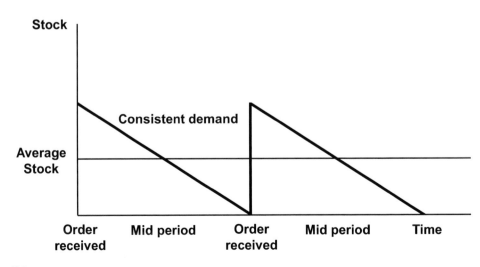

If we decide instead to order twice a year, each time ordering 1500, the average stock would again be Q/2 or 1500/2 = 750.

In the above examples, the order quantity used has been fixed. When the order quantity is not fixed i.e. different sized orders are planned to meet the total demand, the average stock holding is based upon the average of the total orders placed over the year. Suppose we received order quantities of 1000, 1500 and 500. The average order quantity would be (1000 + 1500 + 500)/3 = 1000. Our average stock would then be Q/2 or 1000/2 = 500.

The examples assume that there is no variation in demand, which is even and steady, and therefore no safety stock is required to protect any uncertainty in demand.

The second of the contributors to stock investment is that which results from the protection of uncertainty in supply and demand, together with the service level to be provided i.e. safety stock. In practice it will be seen that on some occasions there will be a requirement to use some of the safety stock and on other occasions the stock will stay above the safety stock level.

The following diagram provides an example of an item that has variability in both demand i.e. not steady and even; and variability in supply i.e. varying lead-times.

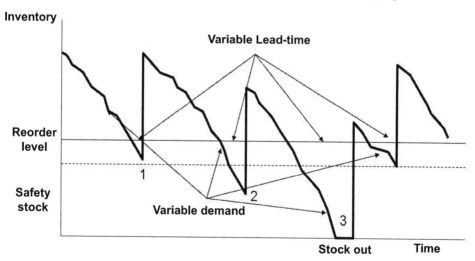

At position 1 on the curve the safety stock has not been used. Some of the safety stock has been used at position 2, and at position 3 all the safety stock was used resulting in a stock out.

If we consider the average position, the safety stock will always be present. Of course, the stock will be rotated physically in the warehouse, but it will remain at the same level on average.

Given the two major contributors of cycle stock and safety stock, average stockholding can be generally expressed, on an item by item basis as follows:

$$Average\ Stock = \frac{Average\ Order\ Quantity}{2} + Safety\ Stock$$

Using our example of three orders a year to meet a total annual demand of 3,000 and assuming that the safety stock required is 20, the average stock investment would be:

$$\frac{1000}{2} + 20 = 520$$

The average stock is measured in the same units as the demand and order quantity. Average stockholding can be converted into stock investment by multiplying the number of units by the unit cost. For example, in the above case if the items cost $100 each our stock investment would be:

Stock Investment = 520 x 100 = $52,000.

This would be the figure that would be shown in the balance sheet of the company. The interest cost of holding this stock at say 10% would be $5,200 and this would appear in the profit and loss account as an interest cost.

In situations where anticipation or speculative stock is also held it would be added to the average stock calculated above.

Free Stock

On a real stock time curve, the quantity of stock that is represented on the vertical axis is the free stock. Free stock consists of several components and is calculated as follows:

Physical stock on hand
+
Stock on order from suppliers
+
Stock in transit
-
Stock allocated to customers
-
Stock reserved for special purposes

1) Physical Stock on Hand
The physical stock on hand is the amount of stock present in the warehouse of a particular item.

2) Stock on Order from Supplier

As orders are placed with a supplier, this needs to be recorded as stock on order. It is possible that several orders may be outstanding from a supplier in which case they need to be totalled to determine the stock on order.

3) Stock in Transit

In some instances the lead-time from the supplier may be long, perhaps involving sea transport. The visibility of stock is important. It maybe that purchase has been made on terms of Delivered buyers' premises, in which case the transit may not be visible. However, if the buyer has purchased goods from a supplier on Incoterms Ex Works (EXW) or Free on Board (FOB); then once the stock has left, it ceases to be stock on order and becomes stock in transit. In all events, the visibility of stock in transit is important and indeed, many organisations do specifically choose EXW or FOB Incoterms for this very reason.

4) Stock Allocated To Customers

Often when a customer places an order a check will be made to determine if stock is available. If it is, the sale is confirmed and the stock is then allocated to the customer to avoid it being resold to another customer.

5) Stock Reserved For Special Purposes

Sometimes it is necessary to build up stock levels for some special purpose. For example, this may happen prior to the launch of a sales promotion. In such a case the stock is reserved so that it will not be used for other purposes.

There are two situations that require extra explanation.

Suppose that we have no stock physically on hand, 100 on order with the supplier and zero in each of the categories. Free stock would therefore be 100. If the reorder level was 90 we would not place an order despite being physically out of stock. Placing a further order would not resolve the problem. The appropriate action is to expedite the 100 that is on order.

In the second situation we have 10 on hand, 0 on order and in transit and 0 reserved for special purposes. If a customer placed an order for 6 it needs to be allocated so that free stock is reduced to 10 − 6 = 4. When the next customer tries to place an order for 5 we can see that there is insufficient free stock to meet the order. If we had not allocated the first order it would still appear that free stock was 10 creating a situation where we over commit.

Let's explore how these mechanics are applied in different types of inventory systems; we shall examine in detail the two main stock inventory replenishments methods (or systems) that are available:
- Fixed Order Quantity or Continuous Review.
- Fixed Order Cycle or Periodic Review.

Fixed Order Quantity System

The first system we will examine is the fixed order quantity system or reorder level system; it is also referred to as the variable order time cycle system and the continuous review system.

This system is the most straightforward inventory system. It works in the following way. When a customer places an order, the stock is allocated and deducted from free stock. The new free stock level is compared to the predetermined reorder level and if it is less, an order is placed. If the free stock level is equal to or higher than the reorder level no action is taken.

When the next customer order is received the process is repeated, hence the name continuous review. Each time an order is placed the same size order is used, hence why it is referred to as fixed order quantity.

The cycle of activity is shown in the diagram below. Note that the free stock level will continue to deplete after the order has been placed during the lead-time, until the order is received.

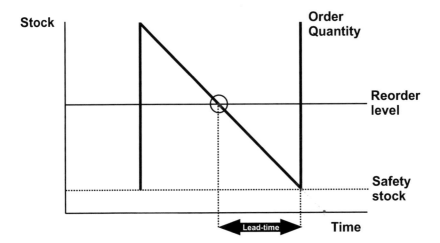

The system is very robust adjusting itself to changing circumstances. Consider for example what happens when demand slows down below the expected level.

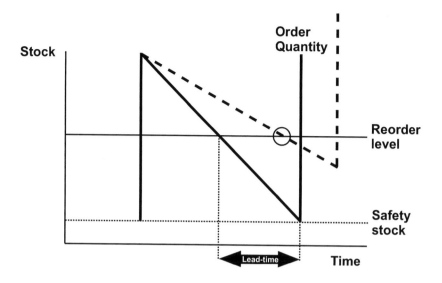

The lower level of demand means that the reorder level is reached later and not so much stock is used once the order is placed.

Conversely, when demand is higher than expected the situation depicted below occurs.

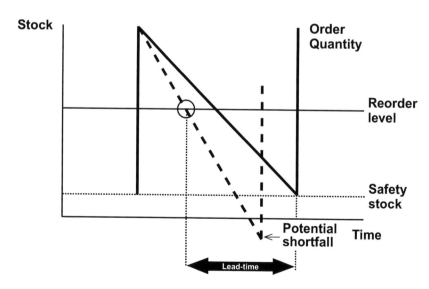

The reorder level is reached earlier, and because demand is higher than expected, more will be used during the lead-time, resulting in a potential stock out.

In order to configure the system, two calculations are required:

1. calculation of the reorder level
2. calculation of the order quantity

1) Calculation of the Reorder Level

The reorder level is calculated as follows:

- Lead-time average demand (which is the average demand that will occur during the supply lead-time).

        +

- Safety stock for uncertainty in supply.

        +

- Safety stock for uncertainty in demand.

At this stage consider what this reorder level means.

Suppose we have an item with a lead-time of 1 week, and that we absolutely knew the demand would be 300 per week, i.e. the standard deviation of demand would be zero.

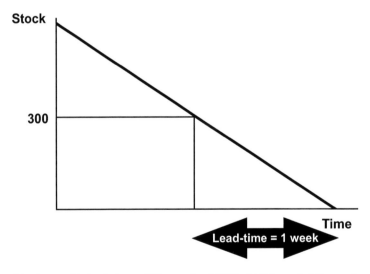

Stock would deplete until it reached 300. At this point the order would be placed and in one week's time it would be received just as the last item in stock was used.

Demand uncertainty

However, life is seldom as perfect and demand can vary and this is measured by the standard deviation, which suppose is 20. Assuming that we have a desired service level of 95% our calculation becomes:

(1 x 300) + 1.64 x 20 = 300 + 32.8 = 332.8

The explanations are as follows:
- The first term (1 x 300) is the amount of stock that will be used on average during the lead-time. This is exactly the same as we calculated above.

- The second term 1.64 x 20 represents the service level factor for 95% derived from the normal distribution table multiplied by the standard deviation.

Recall from the earlier discussion that the situation represented means the following. Given that average demand is 300 and the standard deviation of demand is 20, there is a 95% that demand will be less than or equal to 332.8. There is a 5% chance that demand will be greater than 332.8. The extra 32.8 above the average level of 300 represents the safety stock.

Let's add another level of complexity by increasing the lead-time to 3 weeks. In effect we have the following picture of demand in each of the 3 weeks.

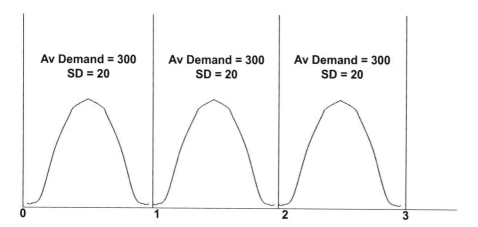

Of course we are not really interested in what demand will be in any single week of the lead-time. We need to know what the pattern of demand will be during the total lead-time. Using a further characteristic of the normal distribution allows the identical distributions to be combined into one, with an average equal to the number of distributions multiplied by the average of the smaller one, and a standard deviation equal to the standard deviation of the smaller one multiplied by the square root of the number of distributions (it is beyond the scope of this book to prove this, but interested people might like to note that this is based on the Central Limit Theorem).

In our example the average demand of the small distribution is 300 and we have a lead-time of 3 weeks so average demand during the lead-time is 3 x 300 = 900. The standard deviation is 20 of the small one, so the SD of the distribution for the lead-time is $20 \times \sqrt{3} = 34.6$.

Hence the reorder point would be 900 + 34.6 x 1.64 = 956.8. The safety stock would be 56.8.

So far we have handled the uncertainty in demand. Now we need to consider the uncertainty in supply.

Supply uncertainty

When we considered the lead-time key concept, we explored how lead-time also follows a normal distribution with an average and a standard deviation. We can use this information to adjust the safety stock further. Let's suppose that our average lead-time remains at 3 weeks but there is a SD of LT equal to 0.5 weeks.

This is a more complicated situation involving the combining of two normal distributions, one for demand and one for lead-time. In this case, these distributions are not identical and indeed are completely independent. In such a situation the combined standard deviation is calculated using the covariance as follows:

$$CombinedSD = \sqrt{(DemandMSD \times AvLT + LeadTimeMSD \times AvDemand^2)}$$

Note that the Demand MSD is the Mean Squared Deviation of demand, and Lead-time MSD is the Mean Squared Deviation of the lead-time. Recall that Mean Squared Deviation is equal to the square of the Standard Deviation. If there is no variation in lead-time the MSD would be zero giving:

$$CombinedSD = \sqrt{DemandMSD \times AvLT}$$

$$CombinedSD = \sqrt{DemandMSD} \times \sqrt{AvLT}$$

$$CombinedSD = SD \times \sqrt{AvLT}$$

This was exactly the same expression we used above.

In our example the combined SD would be:

$$SD = \sqrt{((20 \times 20 \times 3) + 0.5 \times 0.5 \times 300^2)}$$

$$SD = \sqrt{1200 + 22\,500}$$

$$SD = 153.9$$

We can now use this to calculate the safety stock and then the reorder level.

Safety Stock = 1.64 x 153.9 = 252.5

Reorder Level = 3 x 300 + 252.5 = 1152.5

The spreadsheet below provides a complete calculation with formulas in Excel.

1	A	B
2		
3	Calculation of Safety Stock and Reorder Levels	
4		
5	Average demand (wks)	150
6	Lead Time (wks)	4
7	Standard deviation of demand	25
8	Standard deviation of lead time	1.25
9	Service Level	0.98
10		
11	Safety Stock	=NORMSINV(C9)*SQRT(C7*C7*C6+C8*C8*C5*C5)
12	Reorder Level	=C6*C5+C11

Note: the use of the Excel function NORMSINV(%) which calculates the service level factor.

Calculation of Safety Stock and Reorder Levels				
Average demand (wks)	150		Safety Stock	398.5
Lead Time (wks)	4		Reorder Level	998.5
Standard deviation of demand	25			
Standard deviation of lead time	1.25			
Service Level	98%			

In this example if we were able to eliminate the lead-time variation the following would be the position.

Calculation of Safety Stock and Reorder Levels				
Average demand (wks)	150		Safety Stock	102.7
Lead Time (wks)	4		Reorder Level	702.7
Standard deviation of demand	25			
Standard deviation of lead time	0			
Service Level	98%			

Notice the reduction in safety stock. This can be a very useful calculation to do prior to discussion with suppliers who are causing lead-time problems.

There is an alternative way to allow for lead-time variation. Instead of using the above calculations we could examine our table of lead-time history to determine the maximum lead-time that has ever occurred. If this is not available we can estimate it by using average lead-time plus 3 standard deviations (recall the characteristic of the normal distribution where the range of the distribution is equal to the average ± 3 SDs). In our case maximum lead-time would be 4 + (3 x 1.25) = 7.75 wks.

Using this in our spreadsheet gives:

Calculation of Safety Stock and Reorder Levels				
Average demand (wks)	150		Safety Stock	142.9
Lead Time (wks)	7.75		Reorder Level	1305.4
Standard deviation of demand	25			
Standard deviation of lead time	0			
Service Level	98%			

Whilst the safety stock is higher than the 102 if lead-time variation did not exist, it is much lower than the 398 we calculated above.

If this method is used, care needs to be taken to ensure the lead-time is adjusted as improvements are made.

The examples above illustrate a very fundamental point about lead-times. Long reliable lead-times produce less safety stock than short unreliable ones; as has been said: "Uncertainty is the mother of inventory". Inventory managers should always, therefore, strive for lead-time reliability. Once this is achieved, you can look for lead-time reduction, but this should never be at the expense of reliability.

This once again emphasises the importance of knowledge and control of supply lead-times. We know of a company replenishing its stock items needed to facilitate its gas production, who sourced by either importing from many different global locations or by buying in their local marketplace. In placing orders, they only used two lead-times in the calculations, one of 6 months for the imports, and 3 months for the local purchases. The reality, of course, was that lead-times varied with each supplier and, on examination, these were all found to be systematically well under the 3 and 6 months being used.

2) Calculation of the Order Quantity
The usual method used to calculate order quantities in the fixed order quantity system is the Economic Order Quantity (EOQ).

In any inventory management system, the question arises: "How much should I buy at a time?" If you buy in large quantities, the unit price may be low, but you may have a lot of money tied up in stock, and it may require a lot of storage space. If you buy frequent small batches, much less money is tied up in stock, but a lot may be spent on raising a large number of orders and on transport.

The EOQ model shows how that trade-off between the cost of holding stock and the cost of ordering stock is evaluated; it is illustrated below.

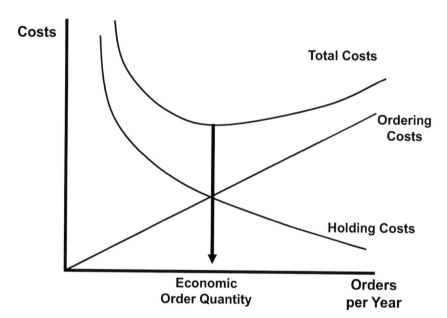

The model is one of the fundamental models of inventory management, first formulated around 1913 at the Westinghouse Company in America. It remains one of the basic techniques for bringing a structured approach to inventory management.

It is a method for calculating order quantities at individual SKU level. Like all models it rests on assumptions, in this case about costs and annual quantities. These assumptions are described in detail below.

The Economic Order Quantity (EOQ) has a direct bearing on the processes used to replenish inventory. Under Continuous Review it determines how much will be ordered when the reorder level is reached. Under a Periodic Review system, as we will explore later, it determines, or at least influences, the frequency or the reorder point in time with which orders are placed.

Under the Continuous Review ordering system, the order quantity is the component of inventory that can be classified as the cycle or working stock. Its purpose is to satisfy the day-to-day demands. In determining the order quantity, a number of factors have to be considered. These ensure that inventory management continue to maintain an economic approach which seeks to minimise the costs of the operation, whilst accepting that the method rests on cost assumptions which cannot always be regarded as totally accurate.

The three costs involved in establishing order quantities are:

a)   Average cost of placing an order.
b)   Average cost of holding stock.
c)   Average cost of running out of stock.

a) Average Cost of Placing an Order
The costs of placing an order include those costs related to:
*   The decision process in identifying the time to place an order, including all the labour and equipment costs.
*   Planning, progressing, and controlling the order.
*   Receiving, inspecting and putting away, together with the administrative costs of notifying that stock is available.

All the above costs are included when considering items purchased from suppliers. However, when the items are sourced from an organisation's own production facilities an additional cost is involved:

*   The costs related to the set-up time and changeover costs together with any initial spoilage costs.

Points to note about ordering costs include the following:

*   The average cost of placing an order can vary enormously from company to company and a cost of £25 - £35 is not unusual. Benchmark figures in literature for order costs can be misleading, for example, quoted figures of £5 - £15 at the lower end and £50 - £75 at the higher end. Quite a variation for alleged standard benchmark figures.

*   The difficulty in establishing the order cost tends to provide a wide range of values and in many companies this is significantly underestimated.

*   Many products may be ordered on one order document. The cost per order line may have to be used as an estimate of the ordering cost.

*   Ordering costs and receiving costs may be very different for different SKU's. For example, chemicals taken into stock may have to be tested. This process may be costly, making the cost per order high.

*   Suppliers may be able to reduce the costs of receiving by clear labelling of pallets and cases.

So that each company can verify its own figures, a practical approach that could be used to estimate order costs would be as follows:

- Estimate the Purchasing department cost by dividing the total department cost by the number of order transaction lines per year.

- Estimate the receiving costs by:
  - Calculating the physical handling costs (e.g. average minutes per pallet x cost per fork truck hour/60).
  - Adding the costs of checking and testing.

b) Average Cost of Holding Stock
The holding cost is usually expressed as a percentage of the unit cost of the item. The main components of the holding cost are:

- Interest on capital.
- All costs related to tax, insurance etc.
- All costs related to the storage i.e. provision of the facilities.
- All costs allowed for deterioration, spoilage and obsolescence.

The value of the cost of holding stock can vary from 15% to 30% per annum, but due to the difficulty in establishing an accurate guide, it could be expected that it is often underestimated.

c) Average Cost of Running Out of Stock
The stocking of an item implies that a cost is incurred whenever the item is not available. The cost of non-availability can be identified in, for example a retail industry, as the loss of revenue or profit from the lost sales and from the loss of customers for future purchases. In other industries, for example oil production, the cost of non-availability, of say a critical spare part, could mean that production is lost at a cost of x barrels at y dollars per barrel.

To establish these costs is extremely difficult, as the assessment can be based on judgement. In general, therefore, although this can be included in the cost equation, it is more generally ignored due to the uncertainty of the accuracy of assessment.

The purpose of calculating an economic order quantity is to balance the costs of ordering and the costs of holding stock, such that the two costs are equal. The purchase quantity that makes these two costs equal is also the minimum total cost for purchasing and receiving.

Note that the "total cost " does not include the annual cost of buying the item, since that is assumed to be the same regardless of the quantity purchased on each occasion. The term "total cost" means the total of the purchasing and receiving costs. Where quantity discounts are being evaluated, then the annual cost of the purchased item, plus the ordering and receiving costs must be considered in total. An example is given later. As the order size decreases the order frequency increases, but the average value of stock held falls. This can be seen in the example below:

Annual Demand	1000		
Order Quantity	100	Orders per year	10
Order Quantity	10	Orders per year	100
Order Quantity	500	Orders per year	2

EOQ Table
A full analysis of establishing an order quantity for a specified stock item can be shown in the following table, where:

Annual Demand	3000
Unit Cost of Item	£12.00
Average Order Cost	£20.00
Average Holding Cost	25%

A	B	C	D	E	F	G
Orders Per year	Quantity Ordered	Average Stock	Ordering Cost	Average Stock Cost	Holding Cost	Total Cost
10	300	150	200	1800	450	650
11	273	136	220	1636	409	629
12	250	125	240	1500	375	615
13	231	115	260	1385	346	606
14	214	107	280	1286	321	601
15	200	100	300	1200	300	600
16	188	94	320	1125	281	601
17	176	88	340	1059	265	605
18	167	83	360	1000	250	610
19	158	79	380	947	237	617
20	150	75	400	900	225	625

The calculations for the above table are as follows:

1. Quantity Ordered = $\dfrac{\text{Annual Demand}}{\text{Column A}}$

2. Average Stock = $\dfrac{\text{Column B}}{2}$

3. Ordering Cost = Average Order Cost x Column A

4. Average Stock Cost = Column C x Item Cost

5. Stock Holding Cost = Column E x Average Holding Cost %

6. Total Cost = Column D + Column F

It can be seen from the above example that the point at which the order cost and holding cost are equal and provide a minimum total cost, is for an order quantity of 200 to be ordered 15 times per annum. This table can also be represented graphically.

EOQ Graph

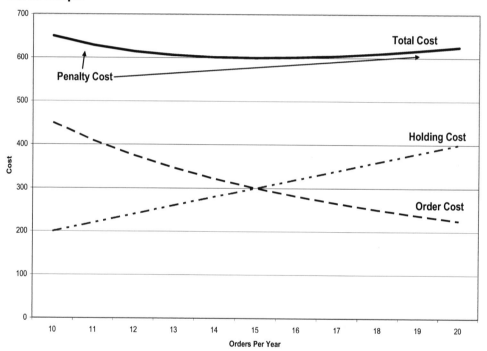

It will be seen both from the table and the graph, that the area around the minimum total cost shows a flat-bottomed picture. This indicates that relatively slight deviations from the minimum cost have little effect on the total cost. For example, an order quantity of 167 as compared with the proposed order quantity of 200, i.e. a 16.5% difference, only represents a 1.5% addition to the total cost.

EOQ formula
To carry out an analysis of each item using the method described above would be extremely lengthy. A formula has therefore been derived which simplifies the

process. The information required is the same as that described for the example and substituted in the following formula:

$$Economic\ Order\ Quantity = \sqrt{\frac{2RS}{CI}}$$

Where:

      R = Annual Demand
      S = Order Cost
      C = Unit Cost
      I = Holding Cost as a percentage

Using the data from the example would give:

$$EOQ = \sqrt{\frac{2 \times 3000 \times 20}{12 \times 0.25}} = \sqrt{\frac{120\,000}{3}} = 200$$

Note that the average cycle stock held (where cycle stock is defined as the amount of stock purchased each time an order is placed) is half the EOQ. In this case, the average cycle stock held would be (200 / 2) = 100. If the number of orders per year is increased so that each order is smaller, then, as the total annual requirement remains the same, the average cycle stock held will be less.

One of the most frequently used methods of reducing inventory levels in the short-term is to reduce order quantities, even where the resulting order sizes are considerably smaller than the EOQ. Ordering costs would then increase, but holding costs would reduce.

It is important to review the values used in calculating EOQs on a regular basis. Demand rates, unit prices, holding and ordering costs can change relatively quickly. A computer-based system should review the EOQ values regularly, but the inventory controller should most definitely review all the parameter criteria regularly; even where computers are used.

From the above formula, it can be seen that any increase in the annual demand and/or the order cost, while maintaining the unit cost and holding cost, will increase the recommended order quantity. Conversely any increase in the unit cost and/or holding cost, while maintaining the annual demand and order cost, will reduce the recommended order quantity.

Effects of Changes in Demand
The changes in demand occurring on an individual stock item held in a specified location (the demand in our example increasing from 3000 to 3300) need to be

monitored, but does not necessarily affect significantly the order quantity. The increases shown above would only require the order quantity to be changed from 200 to 209. Under such circumstances it would be more convenient to maintain the original order quantity and increase the frequency of ordering from 15 times per annum to 16.5.

Other causes of changes in demand can, however, make a more significant impact. Where the change in demand is effected through a change in the number of locations in which this item is stocked, then the splitting of the total annual volume between them, requiring calculation of the EOQ for each location, gives rise to an increased overall average stockholding. Let us illustrate this by an example:

The item used in our example with annual demand of 3000 is now held in 2 locations rather than 1 location with a demand of 1500 per location. From the formula the recommended order quantity for each location would be:

$$EOQ = \sqrt{\frac{2 \times 1500 \times 20}{12 \times 0.25}} = \sqrt{\frac{60\,000}{3}} = 141$$

The average stock per location would now be 70, a total of 140 against the original average stock of 100 i.e. a 41% increase. The order frequency would be 10.6 times per annum per location instead of the original total for one location of 15 times per annum.

Finally, the total inventory cost per location would now be:

Order Cost	£10.6 x 20	= £212
Holding Cost	£70 x 12 x 25%	= £210
Total Cost		= £422

Note that the order cost and holding cost are virtually the same.

Therefore, a total cost for 2 locations of £844 compares with the original total cost of £600. The converse of this also applies when reducing the number of locations to meet the same total demand.

Effect of Changes in Cost
It has already been shown that changes in cost without any other changes, will affect the order quantity using the EOQ formula.

Where there are regular price increases, say annually, it is necessary to establish that other costs have risen at approximately the same rate and in effect cancel each other out. However, one set of circumstances can occur which is worthy of checking, through use of the EOQ formula. This applies to investment purchases where a discount is offered for a bulk buy.

An example of such a calculation would be if the cost of the stock item used in the example was reduced to £9 if a bulk purchase of 500 were made.

From the EOQ formula we would see that the recommended order quantity for an item cost of £9 would be as follows:

$$EOQ = \sqrt{\frac{2 \times 3000 \times 20}{(12 - 3) \times 0.25}} = \sqrt{\frac{120\ 000}{2.25}} = 231$$

Therefore a bulk purchase of 500 would be uneconomic. This can also be shown by comparing the total costs as follows:

Bulk purchase 500 at £9 per unit
Order Cost	= £20.00
Holding Cost £250 x 9 x 25%	= £562.50
Total Cost	= £582.50

Normal purchase 200 at £12 per unit

Order Cost $= \dfrac{£500}{200} \times 20$ = £50.00

Holding Cost £100 x 12 x 25%	= £300.00
Total Cost	= £350.00

This can be seen by comparing the total cost as follows:

A.
Bulk Purchase 500 at £9 per unit	=	£4500
Ordering Cost	=	£ 20
Holding Cost (500/2) x £9 x 25%	=	£ 563
Total Annual Cost	=	£5083
Purchased and Holding Cost	=	£ 583

B.
Normal Purchase quantity of 200 (500 x £12)	=	£6000
Ordering Cost $\dfrac{500}{200}$ x £20	=	£ 50
Holding Cost 200/2 x £12 x 25%	=	£ 300
Total Annual Cost	=	£6350
Purchase and Holding Cost	=	£ 350

Thus the purchasing and holding cost are lower when the purchase quantity is 200. But the overall annual cost is lower when bulk purchase is used.

Summary of FOQ

The fixed order quantity system dictates that every time an order is placed it is for the same fixed quantity. We have seen how to calculate the order quantity and the reorder level to enable the system to be configured. A summary checklist is given below:

Questions	Answers
How is the Reorder Point set?	At a level, which prevents a stock-out during the stock replenishment, cycle (covered in a later section).
What quantity is ordered?	Typically a quantity based on what is called the Economic Order Quantity,
What if the latest transaction takes the stock below the re-order point?	Practices vary – generally the specified order quantity would be ordered if this represented case/pallet on truckload quantities. If single units were ordered, than the specified order quantity plus the shortfall below the reorder point might be issued.
What is the time interval between replenishments?	This varies according to the current rate of usage. If demand increases, time between orders will be reduced.
What are the key parameters driving this method of inventory control?	The reorder point - based on lead time demand. The order quantity.
Why is this system used?	The system is used because it is easy to understand and manage and it requires less safety stock than fixed order cycle systems
What sort of product is it used to manage?	Stable demand medium-to-high volume items.
How often should the key parameters be reviewed?	Probably monthly for high volume items, quarterly for lower demand items.

A simple adaptation of the fixed order quantity method can be applied, called the Two Bin system; this is especially used for low value items.

Two Bin Systems

This is a simple FOQ ordering system typically used for replenishing low value items in, for example, manufacturing and assembly departments and would include items like nuts and bolts, welding tools, cleaning materials, etc.

The stock is kept in two separate bins. When the main stock is used up, a replenishment order is placed. Stock from the second bin is used during the replenishment lead-time. The following illustrates the principles:

Two Bin Systems

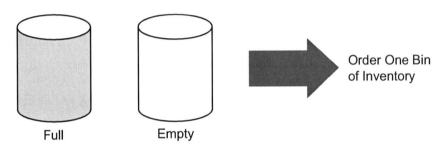

Full	Empty

Order One Bin of Inventory

The checklist for this variation is given below:

Questions	Answers
Why is this system used?	Because it is simple and therefore cheap to administer – very little paperwork.
Which ABC class would use this method?	'C' class items where the average weekly spends is low.
What type of demand patterns makes this a suitable control method?	Regular usage over a long time.
How often should the ordering rules be reviewed?	About every three months.
How is the stock level in the reserve Bin set?	By reference to the reorder level for the item – this reflects lead time and demand rate.
What is the authority to purchase more stock?	A purchase authorisation kept in the reserve stock and actioned when that stock is first used.

Practical use of Fixed order quantity methods

Whilst the Fixed Order Quantity system is simple to configure and operate, there are two issues that reduce its practical usage.

Firstly, the continuous reviewing of the free stock level against the reorder level can be labour intensive, unless a computer system automates the task; as every time a customer order is received, the review must be conducted. This means that it is very difficult to plan the workload of the inventory department.

Secondly, several items will usually be acquired from a single supplier. In practice, it would be preferable to order each item at the same time, so that volume can be consolidated to minimise transport costs. When the Fixed Order Quantity systems are used it is very difficult to do this.

Fixed Order Cycle System

Our second method is the Fixed Order Cycle System or reorder point system. This is also called periodic review, the fixed order time and the variable order quantity system.

In Fixed Order Cycle systems, the time interval between replenishments remains the same, but the quantity ordered varies. In essence it is the complete opposite of the Fixed Order Quantity system.

These systems have the advantage that they allow replenishment to be planned. Where many SKUs are being purchased in large volumes the ability to review requirements and plan orders systematically have many benefits such as the better use of staff, better utilisation of transport, etc.

There are two types of reorder point / periodic review systems:

- The topping up method
- The min-max method

The Topping-Up Method

This system reviews stock levels and places replenishment orders using a constant fixed time interval. At this fixed time period, free stock is subtracted from a maximum stock level to determine the quantity that must be ordered to "top-up" the inventory.

The process of review requires the following parameters to be established:

1) The fixed interval review period.

2) The safety stock required to cover the variability of demand over the lead time plus the review period.

3) The setting of a maximum stock level.

1) Calculation of the Fixed Interval Review Period
This interval can be different for different items of inventory. Based on the ABC analysis of products the pattern might be:

'A' class item - reviewed daily/weekly
'B' class item - reviewed 2-weekly/monthly
'C' class item - reviewed monthly/quarterly

Another way of setting the review period is to use the following formula:

$$Review\ Period = 52\ x\ \frac{EOQ}{Annual\ Demand}$$

For example, suppose we have an annual demand of 26 000 and an EOQ of 2000 the review period would be:

$$Review\ Period = 52\ x\ \frac{2000}{26\ 000}$$

$$Review\ Period = 4$$

Here a review would take place 13 times per year (i.e. every 4 weeks).

2) Calculation of Safety Stock
The periodic review system will require extra safety stock to that needed for FOQ/ continuous review system.

At a review time, we determine the amount of safety stock that will be required to cover demand uncertainty during the:
* Time between this review time and the next one.
* Supply lead-time.
* Unreliability of the supply lead-time.

Whilst the second and third components are similar to the continuous review system, the first one is an additional amount due to the fact that the situation will not be reviewed until the next review interval is reached. In effect this is like extending the supply lead-time. So where in the continuous review safety stock calculation, we had just the supply lead-time, in this system the lead-time is replaced with supply lead-time plus the review period. The full safety stock formula is therefore:

$$CombinedSD = \sqrt{(DemandMSD\ x\ (AvLT + ReviewPeriod) + LeadTimeMSD\ x\ AvDemand^2)}$$

Safety Stock = Service Factor x CombinedSD

The spreadsheet below provides a complete calculation with formulas in Excel.

1	A	B
2		
3	Calculation of Safety Stock	
4		
5	Average demand (wks)	150
6	Lead Time (wks)	4
7	Standard deviation of demand	25
8	Standard deviation of lead time	1.25
9	Service Level	0.98
10	Review Period (wks)	2
11		
12	Safety Stock	=NORMSINV(C9)*SQRT(C7*C7*(C6+C10)+C8*C8*C5*C5)

1	A	B
2		
3	Calculation of Safety Stock	
4		
5	Average demand (wks)	150
6	Lead Time (wks)	4
7	Standard deviation of demand	25
8	Standard deviation of lead time	1.25
9	Service Level	98%
10	Review Period (wks)	2
11		
12	Safety Stock	405

3) Calculation of Maximum Stock Level

At the time that the inventory position is reviewed, the amount of stock that will be required before the position is reviewed again is equal to:

Average Demand used in Review Period and Lead-time plus Safety Stock

Using the example above the calculations are as follows (overleaf):

1	A	B
2		
3	Calculation of Safety Stock	
4		
5	Average demand (wks)	150
6	Lead Time (wks)	4
7	Standard deviation of demand	25
8	Standard deviation of lead time	1.25
9	Service Level	0.98
10	Review Period (wks)	2
11		
12	Safety Stock	=NORMSINV(C9)*SQRT(C7*C7*(C6+C10)+C8*C8*C5*C5)
13	Maximum Stock Level	=C5*(C6+C10)+C12

1	A	B
2		
3	Calculation of Safety Stock	
4		
5	Average demand (wks)	150
6	Lead Time (wks)	4
7	Standard deviation of demand	25
8	Standard deviation of lead time	1.25
9	Service Level	98%
10	Review Period (wks)	2
11		
12	Safety Stock	405
13	Maximum Stock Level	1305

Calculating the Order Quantity

The quantity ordered for each replenishment would be established as follows:

Order quantity = (maximum stock – free stock)

This value might then be marginally adjusted to give case/pallet unit loads.

At a replenishment review the situation might be:

Maximum stock	1305
Less free stock	(600)
Order size	705

The diagram below illustrates the pattern of activity using this system.

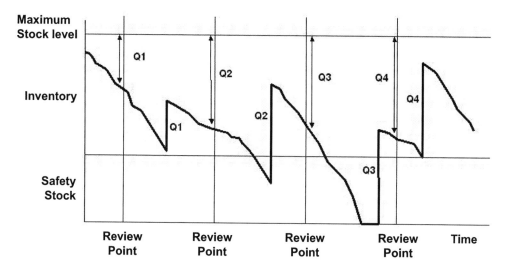

Summary of FOT or FOC method

The summary and checklist of the fixed order time cycle system is given below:

Questions	Answers
Which type of product is this system suitable for?	Items where the reviews are frequent and the lead times short. An example would be the review of stock items held in a warehouse network.
What effect does this method have on safety stock requirements, compared with continuous review replenishment?	Because the safety stock has to cover lead time plus review, more safety stock is needed.
Why does the safety stock have to cover demand variation during lead time plus review?	Because if a review is 'missed', then the stock level would not be reviewed until the next scheduled review, at which time replenishment lead time would have to be taken into account.
Why is it useful to fix a review interval?	Because the review of stock requirements can be structured in such a way that all the products from a particular supplier can be ordered as one delivery, with all the logistics cost advantages that that provides.

149

Is an order always placed at the time of review?	No. If the amount required to reach the calculated maximum stock is very small, then more may be ordered. Also if stock is above the maximum, more would be ordered.
If there is a maximum stock, how could this have been exceeded?	Because earlier orders have been put into stock, and the rate of sale (usage) has declined, perhaps due to seasonal variations in demand.
How would seasonal products be dealt with in this ordering system?	By resetting the parameters which determine the maximum stock level.
Who would set the parameter, and on what basis?	The inventory management team, using demand history, and the latest data on lead times, etc.
How often should parameters be reviewed?	For high volume items every 1-3 months, or at times when major increases or decreases in demand are known to occur
Does this system cope better or worse with fluctuating demands then the Continuous Review system?	Probably worse. If demand suddenly increases, it is likely that the Continuous Review system will pick up the change more quickly because the reorder point will be reached quickly.
What happens if the lead time is longer than the review period?	The calculation of the required order does not change in principle, but it has to take into account stock ordered but not yet received. If lead time is four weeks and the stock if received every two weeks, then there will be 1-2 orders, which have not been received at the time of the review. This must be totally visible to the ordering system.

The 'Min-Max' Ordering System

This is a variant of the Periodic Review System and is used where the stock level is received at defined intervals, but an order is not placed at every review. It would be used where the order quantity is large in relation to the amount of stock to be used between reviews. The effect is to reduce the number of orders compared with the topping-up system.

The system uses a 'minimum' stock level and is calculated in the same way as the 'maximum' stock level of the Periodic Review 'topping-up' system. ((Lead-time + review) x demand rate + safety stock). When the stock is received, if the level is above the minimum level, no order is placed. If the stock is at, or below the minimum at the review, then an order will be placed.

If an order is placed, it is calculated to bring the stock level up to a preset maximum, which is calculated as follows:

$$MaxStock = MinStock + EOQ - \frac{(AvDemand \times ReviewPeriod)}{2}$$

To illustrate, an example follows:

Lead-time	2 weeks
Review interval	1 week
Average demand	50
Safety stock	70
Calculated EOQ	500

Minimum stock level = ((2+1) x 50) + 70 = <u>220</u>
EOQ = 500
(Average demand x Review period)/2   = (50 x 1)/2 = <u>25</u>

Maximum stock level = 220 + 500 – 25   = 695

If, at the review, free stock is less than 220, then an order would be raised to bring the total up to 695.

E.g.   Free Stock = 150

This is below 220, therefore, an order is placed of 695 -150 = 545.

The summary checklist for "Min-Max" is:

Questions	Answers
Why would this method be used in preference to the topping-up method?	Because it allows frequent reviews, but keeps the number of replenishment orders down.
What sort of products would be managed in this way?	Products with moderate to low annual usage, where the order quantity is large in relation to the amount used between reviews.
Why is the 'minimum' stock for this method calculated in the same way as the maximum stock of the topping-up system?	It is a convention that has evolved. It conveys the idea that it is the point below which stock should not fall.
Why is half the review period demand used in calculating the minimum stock?	It has been found to work well in practice.
Would you use this method for high value items?	Probably not because average in stock holding is high.

Finally, please note that throughout this section, we have used the Standard Deviation or the Mean Squared Deviation of the demand pattern. In cases where forecast errors have been tracked, these could be replaced with Standard Error and Mean Squared Error (these were explained in an earlier section of the book).

Comparisons of Fixed Order Quantity/Continuous review and Fixed Order Time Cycle/Periodic review methods

The following comparisons summarise the main replenishments methods discussed above:

Managing Inventory by FOQ or by FOT systems

Parameter	Continuous Review(CR) FOQ	Periodic Review(PR) FOT
How much to order, plus, need to allow for the Free Stock position: The stock on hand, plus any stock expected, less, any stock allocated or being kept for special use.	A fixed order quantity (FOQ) when at the ROL. Typically the EOQ is ordered.	A variable order quantity(VOQ) , (as dependant upon what has been used since the last fixed time check and what is now needed, if any, to bring back to the "up to level"). Allow for Av.D * SLT plus, Av.D * Review Period plus, the Safety Stock calculation
When to order	When at the ROL therefore a variable order time (VOT). The ROL is calculated by the Av.D * SLT plus, the Safety Stock calculation	Fixed order cycle (FOT), as there is a predetermined time when to order. The time is influenced by the EOQ (annual demand quantity, divided by the EOQ, giving the number of orders per annum)
EOQ	Amount to consider ordering when at ROL	Helps in setting the review period frequency of when to order
Assumes/Prefers	Certainty with constant demand, lead times and prices throughout a period. Suppliers have to deliver at any time (as it is a VOT)	Can deal better with uncertainty. Suppliers can make regular planned deliveries (as it is a FOT)
Stable demand	Lower safety stocks	Higher safety stocks as protecting over a longer time period
Seasonal/variable demand	Higher stocks due to big demand swings	Lower stocks
Control	Needs continual / perpetual monitoring of inventory levels, therefore is more responsive	Checked at the review period only

Usage	Most common for low value items and infrequently ordered "C" items. Used by industrial manufacturers.	Most common for high valued and critical "A" items. Used by FMCG industry as gives a rhythm for checking whether to place and order or not.

Managing Inventory by value and volume for independent demand

Value	Low Volume	Medium Volume	High Volume
High Value	1 for 1, poisson distribution	PR: 7 to 14 days	PR: 1 to 7 days with fixed lead times
	Average periods forecasts	Exponential smoothing forecasts with seasonal, trend and error tracking	Exponential smoothing forecasts with seasonal, trend and error tracking
	Parameters reviewed every 3/6 months	Parameters by tracking signals reviewed 4 times per year	Parameters by tracking signals reviewed monthly
Medium Value	CR	CR: Q on EOQ, ROP on av. D + SS	PR: 14 to 28 days
	Average demand forecasts, plan for seasonality	Average demand forecasts	Exponential smoothing forecasts with seasonal, trend and error tracking
	Parameters reviewed every 3/6 months	Parameters reviewed every 1/3 months	Parameters by tracking signals reviewed 1/3 months
Low Value	Two Bin	CR: Q on 6-8 orders p.a. ROP on av. D + SS	CR: Q on EOQ, ROP on av. D + SS
	Average demand forecasts	Average demand forecasts	Average demand forecasts
	Parameters reviewed every 6/9 months	Parameters reviewed every 1/3 months	Parameters reviewed every 1/3 months

Requirements Planning Systems

It is common for inventory planning at distribution depots to be based on an order point system, which specifies, at the product line level, a reorder point and an EOQ. The safety stock element would be based on lead-time and demand variability.

Stock replenishment would be at irregular intervals depending on the rate of usage. If periodic review were to be used, the replenishment would be regular, but of differing quantities.

These **Distribution Requirements Planning (DRP)** systems are designed to be used where there is "independent" demand, the demands placed upon the inventory will come from customers placing orders in a more or less random fashion. The variability in demand will be built into the safety stock levels used in setting reorder points or "order-up-to" levels.

The problem with these methods of inventory management is that they are static. They do not attempt to predict when stock will be required in the future; they merely seek to answer the question "Do I need to order stock now?"

In a multi-echelon system in which a factory supplies regional warehouses, and these are used to replenish local distribution depots, the regional warehouses will respond to orders placed upon them by the distribution depots. If the regional warehouse also uses an order point system for deciding when to place an order on the manufacturing plant, it is also not attempting to predict forward requirements.

An alternative approach is to forecast demands at the distribution depot level. By doing this, and having regard for the need for some level of safety stock, it is possible to plan the input of stock to the distribution depot. This means that the regional warehouse do not require an inventory management system, as these place orders when some level of stock is reached. Its purpose is to move stock through to the distribution depots on a planned basis to meet forecast levels of demand.

The basis of Requirements Planning is that it sets out a time-phased schedule of requirements to meet a sales forecast. This is determined at the actual distribution point from which stock will be delivered to the customer. It is certainly possible for the regional (intermediate) warehouses to be involved in final distribution in their own right. If they are to do this, then they too will be involved in forecasting customer demands.

In this situation, the demands that they place upon the manufacturing plant will comprise the accumulated time-phased requirements of the depots that they service, and their own time-phased demands to meet their own forecast direct customer deliveries.

The Requirements Plan is summary of the total requirements, at each SKU level, of the distribution network over a specified number of future periods. This will provide direct input into the Master Production Schedule, used to plan production in MRP Systems that we will look at shortly.

Manufacturers also use DRP for planning product flows into customer warehouses, for example, a food manufacturer planning shipments to a retail customer's distribution centres to meet the forecasted demand.

Where DRP is implemented, the benefits are likely to include:
- Significant reductions in inventory.
- The priority product requirements are very visible to those preparing the Master Production Schedule.
- Inventory investment is more clearly focused on the products that really matter.
- Forecasting, inventory planning, and MRP can be integrated. In the long-term forecasting, DRP and MRP will be linked to one overall planning system.

As with all other changes in planning methods, and this is a major change compared with traditional reorder point/level systems, it will take time to put in place. Whilst the basic methodology has been available for several years, it is now starting to be implemented more widely as part of Enterprise Resource Planning (ERP) systems.

DRP should be applied firstly to the high volume (A class) products, since it is probable that the low volume products will be centralised in due course. The benefits for production planning will also be more apparent.

Requirements Planning Schedule

Suppose we have a situation where a distribution centre supplies two depots A and B; the requirements planning schedule for Depot A is shown below.

		1	2	3	4	5	6	7
Gross Requirements		20	20	20	20	30	30	30
Scheduled Receipts			60					
Projected Inventory Balance	45	25	65	45	25	-5	25	-5
PIB with receipt	45	25	65	45	25	55	25	55
Planned Order receipt						60		60
Planned Order release				60	60			

Safety Stock = 20, Shipping Quantity = 60, Lead-time = 2

155

The available inventory is 45, and in period one we expect to use 20, leaving 25. In period 2 we expect to use 20 and we have 60 scheduled to arrive, leaving us with 65. In period 3 we use 20, leaving 45. In period 4 we use 20, leaving 25. In period 5 we will use 30, that will leave us with – 5 below the safety stock level. Hence we must schedule 60 to arrive, leaving us with 55. For this 60 to arrive in period 5 we must ship it in period 3 because of the 2 week lead-time. The rest of the schedule then continues.

Assume we have also calculated the schedule for Depot B. The schedule for the distribution centre is completed by adding the various levels together.

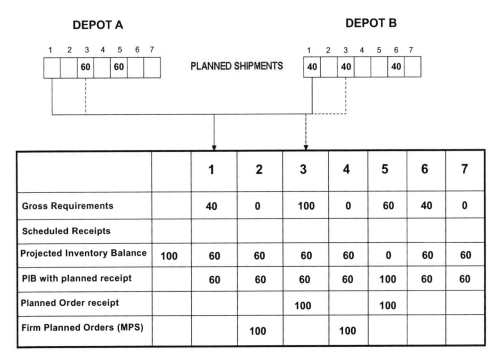

DEPOT A		DEPOT B				
1 2 3 4 5 6 7	PLANNED SHIPMENTS	1 2 3 4 5 6 7				
60 60		40 40 40				

		1	2	3	4	5	6	7
Gross Requirements		40	0	100	0	60	40	0
Scheduled Receipts								
Projected Inventory Balance	100	60	60	60	60	0	60	60
PIB with planned receipt		60	60	60	60	100	60	60
Planned Order receipt				100		100		
Firm Planned Orders (MPS)			100		100			

Safety Stock = 50, Shipping Quantity = 100, Lead-time = 1

The demand at the central location is dependant on the demand at the two lower levels and is derived by adding the two requirements together. The rest of the schedule is derived using the same process described above.

The firm planned orders could then be used in the master planning schedule, to determine when the items need to be manufactured and when materials need to be ordered.

In the example above, the safety stock and order quantity have been pre-set. These can be determined in exactly the same way as the safety stock calculations detailed in the fixed order quantity and fixed order cycle systems. The order quantity could be established by using the EOQ calculation.

In the requirements planning case, the planning horizon must be at least as long as the overall lead-time required for product to move through the supply chain. In the above example, this would have been the total of the supply lead-time from the distribution centre to the depot, plus the supply lead-time from the supplier to the distribution centre. If this is extended further by including the master production scheduling and materials planning at the factory, then this planning horizon can be long. In turn, this could lead to high forecast errors, particularly for items that have a high volatility in their demand pattern. For these reason distribution requirements planning is only usually used for items with low volatility.

Materials planning (MRP/MRPII)

Materials requirement planning systems (MRP) are integrated computer systems planning tools that follow similar process logic to DRP. Used in a manufacturing/production environment, they determine the following:

* What input materials are required?
* How many?
* When needed?

Also used is manufacturing resource planning (MRPII) which follows on from MRP, but adds in production capacity calculations. MRP is also one the parts of ERP (Enterprise Resource Planning) systems, as supplied by the company, SAP. The basics of an MRP system are detailed below:

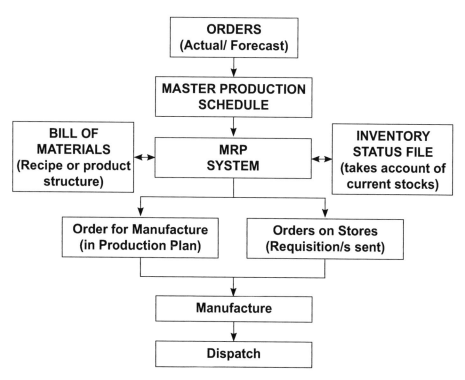

MRP has the following **basic principles:**

- Demand information goes into the master production schedule (MPS) which covers a specific time period and allocates the demand for each product into time buckets of days or weeks.

- The component structure for each product is held in the bills of materials file (BOM), which is the menu of parts and sub-assemblies item-by-item.

- MRP calculates from the top level of the BOM the gross requirements needed. It then accounts for quantities in stock or already on order and then calculates the net requirements for the item. If there are any batching needs, such as a minimum order of 100 items, these are allowed for. Finally the MRP logic calculates against the lead-times for supply and brings forward order dates accordingly. It then goes on to the next level of items until the lowest level of the BOM is reached.

- The output from MRP is a set of time phased materials requirements showing how much and when each item should be purchased.

On the basic principles, MRP is technically robust. However, planning to manufacture to stock (using a forecast) and manufacturing to actual demand (make to order) are not the same. The reality of using forecast orders inputs creates unstable MRP outputs - when subsequent MRP plans are calculated, the new actual orders will mean the MRP system makes adjustments to all of the schedules to reflect these new orders. This results in changes to the plan, because the subsequent actual orders will always be different to the previous forecast.

These plans and replans will cause problems with uncertainties and necessary "firefighting" action to make corrections. To prevent this, it is important to understand that, whilst customer orders may vary in apparent unpredictable ways, the actual end consumer/user demand for most products is pretty stable.

It is useful therefore to identify which products have this underlying consumer stability. For example, 5 % of the line items may account for 50% of demand. This knowledge can then be transferred so that we produce the same volume, but use more frequent regular short runs in a fixed repetitive cycle. This brings in a routine and certainty with consequential reductions in stock levels, both of finished goods and also raw materials/work in progress. It puts a drum beat into the operation; with the buffers reduced, this is a classic application of the Theory of Constraints (TOC). We will look at TOC later.

Meanwhile, those less predictable items are dealt with separately; using fixed planned points to fit into the repetitive cycle, or using a completely separate production process.

A common error in some MRP applications is, once again, the reality of unreliable supply lead-times, and also that the default original lead-time settings, have never been reviewed to reflect subsequent changes. This leads to wrong decisions being made by the MRP application.

From the warehouse/stores perspective, MRP systems will, in theory, give known and predictable receiving times for in bound stocks of raw materials/sub-assemblies etc. with these stocks being only held for a short time. Indeed MRP applications should foster cross-docking activities in stores and warehouses.

4: Inventory and Physical Stock

In this section, we shall look at the physical stock procedures and controls. We will start by examining receipt, product identification and coding, and surplus/ obsolete stock. Next, stock control and records and the varied methods to arrange stock checking programmes are examined, and we conclude by looking at best practices in physical counting and managing stock.

Inventory receipts

Receiving at stores/warehouses is affected strongly by "external" parties and events; for example, the purchasing/ordering policy, the handling unit and the quality of information/documentation. This activity therefore require extensive liaison with suppliers as well as internal departments like procurement.
The following listing represents the key areas of receiving procedures:
*   Establish the correct unloading area; ensuring it is safe and suitable for the operation.

*   Record the arrival of the vehicle and note the security seal number.

*   Break the security seal with the driver present.

*   Ensure the vehicle is safe before staring the unloading.

*   Check the order documentation and record each item against the consignment note/own documentation.

*   Check the goods for condition, possible damage and carry out or arrange for any quality checks or inspections from users.

*   Report discrepancies and condition/quality at once.

*   Assemble the goods in the goods receipt area.

*   Determine the location where goods are to be stored and move them out of goods receipt area as soon as possible.

Further aspects of warehouse operations are beyond the scope of this book; however they are fully explored in *"Excellence in Warehouse Management"* (Stuart Emmett, 2005).

Identifying Inventory

Each company will have a method of identifying products through the use of some form of coding system. The coding system may be unique (for example, the Materials and Equipment Standards and Codes (MESC) 10 numbers coding used worldwide within the Shell group) or it may be a coding system that conforms to industry standards (for example, the UK food industry barcode labelling of products).

Whatever coding method is used, the reasons for it are universal:

- Provides a unique identifier per product line/ item.

- Prevents duplication of stocks; for example by ensuring coding is used in ordering and by all suppliers and customers/users.

- Provides standardisation; for example, coding a "new" product for the first time can identify that similar products already exist and therefore possible duplication is avoided.

- Simplifies product identification for all suppliers, customers and users.

- Can help in determining stock locations; for example within a store holding engineering items where all those products in one main coding category are kept together.

- Assists in pricing and costing; for example with food supermarkets EPOS systems.

Surplus and Obsolescence stock

Surplus goods are those that are of no current use to the company stocking them, but may have a use for someone else, or could be reconditioned economically. Many companies, in the course of their business, will generate quantities of goods that become surplus to the current requirements. A decision is therefore needed on whether they should be re-used, sold or scrapped.

Many companies also have non-moving stock, and when these have no foreseeable future use; then they are declared as dead or obsolete stock. This will involve management and recognition of the problem, with a stock review listing of non-moved items, for example, those, which after one year, are without an issue. Finally, write off procedures will have to be formalised, for example, users have to justify the item's retention. The only acceptable reasons for retaining non-moving stock should be:

- Spare parts for equipment that is still being used.
- Insurance and emergency items.
- For a specific known future use.

Preventing Surplus stock

In order to prevent and minimise surplus stock holding, the following guidelines apply:

- Standardisation and the effective use of product coding to prevent duplications.

- Agreement of procedures to cover the holding of stock.

- Returns from users should only be accepted where there is a ongoing requirement for the item.

- Maintaining of close relationships with customers/users.

- Arranging for supplier buy-back clauses.

- Consignment stocking, where the ownership remains with the supplier until the goods are used.

- Careful selection of spare parts for new projects.

- Consider reducing the variety of products stocked.

Variety reduction
It can be all too easy for business functions to add new products to the companies' catalogue and the stock range of items. This may lead to a proliferation of raw materials or finished products.

Therefore, before embarking on an action that will lead to an increase in the variety of products, the following questions should be asked *(Source: Stock Control IPS 1991)*:
- Do we really need this?
- Do we need it now?
- What will be the effect on cash flow?
- Do we have the storage space?
- Can we use a proprietary item?
- Do we need so many sizes, colours, and shapes?
- Can we replace, not add?
- If this replaces, what is the effect on existing stock and raw materials?
- Can we use multi-language descriptions?
- Can we hold part-processed stocks, and then adapt them to our customers needs?
- What is the development lead-time? Will we miss the market?
- Will this new item change/reduce demand for any of our existing products?
- Is there a shelf life problem?
- Do we have "feet on the ground" forecasts?
- Can this new item be supplied in the quantities we need?

- Does this fit in with our long-term plans?
- Can we adapt existing tooling?
- Do all the departments in our organization know about this?
- Has it been safety-tested?
- What assumptions have been made, have they been tested?
- Can we get this from another division, or from a competitor?
- Can this design replace two or more of our existing designs?
- Can we utilise existing raw materials or components?

Stock Control and Records

Stock control is defined as: "The checking of stock by direct observation and measurement, followed by the comparison and reconciliation to records".

The objectives of stock control can be summarised:
- Ensure the "book" figures agree with the actual physical stocks that are being held (actual/expected).

- Highlight any recurring errors; such as product placed in wrong locations in the store/warehouse.

- Highlight any poor storage conditions, such as damaged stocks.

- Ensure a separation of "powers" between recording and keeping; for example, stock checkers do not report directly to warehouse management.

- Comply with Legal/Fiscal legislation and requirements; for example stock in financial terms is an asset and is therefore valued to determine organisational profitability/taxation.

- Be of assistance in decision-making.

- Get the records right, first time, every time.

Non-accurate records have wide consequences:
- Unforeseen stock-outs as stocks were expected to be available.

- Informal stock piling; e.g. squirrel stores, as users do not believe the records and decide to "do their own thing".

- Excess stock holding; e.g. orders are placed because it is not known products are actually available.

- Informal stock recording; e.g. records are kept by users and are not entered into the overall system records.

- Purchasing direct; e.g. orders "pass by" the system.

- Pickers get frustrated; e.g. they cannot find expected products.

- Orders are not met.

The likely causes of inaccuracies are:
- Data input errors.

- Incorrect recording; e.g. wrong product ID.

- Processing delays on documents; orders placed because recent receipts. have not yet been entered into the system

- Loss of documents.

- Recording part issues.

- Issuing without documents.

- Mismatch between "actual" and the documents.

- Identifying receipts with invoices is difficult.

- Identifying returns incorrectly.

- Poor stock checking.

- Wrong locations.

- Theft, internal (80% of all theft) or external (20%).

- Poor packing/ labelling.

Minimising Inaccuracies
To minimise inaccuracies, the following is needed:
- Creating a climate of high expectations, e.g. a clear goal of total accuracy.

- Training, so that mistakes are not from the lack of knowledge of product and processes; training on the wider aspects of the company and the impacts of making errors.

- Performance monitoring, e.g. measure accuracy by section, department, publish figures, give feedback.

- Limit access to goods and materials to combat security issues.

- Monitor systems, investigate and eliminate errors e.g. review checking process, record and analyse errors, investigate, give feedback and correct mistakes.

- Automate, e.g. bar coding, tagging, scanning, auto identification.

Stock Checking Programmes

Stock checking programmes require the authority to undertake the following:

- Approve the method to be used; e.g. continuous, periodic and or spot checks, (these are explained below).

- Approve the programme details.

- Adjust stock check differences.

- Determine the tolerances; for example:

  - A items 1%

  - B items 2-5 %

  - C items 5-10%

- Adjust unresolved differences.

Continuous/perpetual checking

This method is useful where there are large operations so that stock can be checked continually through the year. This ensures that the workload is more evenly distributed. However, every item can be checked once per year (in some companies, once every three years). It can be manual or automated and is scheduled (secretly) by segmenting, for example as below:

- **A lines:** Fast moving lines, or higher value lines, are counted more often with a lower (1%) tolerance for error.

- **B lines:** Medium movers or medium value lines are counted less often, with a lower (2-5%) tolerance level.

- **C Lines:** Slow movers or low value lines are counted even less often, with an even lower (5-10%) tolerance level.

The following example illustrates the principles:

A lines, 2000 items counted 6 times p.a.	= 12,000 counts
B lines, 3000 items counted 3 times p.a.	= 9000 counts
C lines, 4000 items counted 2 times p.a.	= 8000 counts
D lines, (no movers), 500 items counted 1 time p.a.	= 500 counts
TOTAL	= 29,500 counts p.a.

If 230 days are available p.a. and if a standard checker can carry out 100 -130 counts per day, then 128 counts per day are needed.

Continuous/perpetual checking will ensure that:
- There are fewer mistakes.
- Effort is concentrated where needed on the A lines.
- Stock checking is an ongoing function.
- There are no "shut downs" for stock checking.

Periodic checking
This is used in smaller companies and requires a "shut down" with a known time for stock checking. It will often use untrained people and errors are more often found.

Spot checks can meanwhile be undertaken with both methods, as required. It will be unknown when they will happen, and they are often "security" driven and perhaps only undertaken on specific lines/items.

Resolving Differences
As noted above, resolving difference is an authority matter. Investigation of the difference from tolerances is needed, preferably quickly as there are impacts if the causes are not determined/agreed/corrected.
If the difference is small, then an adjustment is made.
If there is a large difference then the following needs to happen:
- Check any unprocessed items.
- Check any earlier common causes.
- Check again, second count?

If the difference still remains large, then a debit or credit will need to be made to the stock account.

Physical Counting of Stock
There are certain requirements needed for the people physically undertaking the stock checking. These include the following:
- Count and record what is found, and not what the records indicate. This is called "blind checking", as the checkers are blind to any knowledge of what should be there. Their job is to report what they see, not what they expect to see from the records.

- Ensure that what is found agrees with the product coding or identification method used in the organisation.

- Look for any product deterioration.

- Ensure the product is in a suitable location.

- Note / record what they have found, by using manual or direct entry equipment systems.

The problems found when physically counting

These include the following:
- Poor preparation.
- Improper procedures.
- Poor checking of discrepancies.
- Unmotivated counters (people).

The common errors found during stock checks are as follows:

	Recorded wrong	Counted wrong
Shortage	Less received than recorded	Did not count all locations
	Issued more than recorded	Counted wrong items
	Pilferage	Wrong item in location
Overage	Receipt not recorded	Counted incorrectly
	More received than recorded	Counted wrong item
	Issued less than recorded	Wrong item in location

To overcome these problems, appropriate planning and procedures are needed. Planning will need to include the following:
- Date, time, locations.
- Assign Controller and Counters.
- Paperwork is prepared.
- Control of receiving and issuing during the count.
- Prepare the area (housekeeping).
- Written procedures for taking the count.
- Verify the equipment needed.

Procedures during the stock checking are as follows;
- Issue count sheets to counters.
- Counters record count in the first column.
- Count by the unit of measure assigned to the item.
- Issue guidance for partial units and for outers/contents.
- Mark each item location with a coloured sticker to indicate it has been counted.
- Return completed sheets to Controller.
- Compare physical to balance on hand.
- Sort sheets into two piles: (a) recounts (b) no recounts.
- For recounts give a clean sheet to a different counter.
- For no recounts, enter page number in records.
- For the recounts sheets returned, back to 4 above.
- When recounts are not acceptable, set aside for review by senior person.

- Hold a final meeting with all involved to share, review, praise/criticise etc.
- Finalise the report to include:
  - Date.
  - Total number of people involved.
  - Cost of labour involved.
  - Total number of SKUs counted.
  - Accuracy rates.
  - Money adjustments made.
  - Areas of concern.
  - Suggestions for improvements.

Reviewing current procedures/polices

Finally the following stock control key questions can be asked. This will enable a review of an organisations stock control procedures/polices:

- How have stock levels moved in relation to sales?
- Who is responsible for balancing the conflicting issues of stock, customer service and production or purchasing performance?
- Do we have control information for customer service and stock levels?
- Do we set meaningful targets?
- Is our system a burden or an aid?
- Do we have slow-moving or redundant stocks? How are these dealt with?
- Are there regular inspections by senior management of our warehouses?
- Are our housekeeping standards high at all times, or just for VIP visits?
- Do new product proposals explore the implications of additional stock and their effect on cash flow?
- Are our stock records accurate?
- Can our vendors help us, e.g. supplier stockholding?
- What has been done to reduce set-up times?
- Can we hold part-processed stocks to reduce finished inventory levels?
- Are we making use of techniques that will help us such as EOQ, exponential smoothing for sales forecasts etc?
- Do we have cash flow forecasts?
- Is sales forecasting taken seriously?
- Are our terms of credit compatible with our suppliers' payment terms?
- Do our suppliers frequently put us on stop? If so, why?
- Are we always running out of things? If so, why?
- Is the availability of our finished stock reduced by stock reservations for customers?

- Have we fully explored variety reduction?
- Do we have exception reporting techniques?
- Is the computer working for us or against us?
- Do we invest in practical training for our staff?

Source: Stock Control IPS 1991

5: Evaluating Inventory Performance

In part five, we look firstly at how we can assess stock levels, and provide examples on how to do this, along with practical examples for determining stock targets. Finally, we conclude with questions that can be asked to ensure the inventory is continually and proactively managed.

Inventory Assessment

In the earlier sections, we dealt with the technical aspects of managing individual items / SKUs through an understanding of demand, variability, forecasting, measurement of forecast accuracy, and determining recorder points and order quantities.

These tools need to be seen in the context of setting realistic goals for inventory, that are about reducing inventory levels at all stages of the supply chain, without reducing customer service levels.

Stock levels are often arbitrarily set, regardless of the variability of the demand, the reliability and length of the lead-time, the service level required, or the level of forecast accuracy.

Where replenishment is made based on a reorder level or point being reached, the setting of the reorder level and reorder point must be reviewed at the SKU level. The rules for setting these triggers must be clearly defined, understood and reviewed regularly by a nominated individual. Even when a computerised inventory management system is being used, an experienced inventory person must oversee this process.

Where replenishment is based on forecasts, from either in-company manufacturing or from external suppliers, it is the level of forecast accuracy and the frequency of manufacture/purchase that will determine stock levels. It is the task of inventory management to reduce inventory levels progressively consistent with achieving customer service targets.

Having set a target, its achievement has to be monitored with significant deviations reported, so the reasons can be established, and remedies implemented. For example, the introduction of a new, additional product range could be expected to increase stock levels.

Assessing the stock level

How can you set about deciding whether existing inventory levels are reasonable or not? One relatively easy way to assess the existing situation is to look at inventory value as a proportion of the annual value of inventory used. When applied to finished goods the ratio indicates how many weeks of stock cover are available. The result can then be compared with:

(a)   Other companies in the same type of business – a benchmarking exercise.

(b)   Within the company, over a period of several years.

The calculations look like this:

	£m	
Cost of goods sold in year	6.0	A
Year-end value of finished goods at cost	2.0	B

B/A x 52 = Weeks of Cover
Therefore: 2/6 x 52 = 17.3 weeks

Is this good or bad? Well, that depends on the type of business, for example:
*   In companies where goods are purchased for resale such as food, clothing, cosmetics, it would represent very poor performance.

*   In companies where a high level of customer service is expected from a very large catalogue, it may be necessary to hold large stocks.

*   In FMCG (Fast Moving Consumer Goods) retailing, the level of inventory would be around two weeks for the 'best in class' companies; with further reductions being sought by better forecasting, more frequent deliveries into store and by the application of 'cross-docking' at distribution centres. This latter process allows inbound deliveries from manufacturers to be assembled directly into vehicle loads for onward delivery to stores.

Meanwhile, comparison over time might be done like this:

Financial Year	2001	2003	2004	2005	2006	
Cost of goods sold (£m)	5.0	5.2	5.6	6.1	7.1	(A)
Finished goods stock (£m)	0.63	0.74	0.80	0.94	1.13	(B)
Stock turns per year	8	7	7	6.5	6.3	(C)
52/(C) = weeks of cover	6.5	7.4	7.4	8	8.25	(D)

This shows a reduction in stock turns over a five-year period, and a corresponding increase in weeks of stock cover. This is a deteriorating situation.

This methodology can also be applied to raw materials and purchased components, and here the annual usage is related to the value of stocks shown in the balance sheet.

These results can then be compared with other companies in the same industry sector – those 'best in class' companies which are constantly seeking to reduce inventory values at all stages such as raw materials, work in progress, and finished goods by a detailed management at the SKU level.

Models for Implementing Inventory controls

Assuming that you had recently become an inventory manager in a company which purchased stock for resale such as a wholesaler, and you had to improve the inventory controls, how would you start?

The process could be something like this:

(1)   Carry out the simple financial analysis illustrated above, to show whether the situation had been getting better or worse.

(2)   Carry out a detailed analysis at SKU level to show the individual stock turns. This would done as follows:

     (a)   List all the products (SKUs) sold in the last 12 months at cost.

     (b)   Alongside each, show the current stock value of each, also at cost.

     (c)   Calculate for each, the weeks of cover held.

     (d)   Arrange the information in descending order of value. This will typically reveal that 80% of the cost of goods sold will come from 20% of the SKUs (the 'A' class items in Pareto analysis terminology).

     (e)   Review the stock level of the 'A' class items to see that they are neither too low nor excessive. There is always a danger, when reductions in inventory are sought, that the fast moving and main revenue earning products will have stocks which are too low, since they are the items where reductions can be more easily achieved due to high turnover rates. Slow moving products may take a long time to 'drain away', and some may ultimately have to be declared as obsolete/scrapped.

     (f)   Repeat the exercise for the 30% of SKUs which represent the next 15% of usage (the B-class items). It is here that excessive stock levels will begin to show where there is sufficient stock to last, for example, 20 – 30 weeks (whereas for 'A' class items the norm is 2 – 4 weeks).

(g)   The 'C' class items will represent perhaps 50% of the SKUs, and 5% of the usage value. It is particularly in this category that obsolete stocks will be found.

The analysis might look something like this:

	Product Code	Annual Usage Value £ (A)	% of Annual Usage £ (B)	Cumulative % of annual usage (C)	Stock Value £ (D)	Weeks of cover (E) = (D)/(A) x 52
A Items	48976/3	50,000	10	10	2000	2 (Low?)
	28973/4	49,000	9.8 ⟶	19.8	5000	5.3 (High?)
	1876/3	48,000	9.6 ⟶	29.4	3000	3.25
	Continue till 80% of value is reached					

The 'A' class item would typically be purchased weekly; so the stock level should be 2 – 2.5 weeks of cover.

This analysis will quickly reveal whether stocks are reasonably balanced.

The process can be carried out by product category; this is advisable when a wide-ranging inventory of very different values is maintained.

For example, an agriculture merchant would have product ranges for:
     (a)   Bulk materials, chemicals etc.
     (b)   Small implements.
     (c)   Power equipment.
     (d)   Clothing etc.

Since the SKU values of these categories are so different, the above analysis should be carried out for each product 'family'.

This analysis will typically reveal excessive stocks in the 'B' and 'C' classes of each product family. These must be progressively reduced. There may be some items where there has been no usage in the last 12 months. If these can be considered obsolete they should be disposed of.

If the value of these obsolete stocks is still retained in the stock valuation in the company balance sheet, then any write-off of obsolete stock will affect the reported profit for the year.

Carrying out the Pareto analysis, as indicated above, is only an initial step. The next stage will be to review the inventory parameters used to manage the 'A' class items. Low or excessive stock levels may be due to incorrect values for:

(a)   The order quantity (EOQ).
(b)   The safety stock.
(c)   The reorder level or the reorder point.

It will be necessary to evaluate these criteria on an individual SKU basis and all of these processes have been set out earlier in this book.

A further test needs to be applied to establish whether there is clear evidence of seasonality in the demand for a product.

If seasonal variations are clearly evident, then seasonal profiles can be established. This is typically done at product family level. When seasonality is a major influence on the demand pattern, replenishment would normally be based on forecasts, as described earlier in Part 3 Replenishment.

If trying to bring an inventory of perhaps several thousand SKUs under control, where there has been no proper control before, how do you set about the task? In the absence of an inventory planning system, do the simplest possible things. These would include the following:

• Identify the SKU codes and descriptions.

• Develop a process for collecting demand data in monthly or, preferably, weekly intervals.

• Develop a simple model probably based on the use of a spreadsheet, into which all necessary rules and assumptions would be built. These would include:
    - Unit cost for each SKU.

    - Assumption about lead-time, which could vary by SKU.

    - Assumption about ordering costs and holding costs for calculating the EOQ.

    - Assumption about lead-times and required service levels to compute safety stocks.

    - Rules for calculating the EOQ, the safety stock, and the reorder point or 'order up to' level.

Into this model, the demand data for the last twelve months (or fifty-two weeks), would be 'pasted,' together with the existing stock available, and stock on order. This could be updated and reviewed weekly, with orders being placed if 'stock plus on order levels' are at or below the reorder point, or below the 'order up to' level.

The demand data would be used to calculate variability of demand using the standard deviation. This, together with the specified service level, and a defined lead-time, would be used to calculate the safety stock.

As an outline template of the model would look like this:

Product code/ identifier	Demand	Product Data Columns, e.g.	Stock on order + on hand	Calculation of Parameters	Calculation of Order if required.
	12 periods or 13 periods or 52 weekly periods	Unit cost Holding cost Ordering cost Service level Lead-time For each SKU 1 column for each parameter	Also show allocated stock if required.	Reorder point Safety stock EOQ	

Each row of the spreadsheet would represent an individual SKU. Quite large inventories can be managed in this way, especially if they are subdivided into sections for management by individual inventory planners.

This type of model is not, however, forecast based. A forecasting element can be introduced, but it can tend to make the model overly complex when using a spreadsheet. Replenishment based on forecasting, which is particularly a feature of retailing, requires the use of an order planning system which uses forecasts and forecast errors to determine order quantities.

The development and use of a model such as the one described above, is an ideal method to start to bring order out of chaos. The methodology is consistent, if not particularly sophisticated. It is also transparent, easy to understand, and easily updated and improved. The following is also useful when building and using such a model:

Question	Answer
Where does lead time data come from?	From records based on individual order, maybe one lead time will apply to a particular supplier.
How do you deal with lead time variability?	In the first stage of development you probably won't have the data, therefore, inventory planners and the purchasing department have to use experience and common sense.
Is this too simplistic as an inventory planning tool?	Not if this is the first real attempt to bring an inventory under control. It may need to be replaced by a much more powerful system at some stage, but then the users will be much clearer about what the system requirements are.
How does a model such as this help to bring down inventory levels?	- It shows the effect on stock levels of lead time (safety stock) - It shows the effect on 'cycle' stock on existing order size and order frequency. This provides a basis for progressively reducing lead times and possibly, order quantities.
How are the changes to lead time and order quantity, for example, to be implemented?	By highlighting their significance to the purchasing function, and by tackling the issues with suppliers.
How do you decide when the greatest improvements are likely to be made?	By looking at the items where: - The lead times are longest. - The EOQ is significantly below the present purchase or manufacturing batch quantity.

Determining stockholding targets

Arbitrary inventory targets in general terms such as £100 000, three week's cover etc. are of little use, except as a basic 'sanity check'. For example, if every other company like yours has 6 week's stock, and you have twelve week's, something is probably wrong. But even then, you need to embark on a review which will look at all products in a systematic way.

It is clear from preceding sections that lead-times, order frequency, and batch sizes will all influence the overall stock values. For example, if you place large orders infrequently, you will have a lot of stock; if you have long lead-times, then the safety stocks will need to be higher.

At any moment in time, very few of the items in an inventory will be at the 'average inventory' level, since there is a constant inflow and outflow of items. However, over the whole inventory, the total value (calculated units x unit cost) should be something like the calculated value (i.e. calculated on a SKU by SKU basis).

This should be frequently tested.

It will probably be found that the calculated value varies from week to week, but it should be falling as inventory is brought under closer control, for example, by shorter, more dependable lead-times, purchasing/manufacturing batch sizes being reduced and the consistent operation of control parameters.

Problems arising from setting targets by product groups

As an indication of the loss of identification to an individual item when dealing with item groups, the following examples have been constructed:

Item	Target Stock	Actual Stock	Unit Cost £	Target Value	Actual Value
A	50	50	10.0	500	500
B	120	120	50.0	6000	6000
C	150	150	12.0	1800	1800
D	600	550	1.0	600	550
	920	870		8900	8850

From this example it can be seen that:

Target volume = 920, Actual volume = 870, % Actual/target = 94.56%

Target value = £8900, Actual value = £8850, % Actual/target = 99.44%

If we now amend the figures so that:
Item A has a nil actual stock
Item D has 600 actual stock

We would get the following:
Target volume 920   Actual volume 870   % Actual/target 94.56%
Target value £8900   Actual value £8400   % Actual/target 94.38%

With the same target volume and value plus the same actual volume a different picture emerges. First the percentage of value, actual to target, for the group of items shows a significant decrease. Secondly, although the volume actual to target for the group of items is unchanged, one item is in a nil stock position.

Using Stock cover as a Performance Measure
The most common method of measuring stock coverage is by expressing the actual stock in terms of periods covered based on an average demand.

The period can be days, weeks, months etc., for example:

Annual Demand	1200
Average Monthly Demand	100
Actual Stock	400
Stock Coverage	400/100 = 4 months

However, this assumes that at any point in time at which the stock coverage is measured, that average demand as shown is applicable. This would only be true of a stable item, with little or no variation in demand.

Some examples of the effect of trends, demand variation and the methods employed to measure stock coverage are shown below.

Example A

Actual stock $= 1000$

Previous 6 periods demand were 50, 80, 120, 150, 250, and 350.

Average demand $= 166.7$

Stock coverage $= \dfrac{1000}{166.7} = 6.0$ periods

If only the last three periods demand were used to establish the average demand the stock coverage would be:

Stock coverage $\dfrac{1000}{250} = 4.0$ periods

The selection of the number of periods over which the average demand is calculated has an effect on the measurement result.

Example B

If we accept that stock on hand is, in fact, to support future demand, it would then be more realistic to base the stock coverage on predicted demand.

Actual stock $= 1000$

Predicted 6 periods demand is 550, 500, 600, 400, 350, and 300.

Average demand $= 450$

Stock coverage $= \dfrac{1000}{450} = 2.2$ periods

Once again using a three period average predicted demand the stock coverage would be:

Stock coverage $\dfrac{1000}{550} = 1.82$ periods

The 1000 units would cover the whole of the first forecast period plus 90% of the second period ahead, (450/500) = 90%.

Example C
Using groups of items can provide a more distorted effect on the measurement.

Item A – Actual stock 1000 Predicted demand 300; 350; 400; 550

Item B – Actual stock 200 Predicted demand 30; 30; 50; 60

Total A & B – Actual stock 1200 Predicted demand 330; 380; 450; 610

Average demand = 442.5

Stock coverage $\dfrac{1200}{442.5}$ = 2.71 periods

For the individual items the stock coverage would be:

Item A = 2.50 periods
Item B = 4.70 periods

It can be seen that any change in the Item A data will have a more significant effect than that of item B.

Example D
In some instances stock coverage is calculated on a value basis. In this example, using the basic data in example C and a unit cost of £1 for item A and £50 for item B, we can see the effect on the stock coverage achievement by comparison with example C.

Item A Actual stock value £1000 Predicted demand value £300; £350; £400; £550.

Item B Actual stock value £10 000 Predicted demand value £1500; £1500; £2500; £3000.

Item A & B Actual stock value £11 000 Predicted demand value £1800; £1850; £2900; £3550

Average demand value = £2525

Stock coverage $\dfrac{£11\ 000}{£2525}$ = 4.36 periods

For the individual items the stock coverage would be the same as in example C. In this instance any changes in item B would have a greater effect on the total.

Example E
One further method that can be used to establish stock coverage can be described as the stock depletion method.

This assumes that the actual stock will be depleted by the forward predicted demand on a period basis, rather than as an average, until it reaches zero.

Item A Actual stock 1000

Predicted demand 200; 250; 350; 400; 400; 450

Stock coverage 1000 – 200 – 250 – 350 – (400 – 200) or 3.5 periods

Stock balance 800; 550; 200 (200 remains for 50% of Period 4 demand forecast).

Item B Actual stock 200 Predicted demand 40; 40; 30; 20; 50; 70

Stock coverage 200 – 40 – 40 – 30 – 20 – 50 – (70 – 50) or 5.29 periods.

Stock balance 160; 10; 90; 70; 20; 20/70 = 0.29 (29% of Period 6).

The grouping of items and a similar measurement using value rather than volume, will present the same problem in the target setting and also the evaluation/measurement; as has been identified in previous examples.

It is obvious that considerable care and understanding is required in the establishment of targeting and measurement systems and processes. In all cases these should reflect the service and cost objectives set for the inventory system, its management and control. An ability to measure and understand the variances between targets and achievement is important to the whole process. It is good to remember that there is little point in planning if you do not intend to measure, and there is little point in measuring if there is not a target with which to compare results.

Inventory Questions
To paraphrase the management guru Peter Drucker, the problem with many managers is their emphasis on getting a right answer, rather than asking the right question. So an additional way to check on the performance of inventory is to use the following questions; this will help to ensure pro-activity in managing inventory. It should be noted, however, that the division of questions is somewhat arbitrary:

Strategic aspects
- Why do you have inventory?
- What drives the present level of inventory?
- How are inventory levels set?

- How current is the decision on the inventory levels?
- How often are inventory decisions reviewed?
- What direction is inventory being driven, and why is it?
- What are the actual service requirements of customers?
- How does the direction and/or change in inventory compare with the direction and/or change in sales?
- How much of the inventory reflects safety stock?
- Who is responsible for setting and for managing inventory levels?
- Are they the same person/department or not?
- How are excess inventories, and the cost of, reflected in management responsibilities?
- How are the alternatives, inventory stock-outs, and the cost of inventory reflected in management responsibilities?
- How are ICT system algorithms and underlying assumptions reviewed?
- Is customer input used?

Purchasing Aspects
- How are stock levels reviewed?
- Is buying scheduled in accordance with these reviews?
- How are suppliers managed?
- Are supplier lead-times part of the suppliers' performance criteria?

Demand and forecast aspects
- How variable is demand?
- How is forecasting done?
- Is forecast accuracy regularly measured?
- How accurate is it, at the item/SKU level?
- How efficiently is it prepared and submitted?
- How does purchasing and manufacturing handle the forecast inaccuracies?
- Do they overbuy or overbuild to compensate for doubts about the forecast?
- Is inventory forecast to the distribution centre level so the right inventory at the right quantity is carried at each facility?
- Or is the forecast at a macro level with no direction on what inventory, how much inventory and where inventory should be positioned?

Lead-time and methods aspects
- How variable is supplier lead-times?
- How are the total lead-times, including in transit stock lead-times and

internationally sourced items, incorporated in the system?

- How accurate are the free stock inventories that are used in the resulting production planning and sourcing?
- How is supplier reliability and lead-times reflected in inventory planning and management?
- Are additional inventories factored in to buffer for each of these issues?
- How these aspects are factored into supplier selection decisions?
- Does purchasing have purchase order visibility with suppliers to control ordered items at the SKU level?
- Do suppliers understand and collaborate with the inventory philosophy and approach?
- Do products purchased flow to keep inventory in the supply chain or are they irregular, aggregated?
- How are transportation reliability and transit times reflected in inventory planning and management?
- Are additional inventories factored in to buffer for each of these issues?

Warehousing aspects
- Where is inventory stored and why?
- How many distribution centres are used and why? (Each distribution centre means additional safety stock will be carried).
- Are they in the right locations?
- How much obsolete/dead, old promotions and very slow-moving dead inventory is there?
- What is the storage cost for such 'dead' inventory?
- Is inventory often transferred between distribution centres to provide inventory to fill orders? (That is inefficient use of transportation, not good customer service and resulting from wrong forecasting allocation).
- How are goods received and booked in so that errors are prevented?
- How are stocks rotated to prevent out of code problems, product obsolescence etc?
- How is picking accuracy undertaken (to reduce stock inaccuracies)?
- What method of stock control and checking is undertaken?

Inventory KPIs in Warehouses/Stores
Finally, the following table (overleaf) represents the commonly used performance measurements for managing inventory in warehouses/stores, with measurements needed at each holding place for stocks of raw materials, work in progress and finished goods.

Measure	Definition	Calculation
Accuracy	Actual quantity versus system quantity	Actual quantity by SKU/Reported quantity by SKU
Damages	Damages as a % of cost value	Total damage/total inventory value
Days on hand	Average sales days of inventory based on history	Average inventory value/average daily sales (past month)
Storage utilisation	Occupied space in warehouse as % of available storage capacity	Space used/space available
Forecast accuracy	Actual demand versus demand forecasted in a period	% forecast accurate: Actual/Forecast sales per SKU.
Availability.	Quantity required versus quantity issued/delivered	% available: Ordered / Delivered Per SKU.

6: Inventory Strategies

In this chapter, we recognise that inventory is totally central in Supply Chain Management. As supply chain management is a dynamic and changing engagement, varied inventory management approaches have been developed. Whilst some of these are new innovative approaches; other approaches often take one specific aspect of the supply chain (such as time compression), and re-package it using a catchy new name (like Quick Response). This is often also reduced to a two or three letter abbreviation (like QR/ECR).

Such re-packaging can of course be useful: people often focus better and identify more with badges, as these provide a clearer identification of the approach needed and can therefore give direction.

We shall examine in the final part of the book, some of these approaches and these will be presented as being more specific about:
*   The total supply chain (push/pull, QR, ECR, CPFR, lean/agile, TQM).
*   Distribution (postponements, consolidation).
*   Inventory (VMI, CMI, Consignment stocking).
*   Financial (DPP, EVA).

It should be appreciated this division is arbitrary, and overlap will be found. For example, inventory is a common aspect in these approaches, as is collaboration.

Supply Chain Push/Pull options
In Part 1 of this book, we identified, for discussion purposes, the Type I and Type II supply chains. The former was more production led and supply push; the latter was more market led with demand pull.

The Type I supply chain is similar to traditional UK mass production, that has been relatively late in changing to embrace demand driven markets that require producing in smaller, make-to-order batches.

The conflicts between volume and variety are a main consideration in production, and traditionally, high volume with low variety (and low price), was seen as the 'only way'. However, changes have been made in those industries that have remained in the UK; meanwhile off-shoring has been used for much of the former UK manufacturing and production base.

The make-to-stock or make-to-order decision is a classic trade off in supply chain management, that has clear implications for all supply chain activities, not the least of which is the inventory.

Making to Order or Making to Stock is the separation point between forecasting and ordering and gives five positions or 'decoupling points', as shown by the following diagram:

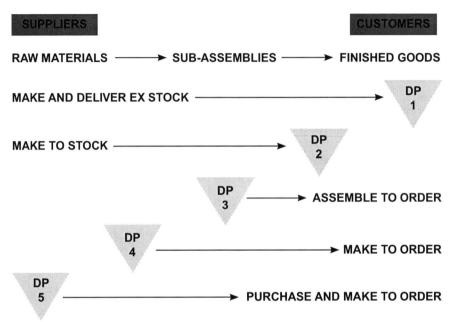

The 1-5 positions are separated by Forecasts and Order activities as discussed below:

DP1) Make and deliver from stock = Forecast driven
Examples are fast moving food products that are held in regional distribution centres, near to retail outlets.

DP2) Make to stock = Forecast driven
Examples are slower moving consumer and food items that are held more centrally in Central Distribution centres. Traditionally this was also the main method used for UK car assembly.

DP3) Assemble to order = Order driven
Furniture and beds are examples of this method of production along with, in recent years, UK car assembly led by Nissan and Toyota.

DP4) Make to order = Order driven
Examples here are PC's and top of the range cars like a Rolls Royce.

DP5) Purchase and make to order = Order driven
High tech and large capital one off items are examples here.

From a production aspect, the following can be found:

DP1: typically continuous flow production with very high volume produced but with no product variation; such as with petrol and steel. Such items are known as "runners".

DP2: typically dedicated line flow production with very high volumes made and with little product variation; the mass production of cars was traditionally a good example.

DP3: typically mixed product line flow with medium volumes produced of medium product variations; the manufacturing of clothes is an example here as is the "newer" method now used for car assembly. Such items are known as "repeaters".

DP4: typically batch flow production with lower volumes of high product variation; job shops like printers, for example.

DP5: typically job shop production of very low volumes but very high product variations; project one-off items like ships being one example. Such items may be called "strangers" as they are not found too often!

These 5 positions give rise to the following supply chain basic options where:
- **"Push"** involves forecast driven activity that pushes and supplies stock towards the customer, where it is held to await the customer's demand orders. It involves the inventory holding of finished goods and is risky, as it deals more with uncertainty in demand.

- **"Pull"** involves actual demand orders pulling stock through the supply chain from the point of supply. It is responsive directly to these orders and involves the products matching exactly what customers order. It involves holding stock of semi-finished work in progress, or even no inventory at all (as with DP5), where raw materials are ordered specifically to manufacture a customer order. There is less risk with this option as nothing is more certain than the customer's order.

The following is a summary of these options:

Activity	MTS(DP1/2) "Make then sell" Forecast "Push" Supply-demand	MTO(DP4/5) "Sell then make" Order "Pull" Demand-supply
Main driver	Forecasts. Structured planning and scheduling.	Orders. Sense and respond using real time information.
Buying	Is for anticipated needs by instructing suppliers. Focus on cost and quality.	Is for daily needs using involved suppliers. Focus on speed, quality and flexibility.
Product	Standardised products. Cost driven.	Can be bespoke and modular. More quality driven.
Customer lead time	Fast and short	Slower
Production	Low cost as uses long production run lengths. High average utilisation.	Higher costs and short run lengths and fast production line changes. Excess buffer capacity is used
Inventory	Cost is in finished goods and uses safety stock. Stock is viewed as an asset and as a protection	Cost is in raw materials and work in progress with little safety stock. Stock is viewed as a liability
Distribution	Storage costs are high with low transport costs (as moving in bulk).	Storage costs are low with transport costs being higher as moving smaller quantities more frequently

The "make then sell" position is well represented by the Henry Ford expression of "you can have colour you want, as long it as it is black", and also by the traditional manufacture/assembly of consumer goods. Nowadays, cars for example, are increasingly "assembled to order" (position three), which involves assembling a specific order from stocks of components/work in progress. This method of production represents, for many, the optimum production trade-off in the supply chain, as final assembly is only taking place on receipt of the order; the final product production being "postponed" until a firm order is received. It also means adopting a more challenging form of supply chain management that has clear implications for the inventory strategy.

Make to order/order pull

The following case study shows how inventory levels can be reduced by only making products to meet specific orders. Therefore only stocks of parts and sub-assemblies are held; these being cheaper than holding stocks of finished goods that are awaiting sale

Case Study: Supply chain lessons from Dell

One company that is building on a history of excellent supply-chain management to meet the Internet challenge is Dell Computer Corporation. Dell uses supply chain management to implement and continuously improve its "direct" model. This model continues to be a major differentiation for Dell in the ultra-competitive PC market.

The Dell "direct" model demonstrates the value and effectiveness of supply-chain integration:
- Dell buys components just in time, benefiting from the latest (i.e. the lower component) prices.

- For Dell, "build-to-order" means exactly that: no resources are committed until a customer order is received.

Through combining these and other supply chain management practices, Dell is able to offer:
- A wide product range

- Competitive prices

- Short delivery lead-times, without sacrificing margins and with minimum inventory

Dell continues to develop and improve capabilities of its supply chain. For example, by the end of 1998, the Dell web site was generating revenue of over $14 million a day, an increase from around $2 million at the end of 1997. The web site makes online ordering quick and convenient by allowing customers to specify the product features they want, and by instantly giving them a price quote.

To further differentiate itself in the corporate market, Dell has created "Premier Pages". These are web sites dedicated to corporate clients that can be accessed by a client's authorised employees to research, configure, and price PCs before they buy. Each web site holds client-specific information, such as preferred configurations and pricing. This information improves order accuracy and simplifies Dell's order entry processes. For customers, the cost of buying PCs is greatly reduced.

Source: Managing your supply chain in the 21st century, PRT&Mc

Quick Response (QR)

QR was originally developed in USA in the 1980s for the domestic apparel and textile industry. The name was 'the badge' used to encourage national suppliers to react faster to compete with lower priced imports. It involves shorter lead-times with reduced stock levels and demand lead-times, so that a faster response could be made to customers order requirements. It requires adjusting the re-order levels and also closer working between suppliers/customers.

Efficient Consumer Response (ECR)

ECR is another USA acronym originally developed for FMCG grocery products. It uses consumer demand to drive the supply chain to deliver exactly when required, by using collaborative approaches supported by ICT. It has a mission statement of "Working together to fulfil consumer wishes better, faster and at less cost" (ECR Europe). ECR operates in two ways:

- As a set of principles and best practice for supply chain management where individual companies work together in collaboration with others, for example between suppliers and customers.

- An industry initiative developing leading edge thinking into best practice tools and techniques, and common standards for implementation.

The potential benefits for a company for adopting an ECR approach identified by the Institute of Grocery Distribution (2002) are as follows:

- Better responsiveness to consumer needs.
- Faster growth.
- Enhanced margins.
- Improved product ranges.
- More effective use of promotional activity.
- Lower levels of stock.
- Greater synchronisation of production.
- Increased integration across the supply chain.
- More rational use of resources.
- Positive environmental impact.

ECR has four main strands: product range and assortment, promotions, new line introductions and replenishment. This latter aspect means examining buying (in terms of managing promotions, and using and coordinating alternative suppliers of identical products), lead-times and forecasting (already discussed), plus collaborative supply chains, warehouse operations like cross-docking and CMI/VMI inventory methods (all of which will be discussed shortly).

Collaborative Planning, Forecasting and Replenishment (CPFR)

CPFR is a collection of business processes that are better enabled by a jointly agreed information system. It aims to change the relationship between suppliers/ customers to create an accurate end consumer driven process and information flow. Suppliers/customers have a common view of consumer demand; they collaborate and coordinate plans, actions and activities through a jointly owned planning system to ensure product availability.

CPFR means that the following has to happen:

- Develop collaborative agreements.
- Create joint business plans.
- Create sales forecasts.
- Identify exceptions to the sales forecasts.
- Resolve these exceptions.
- Create the order forecast.
- Identify exceptions to the order forecast.
- Resolve these exceptions.
- Generate the order.

It can be seen that collaboration is used to resolve the exceptions in forecasts; CPFR therefore looks to build business relationships by focusing on jointly managed processes with common communication tools. In summary, CPFR allows for pre-planning rather than reacting and uses ICT/ internet technology to reduce inventory and expense, while increasing sales and improving customer service. CPFR looks to improve the forward visibility of requirements across the entire supply chain by effectively and collaboratively making forecasts a dependant demand driver.

Lean and Agile approaches

Lean: *(Webster's dictionary: containing little fat)*

This represents efficiency and eliminating waste by enhancing the flow between source/user to satisfy a known and predictable demand, for example, as with MRP and with J.I.T. in car manufacturing where suppliers are selected for product quality and reliability as well as cost.

In the car industry, it can be seen as concentrating more on the supply chain, focusing on "stock push". Planning and forecasting can be the main driver, with Economic Batch Quantities/ Make to Stock production methods. As it can take up to 18 hours to build a new car, but up to three months to get the car to consumer, these post production times are currently being targeted under "the three day car" initiative (this being the lead-time from building/assembly to the consumer).

Lean can be seen as the response to dealing with the perceived uncertainty in demand, leading to efficient supply. It is the supply side that is Lean; the demand side may, however, be Fat.

Case Study: Adopting Lean principles: Motor cycle manufacturer, Ducati, leans hard into a fast bend

Lean principles have always influenced thinking at Ducati. While other motorcycle brands were busy adding power and weight to their machines, the Italian manufacturer always believed in keeping weight to the minimum to improve stability when a bike is leaning hard over into a fast bend. Now the company has embraced lean principles throughout its manufacturing process as part of a major turnaround in its operations. And the results are impressive: production costs down by up to 25 per cent, throughput time shortened by 50 per cent and motorcycle build quality, before delivery, increased by 70 per cent.

These figures are the culmination of a three-year efficiency drive led by Giovanni Contino and Filippo Pellerey, joint managing directors of Ducati Consulting, which was set up to oversee the project. The move to lean manufacturing followed the acquisition of Ducati in 1996 by the Texas Pacific Group (TPG). The new management wanted to increase production volumes from 12,000 bikes a year to 40,000 within five years. This would have to be achieved in the existing factory space, and without increasing the number of employees.

Ducati's solution was to outsource as many non-core activities as possible and focus its own efforts on assembly and research and development: "We wanted to eliminate all non-value-adding activity, eliminate waste and improve quality, all without any major new investment," says Pellerey. "We decided that outsourcing and embracing lean principles were the keys to achieving these targets.

"We started by adopting the kaizen philosophy and just-in-time methodology, whereby you can achieve major change without big investments by taking it one step at a time. We conducted a careful analysis of our production processes, which revealed all of our problems. For example, in the machining shop the machines were laid out in such a way that components had to follow a long and tortuous path to get to the various operations.

"So we improved the material flow and the factory ergonomics and devised a total productive maintenance approach to improve machine reliability. Some of the most significant results in that department included an increase of up to 12 per cent in machine reliability and a reduction of 23 per cent in hourly costs."

The Ducati team also changed the flow logic for the production lines from 'push logic' to 'pull logic', using assembly kits carrying the materials needed for only one engine or one vehicle. The kits are made up in areas known as supermarkets, that are themselves supplied via a Kanban system. This has reduced inventory, obsolescence and error rates and improved flexibility. In combination, these changes have reduced defects by 70 per cent over the past three years.

"As we worked through all these changes, we found that we could cut the cost of our product by 25 per cent, which was a great start." Pellerey said. "Since only eight per cent of the cost of our product was produced internally, it was necessary to extend, develop and implement the Kaizen philosophy and the J.I.T methodology to the supply chain."

Since the greatest potential for improvement lay with the supply chain, the team was joined by Giovanni Contino, who at the time was Ducati's purchasing and logistics director. He started to export the company's new lean culture to its suppliers.

"We had 380 suppliers, and the lean philosophy was new to most of them," Contino said. "We had to select only those suppliers who could follow our new approach, and so we ended up cutting back from 380 to just 175. To get them on board, we introduced an integration programme that involved Ducati people and supplier staff working in teams.

"We considered our suppliers an extension of Ducati and so it has been necessary to connect them by the Web to exchange and accelerate the flow of information like production planning, parts price lists, invoices, and quality reports and so on."

Sixty percent of Ducati' procurement comes from Italy, because of the long auto ve in Northern Italy, 25 per cent from other EU countries and the rest from Japan. At the moment, the first 100 suppliers are directly connected to Ducati's IT network which is based around O e-business suite. The next step on Ducati's journey is to move closer to the concept of a demand-driven supply network (DDSN). "Right now, that's something we know we want," Contino said. "We want anyone who desires a Ducati motorcycle to be able to walk into a dealer and get one in the shortest possible time, but that will require further development of the information process between our dealer network and the factory. We are working on that now."

Source Logistics Europe July 2005 Automotive Special Report

Agile: (Webster's dictionary: nimble)

As demand can be difficult to predict, there is the need to have a rapid response to the end market demand. Demand drives the supply chain, for example Efficient Consumer Response (ECR) in food retailing where suppliers are selected on speed and flexibility as well as cost.

With food retailers, they can be seen to concentrate more on the demand chain (or pipeline), with "demand pull". The end marketplace (the consumer), is the ultimate demand driver, and, with such certainty, this enables Make (MTO) and Assemble to Order (ATO) production. In turn, this can also mean having modular product structures with postponement until the latest possible time, for example, customisation, kiting, and assembly in Distribution Centres (DCs). Everything that is bought, produced, moved, and handled is in response to a known customer requirement.

Lean/Agile Conclusion
The main change needed to be agile is to get close to the market real time demand. Once this is achieved, other challenges will remain for efficient and effective Supply Chain Management. These include:

- creating value from the customers perspective.
- identifying the value stream.
- highlighting non value added work.
- sharing information.
- process integration by smoothing the supply/demand chain.
- forming a network of companies who work closely together.

These all remain as important challenges and required areas for change to the past traditional ways of supplying products to markets. Indeed, for the car assembly industry, such challenges are conceptually similar to those initially experienced when they changed to J.I.T. supply from the previous bulk buying and large stock holding processes.

The terms need not be mutually exclusive. Within a Total Supply Chain viewpoint, being Lean and Agile is both efficient and effective, as both Supply and Demand respond by pulling to the end market consumer demands in real time. "Leagility" is a term which has been developed to describe the combined lean and agile viewpoints.

Quality Management
Quality Management has many parallels with Supply Chain Management, and is therefore very supportive in aims and ideals. Quality management represents the involvement and commitment of everyone, in continuously improving work processes, to satisfy the requirements and expectations of all internal and external customers. It is, therefore, somewhat fundamentally similar to Supply Chain

Management; as will be seen in the ten basic principles of Quality Management:
* agreed customer requirements.
* understand and improve customer/supplier chains.
* do the right things.
* do things right first time.
* measure for success.
* continuous improvement is the goal.
* management must lead.
* training is essential.
* communicate more effectively.
* recognise successful involvement.

There are several options available to use to further these principles:
Kaizan means continuous improvement in a gradual and ordered way. It has an objective of the elimination of waste in the processes, components and functions. It has two parts: one being improvements and change and the other being to do this in an ongoing and continous manner.

Total Quality Management (TQM) is an approach towards larger scale company change, and improves existing process and functions. TQM needs strong direction and leading from above, as it needs commitment and involvement from all. As such, middle management in traditional command and control structures can often be a barrier to TQM, as the managers fear a loss of control as their jobs become largely superfluous as involvement spreads below them.

Six Sigma involves statistics, as in the use of the word sigma, which is another word for standard deviation. Statistics are used to establish company benchmarks, which assist in work processes being continually improved to meet the customers' expectations. The goal is to reduce the chance of failure to only 3.4 in a million opportunities (this is six sigma/standard deviations). Whilst this may be unattainable, it does indicate that six sigma, like quality generally, often represents the journey towards a destination. The six key concepts of six sigma are:
* Critical quality: what actually is it that matters to the customer?
* Defects: what happens when fail to deliver what the customer wants?
* Process capability: what can the processes do?
* Variation: what is the customer's perception and how does this differ from the critical quality?
* Stable operations: what has to be done to ensure consistent and certain processes?
* Design for six sigma: what is involved in designing to meet customer needs and to get process capability?

The Seven Wastes
The Seven Wastes from Quality Management are as follows:
- Overproduction: for example, having excess finished goods stocks from 'production only' economies of scales, especially found in make-to-stock scenarios.

- Waiting: for example, time spent having to queue for a machine to finish its cycle.

- Transporting: for example, when moving work in progress (WiP) around for finishing; the transport cost is a waste and adds no value to the finished product.

- Inappropriate processing: for example, from over specifying /engineering.

- Unnecessary inventory: for example, having more stock than the required minimum.

- Unnecessary/excess motion: for example, from having movement that does not contribute in getting products to customers.

- Defects: for example, having to correct faults and defects.

Some observers have noted that there is also an eighth waste: not using people's innovation and creativity - it needs people to look at the above seven wastes and then create improvements.

Postponement
This represents coordinating and delaying the 'buy/make/move' activities so that they take place as close as possible to the 'sell' demand. Used especially for high value goods that have a high demand uncertainty, postponement involves, for example, assemble-to-order at distribution centres (or a partner downstream) located close to customers and who customises product to meet the specific order.

Cross Docking
In some supply chain operations, both receiving and dispatching may occur almost simultaneously. This is often known as cross docking as goods effectively move from the receipt dock area to the goods dispatch dock areas, without incurring any long term storage.

Product flows through the warehouse more quickly and easily, with stock being held in transit for only minutes (as a minimum) to a few hours as a maximum.

There is less movement and less cost incurred in the warehouse operations, with reduced lead-times, minimised handling and virtually no storage holding costs.

Cross docking will require that the following conditions are satisfied:
- Integration and coordination of the appropriate supplier/ customer interfaces. EDI/email, scanning and bar code technologies can be most useful enablers.
- Destination is known, ideally before, but at the latest by when the goods are received.
- Customer is ready to receive the goods.
- Product data recognition; to facilitate quick checking/verification.
- No long timescales for any quality control or checking, on receipt.
- Good quality information; (for example, with advanced knowledge and EDI/email).
- Co-operative supply chains.
- Disciplined deliveries.

Cross Docking will therefore be sensitive to any of the following:
- Non receipt of suppliers deliveries
- Short receipt on suppliers deliveries
- Late arrivals of suppliers vehicles, bad weather, road traffic delays
- Last minute changes in customer orders

Case Study: Stock reduction by cross-docking

Company:
- Retailer of apparel, household merchandise
- £500 million per annum turnover
- 3 RDCs
- Product sourced 50% overseas and 50% UK
- All products bar coded

EDI with UK Suppliers:
- Used with suppliers for order call offs
- Suppliers give stock availability
- Call offs given per RDC to supplier
- Tracked at key points
- UK stock is cross-docked

Supplier Lead-times:
Day 1: call off
2: schedules for collection
3: collection by retailer
4: RDC
5: store

Reasons for Success:
* Lead-time disciplines clearly stated and agreed
* Commitment of all involved
* Multi disciplined internal team of purchasing, store merchandising, logistics and store operation

Consolidation

This is used to obtain the benefit from economies in scale, especially of transport. Retailers for example, have primary consolidation centres (PCCs) located in regions near to suppliers where stock is held pending, being 'called forward'. It is then consolidated with other supplier's goods at the PCC into a full load, delivered to each of the retailer's nationally located regional distribution centres (RDCs).

Stock holding is, therefore, effectively externalised in the transport chain and only enters the user's supply chain when the stocks are called forward. At the RDCs, products are either placed into stock, or are immediately cross-docked on receipt for final delivery to the retailers individual stores.

Vendor managed inventory (VMI)

VMI involves suppliers holding stocks at their customer's premises. It requires the sharing of information from customers, so that the supplier has visibility of the customer's demand and usage. Then, the supplier is able to control stock levels in the customer's premises, and manage inventory for the customer; the supplier makes all replenishment decisions, monitors customer inventory levels and possibly directly processes customer demands. VMI can be especially useful when there is stable demand.

Customer ownership and the payment to the supplier is only is made when the stock has been used/sold. For the customer, this clearly reduces costs, reduces the risks of buying goods that will not be used/sold, and improves cash flows. For the supplier, VMI ties in the customer with longer term relationships; this, however, is at the expense of delayed payments and potential product returns.

Case Study: Vendor Managed Inventory: Changing relationships, moving inventory

Sales forecasting has never been an exact science: enter Vendor Managed Inventory (VMI), a planning process used to move stock through the supply chain. Using VMI as a method of continuous replenishment, vendors control the flow of inventory into the retailer's distribution network to replenish the retailer's stock to pre-determined inventory levels. Using daily information from the retailer's EDI system, the vendor is in control of the process from arranging shipments to building loads and cutting purchase orders. Of course, retailers, as the other half of the VMI relationship, agree to hand over their information and be full participants in the forecasting process.

The method is similar to continuous replenishment planning (CRP), except the vendor is in charge of what to ship and when. The reason why the vendor is in an excellent position to manage inventory for the retailer revolves around the fact that vendors are a middle link in the supply chain and can track needs from both ends - from raw material to the end consumer.

One other main advantage, from the retailer's point of view at least, is that the supplier comprehends its own product better than anyone, while the retailer would normally have to keep track of numerous products, thus not understanding their replenishment needs.

On paper, the process seems simple to implement, but in the real world of personalities and professional relationships, there are many obstacles to climb. In short, trust is very important for the VMI model to succeed.

Still, since there are companies using VMI, there must be some strong reasons to do so. When VMI works, it means less inventory sitting in a warehouse and that's good news for the supply chain as a whole. No longer would resources, personnel, time and money be spent on loading inventory that would merely sit in a warehouse collecting dust until an inevitable promotion. As a result, the products would be fresher.

The main advantage of using VMI may be more intangible than dollars and cents, or a cutback in purchase orders. Instead, personal relationships that bridge former gaps in communications between vendor and retailer are what can really spell success for VMI.

"You see, VMI changes the paradigm. It's definitely a different type of relationship with your customer. It's based on mutual trust and it's got to be there to succeed". The goal is to let the consumer drive the replenishment, VMI gives the supplier information that is one step closer to the consumer - hence replacing inventory with information. Loading is not an option under the VMI plan. The buyer's role changes even more dramatically as they're no longer focused on crunching numbers and creating purchase orders. That becomes the supplier's role. The buyer's role becomes one of policing what the supplier is recommending or sending and providing insight into her/his particular business while collaborating on the forecast. There has to be a strong education program within the organization on, what is VMI? How does it work? What are all the commitments that have to be made by all the players on both sides of the fence? Then, how does that get you to your end goal - minimizing inventory in the supply chain?

For Lever Ponds, education seems to have paid off. Over the past two years, since VMI's inception, the company has seen great success. Some customers report 30 to 40 per cent reductions in inventory, but the most impressive statistic of all relates to forecast accuracy, which has gone from non-existent to 75 per cent.

While VMI may not be with us long term, it is one stepping stone towards implementing an overall structure of interconnecting links that will only make individual companies' operations and the entire supply chain stronger.

Source: www.infochain.org

Case Study: Entertainment UK and VMI

With 1, 000 plus new product releases every month, there are winners and losers in the home entertainment sector when it comes to knowing which CDs or DVDs to stock.

Entertainment UK (EUK), part of the Woolworths Group, is one of the largest retail wholesalers of home entertainment products, supplying Britain's best known retailers with nearly a quarter of the UK's music and video, as well as supplying direct to the public via the Internet, kiosks and catalogues. The entertainment wholesale and publishing businesses saw operating profit rise last year by 16% to £49.3M. The EUK retail operation saw overall sales rise 10% to £1.2Bn.

With customers including Tesco, Woolworths, WH Smith and MVC, EUK has been an innovator in the use of a vendor managed inventory model working on behalf of retailers to ensure that each gets the appropriate product selection, in the right quantities, at the right time. CDs and DVDs have short product lifecycles, so EUK requires accurate demand forecasting to prevent exposure to any stock loss and lost sales in a £5.5Bn market.

EUK acts as an intermediary between entertainment suppliers, like Warner or Universal, and retailers aggregating products from multiple suppliers into single store shipments. However, it identified that the efficiency of its supply chain had substantial room for improvement, leading to rising returns and escalating distribution costs.

This was partly put down to inappropriate functionality in certain systems. EUK chose TXT e-solutions to introduce new forecasting and new replenishment software. Competences and understanding of the retail sector's logistics were also key reasons in driving the choice.

Together with EUK's market intelligence for predicting best sellers, and historical EPOS sales data for nearly 3,000 stores, the TXT solution produces as many as 100,000 store replenishment orders a day. To ensure that the shelves remain fully stocked and stores are automatically replenished, information exchange must be fast with retailers and suppliers, and there is only a three-hour processing window each night for forecasting and demand planning.

The initial forecast and allocation is a really critical process in such a highly seasonal and volatile market. This led to intelligence and innovation within the underlying forecasting engine, such as the use of historic profiles (mined from the data warehouse) and the simultaneous analysis of store seasonality, daily selling patterns, market seasonality and product clusters, for instance. TXT offers merchandise planning and replenishment solutions focusing on products with a very short lifecycle and sometimes no history. Under these circumstances, sales forecasts, allocation and replenishment management is carried out using techniques which can incorporate sales trends, store behaviour, seasonality as well as best practice forecasting capabilities. The initial allocation and the daily re-forecasting and replenishment allow them to determine the right product in the right store at the right time in a fast moving environment.

EUK's vendor-managed inventory (VMI) initiative maximises sales whilst controlling movements of stock up and down the supply chain. For most customers, VMI involves integration to both head office and in-store back-office systems, so everyone can effectively share trading data and get a single version of the truth. It uses EDI (Electronic Data Interchange) technology combined with TXT forecasting and replenishment systems to maximise on-shelf availability; minimise stock keeping costs; plan for seasonality fluctuations; provide regional and individual store focus; and provide a pre-ordering facility.

The company also boasts a new 29 500sq m distribution centre (DC) in Greenford, Middlesex, which is capable of despatching in excess of 200 million units per year with more than 99.9% accuracy. Early tests during 2004 in a pilot customer revealed that not only were stock turns improved (typically by 25%), store returns levels fell by 20%, and store availability was maintained above 98%. Now that the technology has been fully rolled out, the retailer's in-store inventory has since been reduced by about 23%, whilst in- store availability has remained strong. During the peak sales period at Christmas, EUK sales rose by about 3%, while returns dropped by about 8%.

Annually, a returns reduction of around 20% is anticipated and already well on target. The impact of this on the distribution centre and supply chain costs is significant, given that returns costs are about twice that of outbound. Pence per unit DC cost reductions have already been recorded.

Other benefits include improved store availability through use of local trends at regional and store- specific level; improved customer activity planning, and in-store execution, through provision of the future inventory picture; and earlier customer communication of upstream supply issues.

EUK has already seen significant bottom-line benefits driven from the advances made in re engineering its demand planning and forecasting processes with TXT. The project is proving extremely successful in a very competitive industry. EUK is well on target to achieving its objectives of improving service with lower costs and lower inventories.

The project's success has encouraged EUK to look at technology for incorporating the promotional impacts on stock management, given that advertising or a celebrity endorsement can have a huge impact on influencing sales. The implementation of TXT's promotion planning module is about to start, with a go-live date set for early 2006.

Source: Logistics Manager July/August 2005: Keeping stock on track

Consignment Stocking

This is another arrangement where a supplier keeps stock on the customer's premises; the stock is only drawn upon when the customer needs materials for example, as with maintenance, repair and operating (MRO) items. The product remains in the ownership of the supplier and the ownership only passes at the time of use.

It is similar, therefore, to VMI, however the visibility of information and control of replenishment is different; this remaining with the user/buyer in consignment stocking. Consignment stock is therefore managed by the customer and not the supplier. This is the main difference with VMI where the supplier manages the stock.

It is important to formalise an agreement between vendor/supplier and buyer/customer/user. This will cover such aspects as:
- What products are consigned?
- Who is responsible for stock checking?
- Length of the arrangements.
- Who arranges insurance cover?
- Who pays for damages whilst in stock?
- Exactly when does ownership pass?
- What happens to unused stocks?
- How can the supplier get access for inspection and checking?

Co-managed inventory (CMI)

CMI involves joint working of suppliers with customers to satisfy demand by cooperatively managing inventory, rather than handing the day-to-day management over totally to suppliers (as happens in VMI). It is a cooperative approach, with information exchange using appropriate systems like EPOS/EDI/E-mail, combined with developing better relationships, such as using cross-functional teams.

The following case study illustrates CMI

Case Study: Effective implementation of Co-Managed Inventory

From May 1995 to April 1996, Summerfield Stores Limited carried out an extensive pilot test on CMI. The trail was carried with twelve leading suppliers of ambient, branded products including several suppliers who compete in the same product category.

Project Establishment and Objectives
Summerfield's main objective was to test and measure the concept of CMI within a reasonably low risk environment, to measure its benefits and to define and establish the new business processes and technical infrastructure on which to base a production roll-out of CMI. No effort was made to restrict the trial to products and categories that were thought to be suitable for CMI.

Supplier Objectives
The theoretical benefits of CMI have been well documented, though largely based on US retail experience of VMI, which has tended to be supplier driven. The benefits of CMI were expected to be:
- Increased sales.
- Reduced inventory — with increased stock turns.

- Improved service levels — with reduction of stock outs.
- Improved forecasting.
- Increased focus on promotions and 'New Product introduction' (NPI) process.
- Moving from push towards pull, driving the supply-chain from a single data source.

The suppliers also saw the trial as an opportunity for:

- Evaluating the cost of CMI processes — gaining a better understanding of the total supply-chain by getting closer to true consumer demand.
- Reducing lead-times.
- Improving load building efficiency.
- Progressing their strategic supplier partnership with Somerfield.
- Measuring costs better, by product and product category.
- Becoming more forecasting focused.

Service Levels and Targets
Somerfield set a service level performance target of 98.5%, measured on case fill from the Ross-on-Wye RDC to store. The choice of the depot-to-store service measurement had some interesting implications for the suppliers. With CMI, a supplier becomes responsible for having the right amount of inventory available at the right time. It is not enough for a supplier to meet, or exceed, service level targets for delivery to the RDC. Focusing on the store measure forced suppliers to be aware of the total supply-chain, and to think about consumer service rather than customer service. This was one of several areas where the trial has started to prepare organisations in moving towards the processes that will be required for successful adoption of ECR.

Experiences and Results of Live Running
Genuine hard and soft benefits were achieved during the trial, with a range of achievement across the product categories and suppliers. The key performance measures of Ross-on-Wye RDC stock and service levels were measured by Somerfield internal systems, and compared with equivalent measures for the Bridgewater RDC, which was the non-CMI control depot.

- Nine out of twelve suppliers ran in live mode for at least ten weeks.

- Five out of the nine suppliers managed to reduce stock in Ross RDC by between 11% and 25%, compared with Bridgewater RDC. Another supplier experienced only a minor stock increase of 4.4%, while improving service level by 2.5%. The remaining three suppliers experienced stock increases of between 11.6% to 24.7%, without achieving a corresponding service level improvement.

- Four of the nine suppliers managed to improve service levels by up to 2.5%, in a range of 1.45 — 2.48%, and a fifth supplier — who reduced stock by 11% — beat the 98.5% target, but was slightly below the

Bridgewater service level.

- The factors affecting the degree of improvement were identified as frequency of replenishment and product profile. Most suppliers were on weekly replenishment, which obviously limits the stock reduction potential.

- Total inventory — measured as number of weeks — tended to be driven-up by promotional activity; push demand and stock allocation of promotional lines creates some 'noise' in a pull-demand oriented CRP system.

- No single supplier achieved spectacular gains in stock reduction/ service level, and we are convinced that this is because major supply-chain inefficiencies are not present in UK retail grocery, that would allow the type of gains that were initially experienced with VMI programmes in the USA.

Several suppliers did experiment with different order patterns, replenishment frequency and inventory planning parameters. Examples include:

- Raising target service on 'A' class items from 98.5 % to 99.5%.

- Reviewing and amending replenishment multiples, to align with rate of sale. Matching supply multiples to demand takes demand peaks out and lowers average inventory.

- Replenishment frequency — changing from weekly to twice- weekly replenishment.

- Changing order pattern by consolidating their products from three groups into one group.

The major intangible benefits experienced by all of the suppliers were better communications and a greater understanding of the total supply-chain. The trial helped to focus on the business processes and procedures in promotions management and new product introduction, and some suppliers improved their internal communications and understanding in this area. The trial also helped the participants to gain a better understanding of the organisational and cultural issues involved in implementing major business process changes. It has provided a framework which can be built upon to create subsequent ECR improvement programmes.

The main incremental operational cost for each supplier was manpower. The weekly load averaged out at four minutes for each SKU, each week. These resource requirements apply to one RDC, although it was projected that there would be economies of scale across several RDCs.

Overview of Lessons Learnt and Implications

- *Responsibility and Process Change Implications:*

When CMI implementations move from a pilot phase into production, with replenishment to several RDCs or multiple retailers, there are significant process changes. The project, which may have had a somewhat peripheral status within the supplier organisation while it was a pilot, now needs to become more integrated with standard supplier business processes. Ultimately, suppliers will seek to integrate CMI systems into upstream supply-chain management systems.

- *Commercial and Legal Implications:*

The key consideration with CMI is that processes and responsibilities are changed, with the supplier taking on additional tasks, and obtaining skilled resources was a concern for most suppliers. CMI operation provides both parties with a much better understanding of the total supply-chain, including the time, cost and resource required to perform each operation, and which operations add value. Negotiations will continue to be necessary, but both parties have better information and cost base on which to conduct the discussion, and share benefits and costs of CMI. The trial did not reach any conclusions as to how benefits should be shared between retailer and supplier, but this would obviously have to be part of the negotiations prior to operational use of CMI.

Subject to the above consideration, we do not believe that CMI requires any major changes in the commercial terms and conditions of doing business. Successful CMI programmes are built upon a basis of partnership, trust and the exchange of timely and accurate information, rather than on detailed legal contracts. Retailers and suppliers must work together on joint management of stock in order to optimise the total supply- chain, and to achieve the potential benefits of ECR. This working relationship requires a commercial framework that focuses on common improvement goals, benefits and benefit sharing.

- *Organisational Implications:*

The most successful suppliers in the trial organised the CMI project as a logistics or supply-chain development project, and were able to establish a cross-functional team under a strong business project manager. The cross-functional teams, typically, had forecasting and inventory control representation and expertise, and often the same people would be responsible for both functions. Information Systems (IS) and Sales/Marketing input was represented in the successful teams, but did not play the dominant role.

- *Technology Issues:*

As our perception of CMI evolved towards an ECR-orientated view, it became clear that a CRP type solution — whether service or in-house — was not sufficient. A very flexible system is needed, which handles both pull and push product demand, and which supports the most common ECR functions - in particular strong promotions and event management, category management, new product introduction. It is unlikely that this functionality will be found in a single application package.

For some suppliers much of the systems benefit and value of a CMI initiative may lie in receiving the daily demand information, and processing it using existing systems.

Organisations that succeed will do so because they are 'good' at supply-chain management, not technology.

Best Practice CMI Organisation:
Both CMI and ECR projects have tremendous cross-functional business implications. The characteristics of a 'good' supplier CMI programme are:
* Top management commitment, with a powerful business sponsor — possibly backed by an ECR steering committee or similar.

* Cross-functional team culture, with existing logistics or supply-chain function.

* Strong hands-on Project Manager, ideally reporting to Logistics Development or Logistics Operation team.

* Forecasting and inventory control seen as logistics/supply-chain functions, with appropriate representatives as core members of the project team.

* IS and sales and marketing backing for the project, but CMI Project Manager obtains IS and sales/marketing input and resources, as required, during the project.

* Pilot project run by core CMI team; use pilot phase to establish new business processes and support systems.

* Handover CMI operation in post-pilot phase to established operational functions within logistics/supply-chain functions.

Critical Success Factors and Recommendations
We would summarise the characteristics of a successful VMI/CMI programme as:

- *Quality and Depth of Existing Relationship:*

  It is obvious that suppliers and retailers must have a good existing relationship to undertake CMI successfully, as there must be a high degree of trust. The relationship must be intelligent, mature and non-adversarial, even if this falls short of a formal partnership, and the retailer must be willing to share information and benefits.

- *Clear Vision and Objectives:*

  As with any major change programme, introducing CMI requires top management support and commitment on both sides. An initial Research & Development or pilot phase is highly recommended, to lower the risk, and to build-up the necessary trust and confidence. The service supplier may be able to play a facilitative role, as GE did in the Somerfield trial. Pilots should be of limited length, and be seen as Phase 1 of a multiphase programme.

  Improvement goals and measurements should be realistic. Benchmarking current or historic supplier performance against the CMI measurement factors is essential for comparisons of CMI versus non-CMI performance.

- *Organisation and Culture:*

  Prospective CMI/ECR participants should seek mature and stable partners who exhibit the following types of organisation and culture:
  - Open and responsive.
  - Proactive, innovative and willing to change.
  - Willing to take risks, and be prepared to fail.
  - Open to sharing information with partners, and with competitors in a controlled manner.
  - Business process perspective.
  - Empowered individuals.

CMI pilot trials should start with a limited number of participants and products. It is important to choose the right partners and get the processes and issues sorted out, before rolling out to the majority.

- *Choosing the right mix of products, CMI techniques and system:*

    Some products are more suited to certain CMI techniques than others. Therefore, if the objective is to trial CRP, then the product mix should be suitable for CRP; conversely, if the product mix is not entirely suitable, then other CMI techniques will be required — for example, a mix of solutions for push-demand and pull-demand models.

- *Starting with Good Data:*

    Exchanging accurate, complete and timely data is of critical importance to the success of a CMI programme; however; much of the data held by retailers on supplier products s incomplete or incorrectly coded. Front-end data inspection for quality and source is a valuable activity which will save time later.

- *Documenting the current business processes and the new CMI process:*

    Entering into a CMI programme will shine a spotlight on all related supply-chain systems and business processes, and on the way data and information is exchanged.

- *Distribution strategy:*

    Ideally, this should be Distribution Centre (DC), not store based, with forecasts based on consumer Electronic Point of Sale (EPOS) data.

- *Existing Electronic Trading Infrastructure:*

    Retailer and suppliers need to have a reasonably mature electronic trading infrastructure in place to consider CMI.

Summary
The trial phase ended formally in May, 1996, although Somerfield and the majority of suppliers are continuing with CMI based operations in some form. The natural evolution will be from the CMI trial programme characteristics of:
- Retailer sponsored.
- Community project.
- Common service-based CRP-oriented solution.
- Research and Development focus.
- Single RDC to a series of individual ECR improvement programmes with each supplier; with the following characteristics:
    - Joint agreement on improvement goals in the overall supply-chain.

- Flexible systems solution, with backward integration into supplier's own systems.

- Separate techniques and systems for management of pull-demand versus push demand.

- Focus on wider ECR techniques — not just CRP.

- Multiple RDCs.

Conclusion
CMI trials can create an excellent enabling framework for retailers and suppliers to build on, and provide an opportunity to work together in joint management and optimisation of the total supply-chain — a key step on the way towards the goal of ECR.

Extracts from: ILT "Logistics Focus" September 1996 Jane Winters and Tony Lunn.

Direct Product Profitability (DPP)

This is an accounting technique to allocate fixed costs direct to specific products. It therefore attempts to ensure that each SKU can be fully costed and compared to its selling price, so that profit can be specifically identified on a per SKU basis. It therefore removes any average costing, on say a percentage of cost basis allocation, that will often give distorted figures; especially when the range of price and cost variable is high.

Essentially a tool used in retailing it can be viewed as the following:
Sales Less the cost of goods sold
= Gross margin, plus allowances/discounts
= Adjusted gross margin
Less warehouse costs
Less transport costs
Less retailing costs
= DPP

DPP can also be used by suppliers who may wish to reduce their customer's total cost of ownership (TCO). Additionally, in allocating and working out costs correctly, activity-based costing (ABC) can be used.

Economic Value Added (EVA)

Like DPP and Activity Based Costing, this was developed to overcome weaknesses seen in traditional accounting practices. The concept is to deduct from

214

the net operating profit, a charge for the amount of capital employed. A positive EVA therefore means that value is being created, a negative one that value is being wasted and destroyed.

EVA has some critics:

- Capital investment by organisations is reduced, so that the EVA remains more positive

- Use of capital is only one measure and does not cover any other measures that contribute to profit, such as innovation, market standing, people development, productivity, utilisation of other resources, etc.

- Use of human capital and knowledge may actually be more critical than the financial capital of an organisation

Nevertheless, EVA can assist in showing more exactly where any financial capital costs focus needs to be.

Collaborative Supply Chains

As has been noted many times in this section, collaboration is an underlying theme in many of the approaches and methods. Indeed, collaboration is noted in two of Emmett's Supply Chain Rules:

- the format of inventory and where it is held is of common interest to all supply chain players and must be to be jointly investigated and examined and,

- the optimum and the "ideal" cost/service balance will only ever be found by working and collaborating fully with all players in the Supply Chain

This section will examine, albeit briefly, this collaboration aspect.

The **barriers to collaboration** can be viewed as follows:

Barriers	Comments
No trust	Fear here is usually of giving information to competition
Poor communications	Usually meaning there is no up to date sharing and also a comment on the format of communication being used
No "big picture" view	Too focused on "own" issues and problems
No risk taking	Fear of having "all eggs in one basket" and a preference for "playing off"
Prefer power based adversary transactional approach	Annual contracts and three quotes, common in the public sector, continues to perpetuate adversary approaches
Want quick and short term wins	In reality success will depend on time and effort over longer periods
No sharing of benefits	The power view of "keeping it all" whereas all should save from mutual collaborations.
No planning, all "kick and rush"	Collaboration is hard work involving soft skills. It also will need adequate planning
No support for any changing "how we do things"	Top support is important
"Output is king and anyway, we are too busy fire-fighting"	Concentration here is on the "operations" and looking just for short-term efficiency whilst ignoring longer term effectiveness.
Fear of change	Remaining with the "status quo" in times of change and stable turbulence that is akin to the ostrich analogy of burying the head in the sand.
Fear of failure from the existing blame culture	Change to a "gain" culture is needed.

The **benefits of collaboration** in the supply chain have, meanwhile, been noted as follows:

Aspect	Collaboration brings
Forecast accuracy	Increased external visibility will force better accuracy
Lead time	Reductions following sharing and joint improvements
Inventory	Reduced as stock levels fall
Utilisation of resources	Improved in a "leaner" operation with less waste
Costs	Reduced and improved
Service levels	Increased and improved
People	Trust and improved relationships

Rules of collaboration are that real and recognised benefits must be found for all internal and external players. This will involve:
- Business process integration at all stages.
- Support collaboration of all the supply chain components.
- Recognition of the culture(s).
- The importance of people relationships; and when improving relationships.

It is useful to remember:
"It is the soft stuff that is the hard stuff"

"People may be physically present, but are they there psychologically?"

"Only when all people come together is found the power of one"

Fundamentally, what has to be changed? The answer is people first, as well as the following:
- Contracts to simple flexible approaches.
- Intensive management involvement.
- Periodic performance monitoring.
- Internal controls for confidential information.
- Problem solving procedures.
- Supplier is seen as a customer = "reverse customer service".
- Cross functional supplier/customer teams.
- Hub (supply chain managers) and spoke (suppliers/customer) organisations.

Collaboration has been more fully covered in *"The Relationship Driven Supply Chain - creating a culture of collaboration throughout the chain"* (Emmett and Crocker 2006).

7: Inventory improvements and the Supply Chain

In this final part of the book we want to examine how to sustain and manage improvements. We have, in part one and part six, shown the critical interactions between inventory and the supply chain and we will continue this theme in examining improvements and will look at the Theory of Constraints to do this.

We will finally look at some improvement methodologies including process mapping the supply chain, before we conclude with summaries of many improvement methodologies.

The Supply Chain & the Theory of Constraints
A useful overview of the fundamentals of supply chain management is provided by the Theory of Constraints (TOC) of E. Goldratt and detailed in books such as *"The Goal"*. TOC sees that any business is basically about:
*   Money.
*   Sales.
*   The 'rates' of movement involved with these two.

TOC has clear implications for supply chain management and we will briefly look at some of its important contributions.

Money and Sales are connected
TOC sees that "Money and Sales" are connected as follows:
*   **Throughput:** The rate at which money is generated by sales (and by the time it taken to move through the system; i.e. the cash flow).

*   **Inventory:** The purchase of things that are held to maintain the throughout and the holding of finished goods. It is the money invested in things, intended to sell/awaiting sales.

*   **Costs:** The money spent, turning inventory into sales.

TOC notes that how we view these connections has changed in recent years, for example:

	Throughput	Inventory	Cost
Past View	Second	Third	First "The cost world"
View needed Now	First "The throughput world"	Second	Third

This is an interesting perspective as it clearly reverses the view held by those companies who only focus on cost control and marginalise all the other aspects. "Low cost" as an objective, is used especially by those who work in functional silos and ignore the wider implications of such single-minded actions.

The importance of having "more than cost" perspectives is well supported by many recent approaches in supply chain management that do emphasise, for example, that variable customer service comes from varied rates of throughput movement and inventory holding. These are the critical aspects that are, refreshingly, included in the "throughput world" of TOC.

Similarly, procurement approaches on total cost of ownership, whole life costs and total acquisition costs look wider than just the superficial cost aspects such as "cost price."

It can be seen that in the traditional input/output diagram of a business, we have the following:

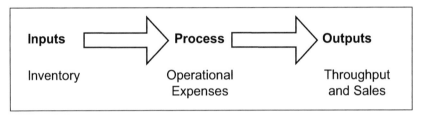

The money flows can also be seen as follows:

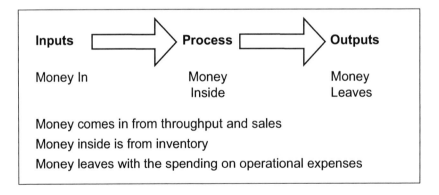

Putting the above together will indicate that the aim of supply chain management following TOC principles will be to:
- Reduce inventory (and reduce the money tied up internally).

- Reduce operational expenses (and reduce the money leaving the company).

- Increase sales/throughout (and increase the money coming into the company).

- Do all the above at the same time and in balance.

Manage the processes

This, of course, is not always going to be easy, especially when dealing with processes that are being independently managed and have opposing objectives and conflicts. A classic supply chain situation! A better "overall total process management" (like effective collaborative supply chain management that we explored earlier), may be needed; especially when we see that a process is "a sequence of dependent events, involving time, which has a valued result for the eventual end user" (another key link here to supply chain management).

Processes are selected portions of larger streams of activity that can be transformational, (for example, in converting inputs to outputs) and can be transactional, (for example, in exchanging outputs for new inputs). Processes interact and are dependant on each other. However they are not always predictable and variability can be found.

The three key features of processes are dependencies, variabilities and interfaces. Looking at each of these in turn, we can see the following:

Dependence
- Is sequential and related (causing "knock-on effects").
- Receives inputs and changes them to outputs.
- What happens "here" causes events "there".
- "A" often needs to be finished, before "B" can start.
- Any process will be as efficient as its most inefficient part ("a chain is as strong as its weakest link").
- The most important factor is therefore the most limiting one.

Variability
- Displays statistical influences (e.g. a normal distribution curve), for example lead-times and demand.
- Is when the "fixed known and expected" can become "variable unknown and unexpected", for example lead-time variablity, non-reliable service perfomance etc.
- Can cause changes from a state of "certainty" to "uncertainty".
- When each part of the process has variability, this causes knock-on effects to other processes, sometimes with catastrophic results; for example, failure to meet planned requirements.

Interfaces
- Are the potential friction points between processes.
- Are often ignored, as our minds concentrate on "the inside of the box" and what happens there.
- However, real dependencies also exist in/at the interface.

Throughput is, therefore, critical in the Theory of Constraints, and is seen occurring at the rate of the last dependency. Throughput is consequently influenced by the fluctuating rates of the other dependencies, and as the chain of dependencies increases (for example with long or variable/ unreliable supply lead-times), then there are going to be:
- Increases in inventory (as we will need to hold more).

- Increases in operating expenses (e.g. from the holding / carrying costs of inventory).

- Decreases in throughput (e.g. the movement slows, service delivery and resulting payment is delayed etc.).

Financial performance
When relating TOC to the normal financial performance measures of companies, (net profit, return on investment and cash flow), Goldratt notes that these are all actually affected by the following operational measures:
- Increases in throughput; (recall that in TOC, throughput is the rate at which money is generated by sales).

- Reducing inventory; (inventory is the money invested, awaiting sale).

- Reducing costs/operating expenses; (money spent turning inventory into throughput).

This view in TOC is therefore very supportive of the importance of the operational aspects, the associated flows/throughputs, and the inventory holding costs.

Making Improvements in the "Cost World" and "Throughput World"
Cost control is only one part of any improvement process. It can be recalled, from the "Throughput World" of TOC, that you cannot control costs without controlling the throughput (1st) and inventory (2nd) that have both caused the costs (3rd). Clearly costs will arise in each process and therefore, to improve costs, we also need to improve the costs in each process.

In Goldratt's view, this gives us only a "local efficiency" in the "Cost World". Alternatively, this can also be seen as cost reductions being made by silo management functions. In TOC, to get "global efficiencies", the requirement will

222

be to make many local improvements that are connected; for example, there are also throughputs in each process and in the supply chain. If a "chain is as strong as the weakest link", the weak link is the blockage (or the constraint). For "global" efficiencies, the linkages are just as important as the flow. This is Goldratt's "Throughput World."

To get improvements here, we will need first to change the weakest link. Improving the other links before this will result in "waste" (already well defined by the Quality movement explored earlier in part 6).

As each link is dependent on the other links, the critical path is the longest path of dependent events in time in the chain.

To summarise therefore:
- **Cost world:** Needs local improvements with each variable link being seen as independent.

- **Throughput world:** Need improvements, first, on the weakest link; with each variable link being seen as dependent on all the other links.

Managing the links and "Drum-Buffer-Rope"
The topic of "weak links," leads us onto another tenet in the Theory of Constraints, that of "Drum-Buffer-Rope". This also has direct connections to supply chain management, as the underlying principle is that a system can only run as fast as the speed of its weakest link (or bottleneck).

TOC observes the role of each is as follows:
- The Drum beats the pace for the whole system (and the bottleneck); for example, in the supply chain, by forecasts and making to stock.

- A Buffer is placed in front of the bottleneck to make sure it is always worked to full capacity; for example with levels of inventory in the supply chain.

- The Rope is the communication (from the bottleneck) on the rate at which material is needed at the front end of the system; for example by "push" scheduling.

Traditionally, therefore, in the supply chain, the drum can be seen as the forecast, the buffer as the high level of safety stock and the rope as scheduling and "push methods". This may mean slow responses, potential wasted throughput, high levels of inventory and higher cost levels.

The role of the drum/buffer/rope can however be seen differently, for example:
- Drum: this becomes the demand and order driver and possibly making-to-order decisions.

- Buffer: this becomes from low to zero levels of safety stock.
- Rope: this becomes visibility, transparency, responsiveness and "pull methods".

By doing these, responses will be made to the throughput actually needed, resulting in lower levels of inventory and lower cost levels. It will also require the examining of trade-offs across functions and breaking down silo management. In summary, the drum-buffer-rope analogy for supply chain improvement will require the following:

1) Identifying the constraints, by finding the weakest link and strengthening it; e.g. physically by removing bottlenecks, e.g. by policy changes (policy is often the core problem).

2) Deciding how to fix the constraints; e.g. physically by adding capacity, or by maximising the capacity etc.

3) Ensuring step 2) is undertaken; e.g. by not only concentrating on the non-constraints.

4) Keeping on with steps 1) and 2) until the constraint is removed.

5) After removing the prime constraint, starting on the next one in the critical path/chain.

The following Case Study shows the use of TOC in improvements that go beyond pure inventory aspects and consider the fuller supply chain:

Case Study: Remploy and the Supply Chain/Theory of Constraints

Three common measures of performance are net profit, return on investment and cash flow. These three financial measures can be impacted upon positively by three crucial operational measures, namely:
- An increase in throughput, i.e. the rate at which money is generated through sales.

- Reduction in inventory i.e. all the money invested in purchasing the product the system intends to sell.

- Reduction in operating expense i.e. all the money spent turning inventory into throughput.

Traditionally, managers have focused on improving sales and/or reducing costs, but rarely on all three of the above measures simultaneously. It was breaking away from focus on part cost-control, looking at whole system benefits (through simultaneous focus on all three measures) that enabled Remploy to transform its performance at a critical time for the company and the country.

Remploy

Any manufacturing company aims to deliver on time, in full and to specification. Remploy secured an order to the MOD. This meant more than doubling their existing production output. Such a contract was also vital to secure ongoing opportunities for training and employment of disabled people who make up 90% of their workforce.

It was clear that a radical new approach was needed to ensure fulfilment of the MOD order. To be specific, how could Theory of Constraints (TOC) methodology, invented by Eliyahu M. Goldratt, be applied to the Remploy supply chain?

Production and supply of garments were not new to Remploy. A central cutting unit (CCU) in Birkenhead supplies four sewing factories in Dundee, Stirling, Cowdenbeath and Clydebank. In all the factories there was abundant stock and work in progress. However, the specifications for their new contract were far more exact; suits of exactly the right size, type and colour were needed urgently.

To respond to the demand, they were required to:
* Dramatically increase flexibility.

* Reduce the lead-time of manufacture and supply.

It was time to question conventional 'wisdom' and challenge preconceptions. For example, the logic of minimising transport costs is rarely questioned. Remploy had managed this cost well, with a weekly delivery of cut pieces transported from Birkenhead, on a run that visited each of the four making-up factories. A central feature of the reviewed approach would be the introduction of four deliveries per week to each factory, quadrupling transport costs. Could this really be an improvement?

The way forward was dependent on a new approach in the factories, which meant a new approach to the supply chain process, both based on the TOO applications. In the factories a system of Drum-Buffer-Rope was implemented. Based upon TOC, there was a shift from 'push' to 'pull' production, according to the demands made by the requirements of the customer order.

It was vitally important to secure buy-in from all the factory workers for these new ways of working, which were clearly likely to provoke scepticism if not direct opposition. There was general agreement that TOC and the Drum-Buffer- Rope approach made good sense, but several concerns were voiced, one of these was that the cutting machine was not suited, technically, to being frequently switched on and off, and as a result, break down.

Another was that delivery of smaller batch sizes might result in the need to stop production lines due to 'out of stock' situations. However, on balance it was decided that the changes should be implemented. The very first step was to stop any further cutting at the CCU for two whole weeks to reduce work in progress.

New ways of working implemented

Reduced work in progress
> This enabled more visibility, for example, of problems around a bottleneck where work in progress would build up. Once seen, such problems could be addressed.

Smaller batch sizes, delivered more frequently
> The cutting machine would produce smaller numbers of each batch before being stopped and adjusted to cut different sizes according to the demands of the order, enabling greater flexibility and a reduction in the lead-time for each garment. This meant that if a sewing factory needed to assemble for example, trousers that measure 32" waist and 32" leg, the correctly cut pieces could be delivered within 24 hours rather than possibly not until a week late with the next delivery. The completion and despatch of the garment from the sewing factory would be correspondingly quicker. Meanwhile, the same factory would not have to store delivered component parts that were not appropriate to the immediate specification of current orders. This reduced work in progress and cash tied up in the business.

Daily measurement
> The schedule of production would be set daily, on the basis of orders placed by the customer.

Gradual rising of the bar
> The 'bar' that identifies production targets would be set low at the start and raised gradually by 5% as subsequent targets were met.

Results

On a return visit 5 months later, the extent of the improvements was immediately visible. There was far more space in the factories, both on the shop floor and in the delivery areas. Whereas in one factory on the previous visit the stores had been choked with 3 week's supply, there was now just one day's delivery. Far less time and effort was wasted in moving and handling stock, as it was easy to locate and identify the low level of stock in the stores. There was much better visibility of work in progress and better control over raw materials and finished goods. The changeover from product to product was smoother.

Contrary to earlier fears, the production line had never had to be stopped as replenishment of stock was both more frequent and more reliable. The transport, a crucial part of the new way of working, had never failed to make a delivery. The cutting machine had withstood being switched on and off without significant increase in break down rates.

Operationally, the results were dramatic. From component parts of a garment being cut in Birkenhead to the finished garment being despatched from a factory in Scotland to the MOD, the elapsed time was now only 3 days. In 3 out of the 4 factories, throughput had increased by 18% or 19%, according to a 4 week rolling average. Output per employee was up by 13.4%. Work in progress in the factories was reduced by more than 50% and in the CCU by 25%. By the end of September production was close to 100% on target, in full. £156,000 had been saved as a result of a reduced need to subcontract.

The increase in cost of transport of about £20,000 was negligible compared to the increased profitability. As well as every employee having increased their productivity, they were far happier and better motivated. Absenteeism in the factories was reduced from levels of 10% down to 3%. Remploy have improved speed, flexibility and variety to such an extent that they are now able to supply new and different products. Through their simultaneous focus on the three key operational measures, they are now able to move in new and innovative strategic directions. Whilst Remploy cannot exactly predict the future, their latest management information provides a sound basis for future strategy.

Extracts from source: Critical EYE Publications Ltd. 2004; Gary Luck Business Director of Ashridge Consulting, he can be contacted at gary. luck©ashridge.org.uk. www.criticaleye.net

Undertaking Improvement Programmes

Here, we will consider various "templates" and checklists that are useful for improvement programnes. It should be noted that these are not intended to be "one size fits all" solutions; they are intended to provide reference points to ensure that all aspects are considered.

Optimising dependant processes

This approach looks at processes that are dependant upon each other and therefore has excellent parallels with the supply chain. An overview of the approach in Balle (1997) follows:

1.   **Determine the Output**
*   Start at the customer end and establish what they do with your output.

*   Never ever forget, that the next link in the chain is always the customer (whether internal or externally located).

2.   **Sketch the Process**
*   Walk through the process, collecting forms, paperwork etc.

*   Challenge each paper process.

3.   **Map the process**
*   Establish the inputs and the outputs.

*   Draw the customer process.

*   Draw in the feedback loops.

*   Determine the lead-times.

*   Time the operations.

4.   **Redesign the process**
*   Look for bottlenecks.

*   Remove them one by one, thereby reducing lead-time.

*   Concentrate on what adds value and reduces waste.

*   Watch for the improvement killers, for example: it's not possible; it's not our job; it should not be like this; the answer is obvious; I am already doing it; I will do it tomorrow etc.

*   Eliminate processes and think parallel.

*   Split processes.

*   Remove unnecessary steps.

5.   **Test and Refine**
*   Check, check and test.

*   Recognise limiting and restraining factors.

*   Expect unexpected reactions to change.

*   Polish the redesign.

6.   Implement and standardise
- Determine: Action/Owner/Deadline/Check up date/Comments.

- Develop best practice checklists.

- Ensure that customer needs have been met.

Method improvements
The following steps are useful to follow, when engaged with improvement programmes:

1.   Pick a job to improve
- Look for bottleneck jobs.

- Jobs that take too much time.

- Jobs where costs are high.

- Jobs that require chasing for materials, tools, supplies.

- Jobs where money can be saved.

- Jobs that can be done faster.

2.   Make a process chart (see the following Supply Chain process mapping example)
- Break the job down into a visual form using, for example:
    - Flow process charts: focuses on distance.
    - Multiple activity process charts: focuses on time.
    - Operator process charts: focuses an individuals.

3.   Challenge every detail
- Study the processes for improvement.

- Challenge every part of the job by asking, in order:
    - What and why?
    - Where and why?
    - When and why?
    - Who and why?
    - How and why?

- Watch for waste.

4.   Work out a better method
- Can we eliminate unnecessary actions? (Watch especially for transport/movements and stock/storage items).

- Can we combine? (For example, inspect "on the job").

- Can we change the sequence? (For example, eliminate back-tracking).

- Can we change the place?

- Can we change the person?

- Can we improve all the remaining aspects?

- Remember the viewpoint: "If I find a job is done the same way as it was one year ago, then I know very well it is wrong".

5.   Apply the new method
- Technical problems: Will it reduce costs, increase productivity, and improve quality?

- Human problems: Remember, people resist what they do not understand and people do not like being criticised. Discuss changes with those affected in advance, explain why and "sell " the change.

- Test/trail, and follow through/review.

Supply Chain Process Mapping

This analyses a supply chain by breaking it down into the component parts/processes and providing a structure for data. It acts as a lens through which to view the process and to focus the efforts on making improvement. When evaluating any business processes, it will be a usual outcome that they do not actually fully work the way which management thinks they do.

Mapping will, therefore, also show, how the informal system, will be different from the formally designed system. It enables a better understanding and will involve questioning those who actually work with the process. It will, therefore, show how it actually works.

Some important aspects on how to supply chain process map are as follows:
- Doing it quickly, is better than doing it slowly.

- Update regularly and often.

- Use the right people (for example with the doers and the decision makers).

- Display the process on cards or post it notes/flip charts.

- Walk and record the real process.

- Enlist the help of people closest to the process.
- Ask questions (see step 5 below).

The following five basic steps may also be used when process mapping:

1. Define that the supply chain / process to be improved.

2. Identify the steps by brainstorming.

3. Display the process in sequence.

4. Change the map to correspond to the actual physical process.

5. Evaluate the process by questioning:
   - What is the purpose of?
   - Where is it done?
   - When it is it done?
   - Who does it?
   - How is done?
   - Why is it necessary?
   - Why is it done then?
   - Why does the person do it?
   - Why is it done it this way?
   - What is the lead-time?

After undertaking the mapping, the above Method Improvement steps can be used. Also the following can be considered:

- Eliminate steps.
- Perform steps in parallel.
- Re-arrange steps.
- Simplify steps.
- Use less expensive operations.
- Use consistent operations.
- Eliminate all waste and non value adders such as:
  - Time spent on correction.
  - Over production.
  - Inventory.
  - Waiting.
  - Non-required processing.
  - Non-required movement.

The minimum result to be expected should be lead-time reductions in any of the processes and as noted many times, this is very important in inventory management.

Supply Chain Mapping: Summary
- Mentally walk and record the processes.
- Display these in sequence on the wall.
- Collect ideas from a discussion.
- Go through the total supply chain step-by-step.
- Starting with the first operation, ask:
  - What is the purpose of this?
  - Is in this value-added?
  - Can it be eliminated?
  - If it cannot be eliminated can it be combined with another?
  - Is there are any other waste that can be eliminated?
- Repeat for all operations.

Improving efficiency
Whilst this approach concentrates more towards improving the efficiency of specific operations, it also has some useful points on improvements generally:

1.   Understanding the operation
- Use input/process/output diagrams

- Recognise that processes transform inputs by altering and ,or inspecting and or transporting and, or storing

- Answer the following questions: Who are the customers/what do they need/what is the product-service/what do they expect/does it meet their expectations/what process is involved/what action is needed to improve the process?

2. Set the right objectives
- Are the strategic/functional/team and personal objectives aligned?

3. Improve work processing
- Identify non-value added/wasted time.

- How can you remove it?

- Control the process by Measuring-Appraising-Acting.

- Manage Risks by Appraisal (likelihood, probability, prioritise) and Contingency Planning ("what if", establish procedures, test, refine, revise).

- Improve housekeeping (for example, by using the 5S approach: sort, straighten, sweep/shine/scrub, standardise, systemise).

- As it is people who make the process work, use job enrichment and empowerment.

4. Increase capacity
- Forecast demand.

- Plan capacity (level/fixed or variable or a mixture).

- Avoid capacity risks by changing the demand and/or the resources.

- Watch for the balance between, low and high utilisation.

5. Continually improve
- Change will come, for example, from new customers/products/ competitors and rising costs/falling revenues.

- Small, continual, incremental approaches will work where there is a culture of continual improvement. The "big bang" approach is not always needed, and when it is, it may be too late.

- Select an issue.

- Identify the process.

- Draw a flow chart.

- Select an improvement measure.

- Look at causes and effects.

- Collect and analyse data.

- Identify major causes.

- Plan for improvements.

- Take corrective action.

- Are the objectives met?

- Write up and standardise the changes that are needed elsewhere.

6. Check the customer perception

- How effective have you been?

- How can you tell?

- Ask the customer how you can improve?

- "Walk it through wearing the customers hat".

- Determinants of service are access, aesthetics, attention given, availability, care, cleanliness, comfort, commitment, communication, competence, courtesy, flexibility, friendliness, functionality, integrity, reliability, responsiveness, security.

Inventory Improvements

Finally, the following give some quick access views and summaries on making improvements to inventory:

Seven Rules for Inventory

1. All inventories should be justified and minimised, with the target being zero inventory.

2. Staff needs training and motivating to correctly identify, locate and count all inventory correctly.

3. Safety stock should only be held to protect variable demand to give customer service, or against variable supply.

4. Orders should only be placed when a stock-out is anticipated.

5. Re-order just enough to cover demand, until the next receipt is due.

6. Focus effort on the few important items and not on the trivial many.

7. ICT can help to remove the "number crunching", but manual checks and reviews are still needed.

Improving Planning

- Establish whether current performance is cost or service driven?

- Conduct an ABC Analysis by value and demand/movement; e.g. focus on the important few not the trivial many.

- Challenge the range and variety of items being held.

- Consider reducing order quantity options; e.g. reorder only enough to cover demand until next receipt, or increase order frequency consistent with EOQ.

- Measure and consider reducing safety stock; e.g. hold only when protects service against variable demand; SLT and SLTV; check service levels are needed; reviews; measure and improve forecast accuracy; reduce number of stockholding locations.

- Reduce raw materials/work in progress stocks; e.g. improve production scheduling; rationalise supplier base with J.I.T; hold consignment/VMI stocks; buy in part assemblies J.I.T; consider standard/common parts.

- Reduce finished goods stocks; e.g. start with high value items and the fast moving items; move towards make/assemble to order; reduce variations, obsoletes, low sale items; make smaller batches.

- Review and check parameters manually and regularly, the target being zero inventories; e.g. Analysis at item level; order more frequently at item level.

- Measure SLT and work with all concerned for short, fixed, reliable supply lead-times with accurate demand forecasting.

- Measure the forecast accuracy.

- Improve communications with all internal players.

- Encourage cross training/learning/working together of all the internal/external players.

The following case study reveals some of the issues involved in optimising MRO inventories:

Case Study: Real World Inventory Optimisation: Focus on Maintenance, Repair and Operating (MRO) Supplies

The following are extracts from a paper presented at "Supply Chain Vitality", the SAPICS 2006 conference by Vince Boswell CFPIM. (vincebozzz@telkomsa.net)

Introduction
Inventory optimisation has become a software-lead initiative, using such expressions such as mix optimisation, heuristic optimisation, multi-echelon, postponement strategy, stochastic optimisation and the bullwhip effect. This

paper will not address any of these software related features of IO. Instead, it concentrates on the aspects of IO, which, if not in place, can lead to sub-optimal results even if the latest technology is deployed. The reasons for disappointing results are numerous. Some of the reasons are simple and logical, and some are complex. Some of the reasons for lack of expected success are:

1. Not understanding that an IO initiative is to balance inventory to meet relevant service levels (which is far more than simply changing reorder levels).

2. The financial implications of the initiative generally entails a direct negative impact on the bottom line when obsolete and high excess stocks have to be written off.

3. Failing to understand the roles of the people who have to be involved from MD to the warehouse packer.

4. Lack of appropriate policies and procedures across all departments in the company.

5. Incorrect and incomplete inventory related master data with the resulting "Garbage in Garbage out".

6. Lack of understanding of their inventory in terms of classification, type, movement, criticality, needed, and nice to have, indicating, therefore, what ran optimised and how.

7. Failure to understand or use the many methodologies that will help to optimise inventory.

This paper will briefly address these factors and give pointers on how an overcome the shortcomings to ensure an inventory optimisation project that meets expectations and is sustainable into the future.

Inventory optimisation defined
Inventory optimisation can he precisely defined as: "To balance inventory to meet relevant service levels"

This means stock is available to meet demand according to the service level for the relevant material. It also implies that there is a balanced quantity in stock that is not too high or too low for the service level set for the material; just the right product, in the right quantity, at the right place, at the right time, at minimal cost. It must also be understood that IO is an initiative that leads to an ongoing way of doing business using beat practice. It is not a part-time inventory reduction project to be carried out by the inventory people with no budget, nor is it Super ABC.

It is very simple to ensure that demand is always met (just have lots of everything), but at what cost.

The problem with many stock ledgers is that there is too much wrong inventory and not enough of the right inventory to meet demand at an optimum cost.

An observation is:
"I receive a lot of phone calls that begin with a client complaining about the lack of space in the warehouse. More often than not, the problem is not too little space, but too much inventory. Most companies have too little 'A' inventory (backorders and customers screaming for those products) and too much 'C' inventory (obsolete stock that nobody wants and nobody has the courage to discard)." **Edward H Frazelle PhD, Author and Educator**

It, therefore, becomes obvious that the reason to optimise inventory is to ensure there is stock on hand to meet varying service levels for different inventories. However, it will be found, that in order to meet this utopian position, many people and resources have to be involved, and it is not just an Inventory Management Department initiative.

Inventory optimisation stakeholders
Another major misconception about IO is that it is an inventory management or materials management task. IO requires input from all departments in the whole company. IO is also a process that should ultimately lead to world best practise being established in all the involved departments with sustainable results. This means more involvement from the MD to the warehouse packer and from the boardroom to the stationery cupboard. The following lists, briefly, the involvement required by the key players in an IO initiative:

MD and President
• Critical to ensure a successful project and that the objectives arc met.

• Must or should be the Project Sponsor.

• Remove obstacles to success.

• Approves expenditure for the project.

• Approves temporary staff if required.

• Give people the courage to discard the unwanted.

Board of Directors
• Ensure their departments do what is expected.

- Understand.

- Innovate.

- Negotiate with '"outsiders".

- Policy approval.

Inventory Management
- Manage the initiative full time including the multi – disciplinary groups involved.

- Suggest policies.

- Administer the inventory.

- Set levels.

- Chase the identification and disposition of obsolete end excess materials.

- Constant liaison with all departments.

- Report.

Procurement
- Buy only what is requested.

- Ensure quality purchased.

- Chase standardisation.

- Manage partnerships or use collaboration methods.

- Outsource possible unnecessary non-core activities such as vehicle maintenance and pump repair.

- Negotiate service level and pricing contracts with suppliers.

Warehousing
- Inventory accuracy.

- Correctly profile incoming and outgoing materials.

- Storage processes, methods, places.

- Two bin systems and carousels.

- FIFO.

- Observation of non-moving material.

- Security.

- Ensure maintenance of materials whilst in storage.

Maintenance
- Decide what can be outsourced.

- Determine what is critical.

- Standardise on manufacturer and / or supplier of MRO materials.

- Update and audit maintenance bills, parts lists.

- Differentiate between maintenance and overhaul requirements for the same material.

- Properly maintain the materials whilst in the warehouse.

Planning
- Plan to minimise inventory, for example by using optimised batch sizes.

- Work closely with inventory management.

Sales and Marketing
- Work on accurate forecasting.

- Obtain customer forecasts.

- Involve all necessary people in thee forecasting process.

- Sell the excess.

- Sell the obsolescence.

Manufacturing
- Make to plan.

- Have inventory reduction in mind.

Engineering

- Standardise on materials, manufacturers and suppliers whenever possible.

- Assist maintenance with outsourcing decisions.

Quality

- Ensure quality of product.

- Ensure quality of process.

- Important element of the supplier evaluation methodology.

Training and Human Resources

- Coordinate all required education and training.

- Recruit the right people.

All the departments in the company have to work together in multidisciplinary groups to optimise inventory, for example, engineering, maintenance, procurement, quality, inventory management work together on standardising on manufacturers and suppliers.

Multidisciplinary groups form a very important aspect of IO. No one department can optimise inventory alone. Invariably it involves two or more departments working together on different elements which will all go together to achieving IO.

Service levels, stock holdings and stock movement

It is essential that the values of inventory, movement patterns and service levels in the different profiles that relate to different classifications, types, classes, codes, material criticalities etc, be known and understood. It is in this area that there is a degree of complexity that requires attention to detail in managing inventory.

One of the most important profiles is that of criticality. How critical is a material to the business? Critical levels should be used in a similar way to that in which ABC is used. Criticality must be determined based on production, safety and environmental considerations. Within these three considerations there should be a scale of 1 to 5 or 1 to 4 on which the material is graded.

In managing MRO up to eight or nine levels may need to be used depending on the number of materials in the stock ledger. The following is a list of possible ABC classifications. The higher up this list the higher the required service level and generally the higher the stock value.

"A" materials can be calculated using the ABC calculation process but should also be manually allocated when necessary, which is a functionality not available in most ERP systems.

In the list below the ABC calculation could manage the A to F categories electronically whilst 0 to J are allocated manually. By allocating the G to J manually, the A to F categories are not 'cluttered" with irrelevant materials.

- A Fast moving, which may or may not include critical and / or insurance materials.

- B Moving.

- C Slow moving.

- B Very slow moving.

- E Slowest moving.

- F Non-moving, in a defined time frame but which still need to be stocked.

- G Highly critical and/or insurance materials that must be held in stock.

- H Dead or obsolete awaiting signature or verification.

- I Buried materials awaiting final disposition.

- J Unknown (Believe it or not, and normally identified by the person who has been in the company for forty years, and remembers it as a spare for a Model T Ford).

The alternative to the manually allocated levels is a system that ignores the G to J materials in the ABC calculation and has a designation purely for materials that have not moved in a particular time frame. Additionally, other material classifications can be used to allocate service levels.

Reorder and order up to levels, ultimately determine the value of stock that will be held. It is therefore essential these are set as accurately as possible. The calculation of safety stock can be based on a simple or extremely complex algorithm depending on the level of optimising required. In the MRO environment, reorder levels cannot always be set using forecasting and average usages and demand is often very erratic, so demand planning is generally not feasible.

Where materials are used in sets or in planned maintenance, the reorder levels and hence average inventory can be very different to materials used only in unplanned maintenance situations. For example, what is the reorder level, for a filter issued one or two at a time once or twice a year in unplanned circumstances, but whenever there is a planned overhaul, thirty are used at a time? In these circumstances, "manual determination" is usually made.

Equally important in deciding how to manage material, is the stock movement pattern. Is it used once a year? Or is it used every month in varying quantities depending upon atmospheric temperature? The answer to these questions can make a difference in how the materials are purchased, how or where they are stored and who may hold them.

Aspects not covered
This paper has covered a number of the important issues that affect the success or otherwise of an IO initiative. However, the following aspects have not been covered or just mentioned briefly but also have a definite impact.

- Forecasting which is a critical factor; software is available today to forecast MRO materials that are very erratic in terms of the number used and the time frame in which they are used. For example, one item is used after seven years with no usage, and then three are used just eight months later. What should the forecast look like and what should the subsequent minimum/maximum or order up to levels be?

- New product introduction; a breeding ground for duplicate materials without a solid management process.

- Inventory accuracy; many books are written on the subject but it continues to be a big problem in many companies.

- Criticality; mentioned briefly above but it is very important and a subject with many facets.

- Service level agreements.

- Repair decisions in-house or outsource and repair or replace; many companies have large in-house repair organisations which suffer frequent stock-outs because the spares range is inadequate, but just down the road is a specialist repair company with a good range of spares.

- End of life planning; proper planning can avoid expensive obsolescence.

- Change management; essential in any to initiative especially as it involves the entire company. Properly done IO will change processes and procedures in many departments in a company.

- Inter-warehouse stock movement and centralisation of high-value slow movers; centralisation of slow movers can lead to very big savings in inventory, however it is s process that inquires very careful analysis and implementation.

- Security of materials in the warehouse and in the field; field examples include copper cable in electricity supply, and water pipes and valves in a water supply environment.

There are many aspects not mentioned here at all, that will also impact IO in one way or another.

Conclusion

Inventory optimisation initiatives are no different to other major business improvement initiatives. The MD and the Board of Directors have a very big role to play in ensuring success. The entire company will have to be involved in one way or another. Company direction must be clearly spelt out in policy formulation and supporting procedures. The foundation for the supporting procedures must be accurate, consistent and complete data.

The nature of materials in the company must be fully understood in terms of classifications, criticality, types, movement and how they are purchased and stored. Additionally maintenance and engineering should attempt to standardise on manufacturer and suppliers in conjunction with procurement and inventory management.

8: Bibliography

Balle, M. *The Business Process Re-engineering Toolkit.* 1997. Kogan Page.

Balle, M. *Systems Thinking.* 1994. McGraw Hill.

Barrar, P and Relph, G. Manchester Business School. *"Overage Inventory"*, a paper presented at the International Symposium on Inventory 20-25 August 1994.

Boswell, V. *Real World Inventory Optimisation: Focus on Maintenance, Repair and Operating (MRO) Supplies,* a paper presented at "Supply Chain Vitality", the SAPICS 2006 conference.

Emmett, S. *Excellence in Warehouse Management.* 2005. Wiley.

Emmett, S and Crocker, B. *The Relationship Driven Supply Chain, creating a culture of collaboration throughout the chain.* 2006. Gower.

Emmett, S. *The Supply Chain in 90 Minutes.* 2005. Management Books 2000.

Emmett, S. *Improving Learning for Individuals and Companies.* 2002. Capita Press.

Goldratt, E. *The Goal.* 1993. Gower.

Luck, G. *Critical EYE Publications Ltd.* 2004.
www.criticaleye.net.

Logistics Europe magazine.

Logistics Manager magazine.

PRT&MC. *Managing supply chains in 21st century.*

Partnerships with People. Department of Trade & Industry. 1997.

Parsons, W. *CIPS Supply Management.* 15 June 2000.

Porter, M. *Gaining Competitive Advantage.* 1985. Free Press.

Signals of Performance. The Performance Measurement Group Volume 4, Number 2. 2003.

Appendices: Poisson Tables

The table gives the probability that _r or more_ random events are contained in an interval when the average number of such events per interval is m.

Where there is no entry for a particular pair of values of r and m, this indicates that the appropriate probability is less than 0.000 05. Similarly, except for the case $r = 0$ when the entry is exact, a tabulated value of 1.0000 represents a probability greater than 0.999 95.

m=	0.1	0.2	0.3	0.4	0.5	0.6	0.7	0.8	0.9	1.0
r = 0	1.0000	1.0000	1.0000	1.0000	1.0000	1.0000	1.0000	1.0000	1.0000	1.0000
■	.0952	.1813	.2592	.3297	.3935	.4512	.5034	.5507	.5934	.6321
■	.0047	.0175	.0369	.0616	.0902	.1219	.1558	.1912	.2275	.2642
3	.002	.0011	.0036	.0079	.0144	.0231	.0341	.0474	.0629	.0803
4		.0001	.0003	.0008	.0018	.0034	.0058	.0091	.0135	.0190
5				.0001	.0002	.0004	.0008	.0014	.0023	.0037
6							.0001	.0002	.0003	.0006
7										.0001

m =	1.1	1.2	1.3	1.4	1.5	1.6	1.7	1.8	1.9	2.0
r = 0	1.0000	1.0000	1.0000	1.0000	1.0000	1.0000	1.0000	1.0000	1.0000	1.0000
1	.6671	.6988	.7275	.7534	.7769	.7981	.8173	.8347	.8504	.8647
2	.3010	.3374	.3732	.4082	.4422	.4751	.5068	.5372	.5663	.5940
3	.0996	.1205	.1429	.1665	.1912	.2166	.2428	.2694	.2963	.3233
4	.0257	.0338	.0431	.0537	.0656	.0788	.0932	.1087	.1253	.1429
5	.0054	.0077	.0107	.0143	.0186	.0237	.0296	.0364	.0441	.0527
6	.0010	.0015	.0022	.0032	.0045	.0060	.0080	.0104	.0132	.0166
7	.0001	.0003	.0004	.0006	.0009	.0013	.0019	.0026	.0034	.0045
8			.0001	.0001	.0002	.0003	.0004	.0006	.0008	.0011
9							.0001	.0001	.0002	.0002

m =	2.1	2.2	2.3	2.4	2.5	2.6	2.7	2.8	2.9	3.0
r = 0	1.0000	1.0000	1.0000	1.0000	1.0000	1.0000	1.0000	1.0000	1.0000	1.0000
1	.8775	.8892	.8997	.9093	.9179	.9257	.9328	.9392	.9450	.9502
2	.6204	.6454	.6691	.6916	.7127	.7326	.7513	.7689	.7854	.8009
3	.3504	.3773	.4040	.4303	.4562	.4816	.5064	.5305	.5540	.5768
4	.1614	.1806	.2007	.2213	.2424	.2640	.2859	.3081	.3304	.3528
5	.0621	.0725	.0838	.0959	.1088	.1226	.1371	.1523	.1682	.1847
6	.0204	.0249	.0300	.0357	.0420	.0490	.0567	.0651	.0742	.0839
7	.0059	.0075	.0094	.0116	.0142	.0172	.0206	.0244	.0287	.0335
8	.0015	.0020	.0026	.0033	.0042	.0053	.0066	.0081	.0099	.0119
9	.0003	.0005	.0006	.0009	.0011	.0015	.0019	.0024	.0031	.0038
10	.0001	.0001	.0001	.0001	.0003	.0004	.0005	.0007	.0009	.0011
11					.0001	.0001	.0001	.0002	.0002	.0003
12									.0001	.0001

m =	3.1	3.2	3.3	3.4	3.5	3.6	3.7	3.8	3.9	4.0
r = 0	1.0000	1.0000	1.0000	1.0000	1.0000	1.0000	1.0000	1.0000	1.0000	1.0000
1	.9550	.9592	.9631	.9666	.9698	.9727	.9753	.9776	.9798	.9817
2	.8153	.8288	.8414	.8532	.8641	.8743	.8838	.8926	.9008	.9084
3	.5988	.6201	.6406	.6603	.6792	.6973	.7146	.7311	.7469	.7619
4	.3752	.3975	.4197	.4416	.4634	.4848	.5058	.5265	.5468	.5665
5	.2018	.2194	.2374	.2558	.2746	.2936	.3128	.3322	.3516	.3712
6	.0943	.1054	.1171	.1295	.1424	.1559	.1699	.1844	.1994	.2149
7	.0388	.0446	.0510	.0579	.0653	.0733	.0818	.0909	.1005	.1107
8	.0142	.0168	.0198	.0231	.0267	.0308	.0352	.0401	.0454	.0511
9	.0047	.0057	.0069	.0083	.0099	.0117	.0137	.0160	.0185	.0214
10	.0014	.0018	.0022	.0027	.0033	.0040	.0048	.0058	.0069	.0081
11	.0004	.0005	.0006	.0008	.0010	.0013	.0016	.0019	.0023	.0028
12	.0001	.0001	.0002	.0002	.0003	.0004	.0005	.0006	.0007	.0009
13				.0001	.0001	.0001	.0001	.0002	.0002	.0003
14									.0001	.0001

m =	4.1	4.2	4.3	4.4	4.5	4.6	4.7	4.8	4.9	5.(
R = 0	1.0000	1.0000	1.0000	1.0000	1.0000	1.0000	1.0000	1.0000	1.0000	1.0(
1	.9834	.9850	.9864	.9877	.9889	.9899	.9909	.9918	.9926	.9(
	.9155	.9220	.9281	.9337	.9389	.9437	.9482	.9523	.9561	.9(
3	.7762	.7898	.8026	.8149	.8264	.8374	.8477	.8575	.8667	.8
4	.5858	.6046	.6228	.6406	.6577	.6743	.6903	.7058	.7207	.7
5	.3907	.4102	.4296	.4488	.4679	.4868	.5054	.5237	.5418	.5(
6	.2307	.2469	.2633	.2801	.2971	.3142	.3316	.3490	.3665	.3(
7	.1214	.1325	.1442	.1564	.1689	.1820	.1954	.2092	.2233	.2(
8	.0573	.0639	.0710	.0786	.0866	.0951	.1040	.1133	.1231	.1
9	.0245	.0279	.0317	.0358	.0403	.0451	.0503	.0558	.0618	.0(
10	.0095	.0111	.0129	.0149	.0171	.0195	.0222	.0251	.0283	.0
11	.0034	.0041	.0048	.0057	.0067	.0078	.0090	.0104	.0120	.0
12	.0011	.0014	.0017	.0020	.0024	.0029	.0034	.0040	.0047	.0(
13	.0003	.0004	.0005	.0007	.0008	.0010	.0012	.0014	.0017	.0(
14	.0001	.0001	.0002	.0002	.0003	.0003	.0004	.0005	.0006	.0(
15				.0001	.0001	.0001	.0001	.0001	.0002	.0(
16									.0001	.0(

m =	5.2	5.4	5.6	5.8	6.0	6.2	6.4	6.6	6.8	7.(
r = 0	1.0000	1.0000	1.0000	1.0000	1.0000	1.0000	1.0000	1.0000	1.0000	1.0
1	.9945	.9955	.9963	.9970	.9975	.9980	.9983	.9986	.9989	.9
2	.9658	.9711	.9756	.9794	.9826	.9854	.9877	.9897	.9913	.9
	.8912	.9052	.9176	.9285	.9380	.9464	.9537	.9600	.9656	.9
4	.7619	.7867	.8094	.8300	.8488	.8658	.8811	.8948	.9072	.9
5	.5939	.6267	.6579	.6873	.7149	.7408	.7649	.7873	.8080	.8
6	.4191	.4539	.4881	.5217	.5543	.5859	.6163	.6453	.6730	.6
7	.2676	.2983	.3297	.3616	.3957	.4258	.4577	.4892	.5201	.5
8	.1551	.1783	.2030	.2290	.2560	.2840	.3127	.3419	.3715	.4
9	.0819	.0974	.1143	.1328	.1528	.1741	.1967	.2204	.2452	.2
10	.0397	.0488	.0591	.0708	.0839	.0984	.1142	.1314	.1498	.1
11	.0177	.0225	.0282	.0349	.0426	.0514	.0614	.0726	.0849	.0
12	.0073	.0096	.0125	.0160	.0201	.0250	.0307	.0375	.0448	.0
13	.0028	.0038	.0051	.0068	.0088	.0113	.0143	.0179	.0221	.0
14	.0010	.0014	.0020	.0027	.0036	.0048	.0063	.0080	.0102	.0
15	.0003	.0005	.0007	.0010	.0014	.0019	.0026	.0034	.0044	.0
16	.0001	.0002	.0002	.0004	.0005	.0007	.0010	.0014	.0018	.0
17		.0001	.0001	.0001	.0002	.0003	.0004	.0005	.0007	.0
18					.0001	.0001	.0001	.0002	.0003	.0
19								.0001	.0001	.0(

Index